CONTENTS

Acknowledgements

The author and publishers wish to thank the following for permission to use copyright material:

Melvyn Bragg for extracts from 'Why dialects are dying beyond our ken', *The Times*, May 1997; Brookside Productions Ltd on behalf of Phil Redmond, creator of Brookside, for extracts from *Brookside*, Episode 1946, Scene 5; Chrysalis Music Ltd for extracts from Mike Scott, 'The Whole of the Moon', music and words by Mike Scott. Copyright © 1985 Dizzy Heights Music Publishing; Faber and Faber Ltd for extracts and whole poems from Sylvia Plath, 'Morning Song' from *Collected Poems*; Ted Hughes, 'Thistles', 'Hawk Roosting' and 'Esther's Tomcat' from 'Lupercal' in *Selected Poems*; Ted Hughes, 'Crow and the Birds' in *Crow: From the Life and Songs of the Crow*; Ted Hughes, 'Otter' in *The Cat and the Cuckoo*; Ted Hughes, 'Wind' in *The Hawk in the Rain*; Seamus Heaney, 'Blackberry Picking' in *Death of a Naturalist*, Seamus Heaney, 'Traditions' in *Wintering Out*, Seamus Heaney, 'A Lough Neagh Sequence II ' Beyond Sargasso' in *Door into the Dark*; Seamus Heaney, 'Follower' and 'Digging' and extracts from 'Punishment', 'Anahorish', 'Brough', 'Gifts of Rain' and other poems in *New Selected Poems*; T S Eliot, *Murder in the Cathedral*; and Brian Friel, *Translations*; Guardian Media Group plc for extracts from a review of *Othello* by Susannah Clapp, *The Observer*; 21.9.97; The Independent for extracts from Arnold Kemp, 'Triumph of black English gives new cred to street talk', *The Independent*, 22.12.96; News International Syndication for extracts from Giles Whittell, 'Black American slang wins place in classroom', *The Times*, 21.12.96. Copyright © Times Newspapers Ltd 1996; News of the World for an extract, 'Gaz-aagh!', *News of the World*, 26.5.97; W W Norton & Company Ltd for E E Cummings, 'I(a' from *Complete Poems 1904–1962*, edited by George J Firmage. Copyright © 1991 by the Trustees for the E E Cummings Trust and George James Firmage; Oxford University Press for Craig Raine, 'A Martian Sends a Postcard Home' from *A Martian Sends a Postcard Home* (1979). Copyright © Craig Raine 1979; Peters Fraser & Dunlop on behalf of the authors for Roger McGough, 'Watchwords', 'Autumn Poem' and two 'Haiku' from *You at the Back: Selected Poems 1967–1987*, (1992) Penguin Books. Copyright © Roger McGough; and for extracts from Richard Curtis, *Blackadder* episodes; Random House UK Ltd for extracts from Anton Chekhov, *The Cherry Garden*, trans. Michael Frayn (1995) Methuen; Graham Chapman et al, *Monty Python's Flying Circus, Vol. 2*, Methuen; and Robert Frost, 'The Road Not Taken' from *The Poetry of Robert Frost*, ed. Edward Connery Latham, Jonathan Cape; The Times Higher Education Supplement for extracts from Christie Davies, 'The Last Gasp of a Dead Tongue', *The Times Higher Education Supplement*, 4.7.97. Copyright © Times Supplements Ltd 1996.

Every effort has been made to trace the copyright holders but if any have been inadvertently overlooked the publishers will be pleased to make the necessary arrangement at the first opportunity.

Introduction

This book is aimed at the increasing numbers of students and their teachers who are tackling one of the new English A-level courses combining Language and Literature. On these courses, you may well have to combine the study of a number of literary 'set texts' with a wider ranging survey of areas of linguistic knowledge. So, you will have to understand how literary and linguistic study can both enrich your responses to what you read. You may also have to undertake pieces of research or project work, or produce pieces of your own writing for coursework.

The next generation of English Language and Literature courses will demand that you do not think of your study of language and your study of literature as two separate strands of the courses. Instead, these new syllabuses will insist on the challenge – how can your study of set texts be linked up with the linguistic aspects of your course to produce a fully integrated programme of work?

This is what *English Language and Literature: An Integrated Approach* sets out to do. It approaches the kinds of set Literature texts which are likely to appear on your course in ways which lead towards the linguistic topics and skills which you also need to cover. So, each chapter is centred on approaches to a couple of 'core' texts which, apart from being notable works of literature, are also interesting platforms from which to launch a series of investigations into key aspects of language. Each chapter includes numerous exercises and activities for you to work through and suggestions for research and writing projects which you could develop as pieces of coursework (according to the requirements of the syllabus you are following). We start from the set texts, shoot off in various linguistic directions, before returning to the texts themselves and bringing to our study of literature the insights which result from also being students of language.

Of course, the actual texts prescribed for study may differ from year to year, so each section also includes some suggestions for applying the approaches adopted here to some popular alternative A-level texts.

English Language and Literature complements the previous two titles in this series, Howard Jackson and Peter Stockwell's *The Nature and Functions of Language*, and Urszula Clark's *An Introduction to Stylistics*. This book touches on several of the topics covered in these companion texts, but in basing our investigations around the study of literary texts, approaches them from a number of different angles. Nevertheless, you may wish to pursue further some of the linguistic issues we raise here by referring to the relevant sections of these books.

We start in Chapter 1 with a survey of some of the huge variety of language we find around us, and begin to make the distinction between what we call 'literature' and other kinds of text. Chapter 2 takes as its core texts Mark Twain's *The Adventures of Huckleberry Finn* and Alice Walker's *The Color Purple*, and explores the nature of narratives in many different forms – in speech as well as in writing, in non-standard as well as in standard forms of the language – before suggesting a number of writing activities for you to try.

Chapter 3 focuses on verse, and places the poetry of Ted Hughes and Seamus Heaney at its core. From there we will consider some linguistic approaches to textual analysis, and apply these to a range of verse in everyday life, from advertising jingles to pop songs. You'll try some verse-writing techniques of your own, too, before returning to the 'core' texts and considering some of the linguistic issues raised by Heaney's poetry in particular.

In Chapter 4, we switch our attention to the language of conversation and the uses which dramatists and scriptwriters make of it. Our core text here is Brian Friel's *Translations*, but we start by examining talk in natural, everyday contexts and in the media (including the language of humour) before considering the uses made of conversations by dramatists. We return to examine closely a number of the important linguistic issues raised by Friel's play.

Dialogue remains our topic in Chapter 5, but our core texts – Shakespeare's *Othello* and *The Tempest* – allow us to branch out in some new directions. We use the texts as starting points for exploring language change, the language of persuasion and the range and power of insults and linguistic taboo.

Each chapter includes numerous suggestions for learning activities; many of these are followed by commentaries with which you might like to compare your responses and analysis afterwards. You may find some of the terminology (in bold) in the main text and in the commentaries useful for describing precisely features of language in the texts. A final section in each chapter offers a summary both of the technical terms used and the key concepts covered, as well as suggestions for further reading and extension activities using other texts. We hope that for both teachers and students, *English Language and Literature* will prove to be a starting-point for many fruitful investigations and projects.

Good luck!

A note for teachers

The rise in popularity of A-level English syllabuses which allow for the study of both Language and Literature has created exciting opportunities for the integration of literary and linguistic approaches. Even if the 'first generation' of such courses, such as AEB's 623 and NEAB's English Language and Literature, have not always demanded complete integration, the new 'combined' syllabuses certainly will. It is my belief that even with the existing syllabuses, judicious selection of linguistically interesting set texts and imaginative course design can produce many exciting possibilities for using linguistic and literary approaches mutually to enrich each other. It is my hope that the kinds of approaches and activities developed in *English Language and Literature* may become even more fruitful as the 'new generation' of syllabuses comes on stream. So, whatever 'core' texts may be studied, teachers will no doubt be able to apply some of the methodologies demonstrated here to their own course.

Although there are certainly places in the investigations contained in this book where it would have been useful to use the symbols of the International Phonetic Alphabet (IPA), I do not attempt to introduce it or its use to students here. If you wish to encourage students to use the IPA in their discussion of, say, the relationship between sounds and spelling in the representation of accents, I refer you to the relevant sections of our companion volume *The Nature and Functions of Language*, by Howard Jackson and Peter Stockwell, also published by Stanley Thornes.

1 The spice of life: the variety of language and literature

1.0 Introduction

You are about to embark on a course of study which asks you to look more closely than ever before at your own language, its hugely varied uses and its rather special application which is called *Literature*. Traditional English Literature courses select from the bewildering diversity of language which we all experience only a very small amount as material for reading – and even having limited the scope of your study to poetry, fiction and drama, such courses limit even further your choice to those works which are deemed 'worthy of serious study'.

However, as students of English Language, or English Language and Literature, the whole world of language is available for you to study, so we need to start our investigations by reminding ourselves just how many and diverse the uses of language actually are.

ACTIVITY 1 LANGUAGE AROUND US

We are surrounded by language in many forms, and we both consume it (as listeners and readers) and produce it (as talkers and writers) in many different situations daily, ranging from the casual conversations with friends in which we participate, through to more formal situations – such as examinations – in which we read and write in isolation.

1 Thinking about both spoken and written forms of the language, list on a (large!) sheet of paper as many of these different occasions as you can think in a typical 24-hour period.

2 Repeat the exercise for someone other than yourself – perhaps someone older, or in a particular kind of job, or living in very different circumstances (e.g. an airline pilot, a retired pensioner, a police officer, someone with a visual or hearing impairment, etc.).

3 Now go back to the different language occasions you have listed and try to
   define for each one the primary purpose for which language is being used.
   What differences and similarities do you find between your own language
   uses and those of your second subject?

COMMENTARY
In the view of many biologists, the development of language in humans has been
the crucial factor in accelerating our evolution as highly social and civilised
beings. Here is Richard Leakey on the subject:

> There is no question that the evolution of spoken language as we know it was a
> defining point in human prehistory. Perhaps it was the defining point. Equipped with
> language, humans were able to create new kinds of worlds in nature: the world of
> introspective consciousness and the world we manufacture and share with others,
> which we call 'culture'.
>
> [The Origin of Humankind, p. 119, 1994]

Certainly, it is almost impossible to imagine a human life outside of and without
language. There may be some interesting differences in the kinds of language
used by different people, as your findings suggested, but all of us, unless we are
in very abnormal circumstances, use language continuously for a variety of
purposes. It is helpful to think of these under four main headings:

- giving and receiving information e.g. a report or a lecture
- giving and taking instructions e.g. a DIY manual or an army drill
- persuading – and being persuaded e.g. an advertisement or a political
  broadcast
- giving enjoyment and entertainment e.g. a joke or a poem.

Even in extreme isolation – marooned on a desert island or living the life of a
hermit in a cave – humans live through language. Some people report that they
often dream in words, and you might even have listed 'thinking' as a use of
language. There is considerable controversy among psychologists about the
precise role of language in thought, but the relationship between the words we
use and the way we think is a subject to which we will return when we consider
the language of poetry (see Chapter 3, Section 3.3.3).

ACTIVITY 2   LANGUAGE PIE

Having briefly surveyed the range of language use in our lives, now let's consider
how much of our waking time we spend consuming or producing language of
different kinds.

Your task is to represent your varied uses of language in the form of a pie chart,
which reflects the proportions of your day which you think you spend in different
linguistic activities. For example, if you believe 50 per cent of your language use
in a day is taking part in informal conversation, this will be half of your pie!

See Figure 1.1 below as an example – but decide on your own ways of
classifying your different uses of language. Make sure, however, you include a
segment which you entitle Literature.

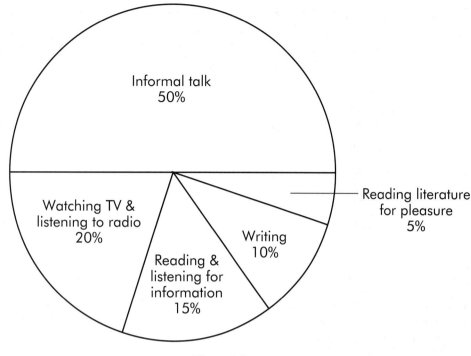

Figure 1.1

COMMENTARY

The relative sizes of the portions of your language pie will obviously reflect your own lifestyle, occupation and individual personality. However, deciding how to complete the chart may well have thrown up some tricky questions: first, there are many different ways in which we can classify language. You may have divided 'informal talk' into such functions as joke-telling, gossiping, moaning, etc. – or distinguished between the different kinds of writing you may have to do during the day.

Secondly, there is the question of deciding what counts as Literature. Presumably you would include any reading you do of your set texts for English – novels, poems or plays. But would you also include that Stephen King or Virginia Andrews story you have by your bedside at the moment? Does watching the latest film version of *Romeo and Juliet* count? And what about those song lyrics on the latest Oasis CD – they can't count as Literature … can they?

Just what *does* it take for a piece of **text** to graduate as Literature?

1.1 Language or Literature? Describing texts

In fact, the definition of Literature is far from simple – as we shall discover. After all, literature – with a small 'l' – can simply describe anything that's written down, but Literature (upper case!) seems to be reserved for a particular kind of written language. Then there's the question of who decides when a particular book, poem or play 'makes the grade' and receives the ultimate accolades – a capital L and inclusion on the set-text lists of Examination Boards!

In the next activity, you will explore some of these problems in practice.

ACTIVITY 3   DESCRIBING TEXTS

1 Read each of the following extracts A–M carefully. They represent a wide
   sample of language in use, both spoken and written, modern and historical,
   literary and non-literary.

2 Your task is to organise the texts into no more than **five** groups, using any
   means of classification which you like. In doing so, consider how useful the
   category of Literature proves to be.

   Complete Table 1.1 as you do so. Give each group a title which summarises
   what the texts have in common, and give more details in the 'Common factors'
   column. You may wish to include the same extract in two or more groups.

   (**NB**: Linguists use the word 'text' to apply to any passage of language, even if
   it is spoken. It is this wider use of the word which will be used throughout this
   book.)

Table 1.1: Classifying texts

Group no.	Title of group	Texts included	Common factors
1.			
2.			
3.			
4.			
5.			

Extract A

*Endless time, patience and
passion, yet probably gone
by the evening end.
A new view of California.
A new collection of wines.
From the family of
Ernest and Julio Gallo*

Extract B

*I went – I started erm – middle o' night and er – rang the erm midwife – an she said er
– how y'gonna get to Thorn St? And I said – oh, we're going on his motorbike – she
said – you can't do that – and er – so we had to walk – from Watson St to Thorn St
which is about – ten minutes – at 4 o'clock in the morning – and knock my mother up.*

Extract C

M: *Dot! How are you? Long time no see.*

D: *Oh hello Mark. Hey, have you seen all the rubbish laying in the street? People drop it when they like where they like, they ain't got no respect.*

M: *I know, Cathy's on the warpath.*

D: *She ought to be, it's disgusting. (Pause) Oh Mark. (Pause) I was ever so sorry about your dad. Your mum told me all about it, oh it was terrible.*

M: *Yeah. I still miss him.*

Extract D

When that Aprille with hise shoures soote
The droghte of March hath perced to the roote
And bathed every veyne in swich licour
Of which vertue engendred is the flour;
Whan Zephirus eek with his sweete breeth
Inspired hath in every holt and heeth
The tendre croppes and the yonge sonne
Hath in the Ram his half cours y-ronne
And smale fowles maken melodye
That slepen al the nyght with open ye
So priketh hem nature in hir corages
Than longen folk to goon on pilgrimages …

Extract E

There was a poor farmer who had three sons, and on the same day the three boys went to seek their fortune. The eldest two were sensible industrious young men; the youngest never did much at home that was any use. He loved to be setting snares for rabbits, and tracing hares in the snow, and inventing all sorts of funny tricks to annoy people at first and then set them laughing.

Extract F

Twas in the year 1898, and on the 8th of June,
A mother and six children met with a cruel doom
In one of the most fearful fires for some years past –
And as the spectators gazed upon them they stood aghast.

The fire broke out in a hairdresser's, in the town of Scarborough,
And as the fire spread it filled the people's hearts with sorrow;
But the police and the fire brigade were soon on the ground,
Then the hose and reel were quickly set round.

Extract G

Gaz-aagh!

GLENN HODDLE last night blasted the brutal tackle which could rule Paul Gascoigne out of England's crucial World Cup Qualifier in Poland.

Gazza, making his comeback in England's 2-1 win over South Africa at Old Trafford, was stretchered off with a serious calf injury following a wild challenge by substitute Linda Buthelezi.

Extract H

Miranda: ...*When thou didst not, savage,*
Know thine own meaning, but wouldst gabble, like
A thing most brutish, I endowed thy purposes
With words that made them known; but thy vile race,
Though thou didst learn, had that in't which good natures
Could not abide to be with; therefore wast thou
Deservedly confined into this rock,
Who hadst deserved more than a prison.

Caliban: *You taught me language, and my profit on't*
Is, I know how to curse. The red plague rid you
For learning me your language.

Extract I

... that was a certainty, it was gony get worse. He needed to do better, he really needed to do better. His entire approach had to be changed. The whole set-up. Everything. He had to alter everything. There was all these different things needed doing and he was the man. Naybody else. If he didnay do them they wouldnay get done. They wouldnay get done if he didnay do them. Ye had to accept it. It's like he wasnay accepting it. It's like he was going about as if he wasnay blind, as if he didnay think of himself as blind but was just meeting up with all these obstacles and fucking things he kept fucking bumping fucking into.

Extract J

A certain man went down from Jerusalem to Jericho, and fell among thieves, which stripped him of his raiment, and wounded him, and departed, leaving him half dead. And by chance there came down a certain priest that way; and when he saw him, he passed by on the other side. And likewise a Levite, when he was at the place, came and looked on him, and passed by on the other side. But a certain Samaritan, as he journeyed, came where he was: and when he saw him, he had compassion on him, and went to him, and bound up his wounds ...

Extract K   *And all the roads we have to walk are winding*
And all the lights that lead us there are blinding.

Extract L

Up; making water this morning (which I do every morning as soon as I awake) with greater plenty and freedom then I used to do, which I think I may impute to last night drinking of Elder Spiritts. Sir Batten and I sot a little this afternoon at the office; and then I by water to Deptford and there mustered the yard, purposely (God forgive me) to find out Bagwell, a carpenter whose wife is a pretty woman, that I might have some occasion of knowing him and forcing her to come to the office again.

Extract M

A: *We eloped. Yeah, we eloped*
B: (laughs)
A: *We went on to have six!*

B: *Six!*
A: *Yeah. One after the other.*
B: *Did you?*
A: *Yeah.*
B: *You and Him?*
A: *Yeah, yeah.*
B: *One after the other.*
A: *Mm.*
B: *Six children*

COMMENTARY

There are many possible solutions to the problem, of course – the most important point is to be clear about the different ways it is possible to group texts together. In sorting these texts for yourself, you will certainly have used some of the categories here.

▷ As we consider each category, try to identify some examples – either from Extracts A–M, or elsewhere – which illustrate each of the descriptions offered below.

Purpose

Texts may be defined in terms of what appears to be their primary **purpose**. There are many ways of defining the purposes of a text, but it is useful to consider these under four main headings:

- to inform
- to instruct
- to persuade
- to entertain.

However, this may not always be straightforward, as there may be more than one purpose behind a single use of language.

▷ Think of some examples of texts which have more than one purpose (e.g. an advertisement may be primarily about persuading you to buy a product – but in order to do so, it may also seek to entertain you).

Mode

A simple distinction can be made between whether a text is in spoken or written language. This is called the **mode** of the text. Even here, there are problems in classifying texts which are written to be spoken aloud, or speech which is uttered in the knowledge that it is being recorded.

▷ Can you think of some of these?

Fiction or non-fiction

You may have felt it useful to distinguish between whether the material in the extracts is 'real' or invented – in other words, whether it is **fiction** or **non-fiction**.

▷ There may well be texts which it is impossible to categorise so simply. Can you suggest some?

Medium

We can classify texts according to the **medium** in which they are transmitted – for example:

- radio
- television
- cinema
- theatre
- magazine
- newspaper
- pamphlet
- spontaneous conversation
- book.

▷ Are there examples of the same text being transmitted in more than one of these media?

Audience

It is always useful to understand language in terms of the **audience** for whom it is intended. This may be defined in terms of:

- age group
- gender
- social background
- historical period
- the special interests/knowledge of the intended readers/listeners.

▷ For which of Extracts A–M is it most difficult to define the audience?

Genres

Whatever the medium of a text, different kinds of communication – or **genres** – have their own rules and conventions. To understand why a pair of actors should suddenly burst into song in the middle of a romantic love-scene, for example, we have to know about the genre of 'musicals'.

There are various genres of fiction and non-fiction, speech and writing, and a list of some other genres might include:

- letter
- novel/short story
- poem
- song lyric
- report
- article
- science-fiction film
- joke
- interview
- TV police series

▷ Add more genres to the list – thinking of TV, film, and everyday speech as well as print-based forms.

▷ Try to define the rules or conventions of one or more of these genres.

Register

The language of a text may be distinctly formal, or informal, or contain expressions associated with a particular subject or specialist area of knowledge. This is known as the **register** of a text.

▷ Which of the extracts A – M would you describe as being in an informal register? Which use vocabulary belonging to a particular topic or area of special interest?

▷ Imagine that a fault has developed with the engine of your family car. Express this idea in as many different registers as you can manage.

Time

Texts can easily be classified according to the **time** in which they were spoken or written. Just as geologists define fossils according to geological eras, linguists have defined the main periods of English as:

- Old English (or Anglo-Saxon) – approximately 5th to 12th centuries
- Middle English – approximately 12th to late 15th centuries
- Early Modern English – approximately early 16th to 18th centuries
- Modern English – 18th century to the present day.

We shall discuss this in more detail in Chapter 5, Section 5. 3.

▷ Some kinds of modern speech and writing preserve forms of the language which strike us as old-fashioned (or archaic) and have in most other contexts died out. Can you suggest any ?

Levels of analysis

Whichever ways of classifying the extracts you have used, as you came to a judgement about what kind of text each extract was, you will have used different kinds of linguistic clues. You will have considered:

- how the text is organised and presented on the page (its layout and appearance, or **graphology**)
- how the texts has been spelled and punctuated (its **orthography**)
- what kind of vocabulary has been used (the **lexis** of the extract)
- how words and phrases have been combined and constructed into sentences (the word order, or **syntax**, and **grammar** of the pieces).

These distinct levels of analysis will be very important when we start to describe texts in more detail – see Chapter 2, Section 2.6 and Chapter 3, Section 3.2.

▷ The importance of each of these factors in helping you 'place' each extract will have varied. For each one (graphology, orthography, lexis, syntax and grammar) identify one extract in which that factor was particularly important in helping you classify it.

Literary or non-literary

Since we are exploring the distinction between texts which may be described as English Literature and those which cannot, perhaps we can classify our extracts as either **literary** or **non-literary**. As you have considered each of the extracts, however, perhaps you have become aware that this distinction is neither clear-cut nor always easy to apply.

Extract A [Advertisement for Gallo Wines, *Observer Magazine*, May 1976]
You might have been tempted to describe this as 'literary' because:

- the way the lines are organised on the page (i.e. its lineation) gives something of the appearance of a poem
- it contains some patterns which we often find in 'literary' language – the group of three ('time, patience and passion') including the alliteration of 'patience' and 'passion', and the repetition of 'A new …' at the beginning of lines 4 and 5.

However, skilful and 'literary' as Extract A's use of language may be – it appeared opposite a photograph of carefully sculpted dolphins in the sand of a Californian beach – few of us would describe an advertisement as Literature!

Extract B [Transcript of unscripted story told and recorded in October 1996]
The hesitations and rather disconnected nature of this text mark it out as natural rather than scripted language. So, even if you classified it as 'story-telling' (or **narrative**), and noted the attempt made by the speaker to make the story interesting by recreating the dialogue spoken in the situation she is describing, it is unlikely you would define this as Literature.

Extract C [Extract from BBC 1 television's 'Eastenders', recorded April 1997]
Unlike Extract B, this dialogue does not contain what we might call the **non-fluency** features of spontaneous speech (hesitations, repetitions, slip-ups, etc.), and is the work of a scriptwriter. S/he has been quite skilful in exploiting many of the features of casual speech to create a fairly realistic dialogue (as we shall see further in Chapter 4, Section 4. 4).

Nevertheless, some people might hesitate to call 'Eastenders' Literature, either because it is written for a relatively new medium – television – or because it is not considered 'serious'; indeed, its inclusion on some Media Studies syllabuses has provoked attacks in some newspapers on 'falling standards'.

Extract D [Geoffrey Chaucer, opening lines from *The Canterbury Tales*, c. 1387]
The unfamiliar spellings and vocabulary are the aspects of this text which probably strike you first – but you will also have noted the pattern of paired rhymed lines (i.e. **rhyming couplets**) and lineation characteristic of verse. It is unlikely that you classified this as narrative, because it is not in the past tense which story-tellers generally adopt (but not always! – see Chapter 2, Section 2.2).

However, it is in fact the opening of the one of the most famous narratives in English – *The Canterbury Tales*. A group of pilgrims trekking on a religious pilgrimage to Canterbury pass the time by holding a story-telling competition. Is it truth, or fiction?

Most scholars believe *The Canterbury Tales* is not an account of an actual journey, and the author's status as the 'father of English Literature' makes this text incontrovertibly Literary! But – if it was simply a documentary account of a real journey, told in prose, would it be?

Extract E ['Jack the Cunning Thief', from J Jacobs (ed.), *Celtic Fairy Tales*, 1994]
The simplicity of the opening, and the recognisable formula (traditional stories involving sets of three are very common – see also Extract J) identify this easily as a 'fairy tale' or 'folk tale'. Stories such as this often have a very long history and stretch back to the time when tales were passed down the genertions in an oral, rather than written tradition. Nowadays, however, we are likely to associate such tales with children. We probably assume it to be fictional, but because such tales have come to enjoy only relatively low cultural status, the term 'fairy tale' is often used pejoratively – we may hesitate to describe it as Literature. However, it may make us consider whether Literature has to be written down at all. Is there such a thing as 'Oral Literature'?

Extract F [William McGonnagall, 'The Disastrous Fire at Scarborough', in *More Poetic Gems Selected from the Works of William McGonagall*, 1972]

The rhyming pattern and lineation mark this out as verse. But is it Literature? You may have raised a couple of objections. If you believe Literature to be mainly about imagined or fictitious events, you might point out that McGonnagall commemorated real events – mainly disasters! – such as this one (a fire at Scarborough) rather than inventing stories.

Secondly, McGonnagall's verse is generally held to be so bad that it only deserves to be called **doggerel**. Would you agree?

Extract G [Report in *The News of the World*, 26 May 1997]
On the face of it, this is a very familiar type of tabloid news report of an actual event. However, although clearly not Literature, there are aspects of its use of language which could be considered literary.

First, the play on words (Gaz-aagh!/Gazza) so beloved of headline-writers is equally the resort of poets (even Shakespeare sometimes made bad puns about people's names!). Then there is the deliberate dramatisation of the event through the use of words like 'blasted', 'brutal' and 'wild'. Would this kind of language be so out of place in a poem or in a speech from a play?

Extract H [William Shakespeare, *The Tempest*, 1611]
First, Shakespeare has become such an established figurehead for English Literature that we may not even question his unique status. His works are prescribed reading for almost all GCSE and A-level English Literature syllabuses. Few would deny his enormous skill as a playwright and poet, but he is also revered as a sort of national symbol representing all things English, in a way which sets him apart from other writers – who some would argue have been equally gifted!

Secondly, the traditional medium for dramatic literature was, and is, the theatre. Shakespeare dominates the theatrical landscape still, but modern writers for the stage generally avoid the highly artificial verse of Shakespeare's language in favour of something closer to the natural speech of our day.

As technologies have developed in the twentieth century, however, the theatre has become something of a minority activity compared with film and television. Film and TV scripts do not yet appear on English Literature syllabuses. Should they?

Finally, it is interesting that the character Caliban celebrates the power of cursing – and does, indeed, curse magnificently throughout the play! Some readers believe that 'literary' language should rise above such vulgarity – as the author of Extract I, James Kelman, was to discover some 380 years later !

Extract I [James Kelman, *How Late It Was, How Late*, 1994]
This is clearly a narrative, but not in the standard form of English which is normally associated with the written word. You may have been deceived by the writer's skill into thinking this is the transcript of natural speech; in fact, it is an extract from a novel which caused great controversy when it was awarded the 1994 Booker prize for fiction. Some critics objected violently, taking the view that a novel (written in Glaswegian dialect) containing such a large number of swear words could never be described as great Literature. Would you agree?

Extract J [St Luke's Gospel, Chapter 11, verses 30–34, Authorised Version, 1611]
This is a well-known **parable** (symbolic story) supposedly told by Jesus and

recorded in the Bible. It is clearly a narrative, and may well be fictitious, but is it 'literary'?

It has much in common with the structure of the traditional folk tale in Extract E, since it follows the traditional set-of-three (or **triadic**) structure (it is the third passer-by who stops). But the unique spiritual status of the Bible in Christian cultures makes it difficult to read *simply* as a work of Literature.

Extract K [Pop lyric from Oasis, 'Wonderwall', 1995]
Arguments may rage about the relative merits of popular songwriters. Some, like 1960s and 1970s stars Leonard Cohen or Jim Morrison of the Doors, claimed for their lyrics the status of 'poetry'. Whilst songwriters clearly exploit many of the features of poetic, literary language – patterns of rhyme and rhythm, plays on words, similes, metaphors and other **figurative language** – some people would claim that the impact of their words depends too much on the effectiveness of the accompanying music for them to be seen as Literature in their own right.

This is not the view held by Professor Christopher Ricks, however, who raised the status of Bob Dylan's lyrics by making them the subject of lectures at Cambridge University in the 1970s.

Extract L [Samuel Pepys, *Diary*, for 9 July 1663]
As with Extracts D, H and J, the unfamiliarity of the language of this text draws attention to its age. For all that, though, it is recognisably a diary – a form of writing which can hover between an individual's private literature and a reading public's Literature. The events recorded by Pepys are believed to be true, and so provide an important historical document of his times. Enthusiasts for his writing also praise his use of language, yet the non-fictional nature of the material has sometimes seemed to disqualify him from the category of Literature.

However, many other 'literary' writers have used the diary form to good effect.

Extract M [Transcript of conversation recorded in April 1997]
Did you think this text was scripted, or unscripted dialogue? It could easily be an extract from a modern, realistic drama for either stage (Literature!) or screen (literature?), as the usual non-fluency features of natural speech do not appear.

In fact, it is a transcript of real speech – a hairdresser and her client quite unselfconsciously using language in ways that a playwright would deliberately have to imitate.

1.2 The canon

If one thing emerges clearly from all of this, it is that the question 'What kinds of text do we mean by English Literature?' leads to all kinds of confusion! The traditional notion of Literature limits itself to texts which:

- are written down – usually in a 'standard' form of English
- use language in distinctive ways – using simile, metaphor and other figurative devices
- use respected genres of poetry, drama and prose fiction (so genres such as detective fiction, science-fantasy and pantomimes are excluded)
- deal with 'serious' themes, even if giving them comic treatment
- offer perceptive insight into human life
- are mainly fictitious
- are approved of by university academics
- repay careful and detailed study.

This select collection of texts has become known as 'the **canon**', and has often formed the basis of English Literature courses in schools and university. Nowadays, however, things are not so simple, as we have already discovered. Teachers and academics often disagree about which texts should be studied, some even challenging the unique position of Shakespeare.

There is no doubt that Literature – whatever we think it should include – is a special application of language to which we give a privileged position. However, as your language pie-charts in Activity 2 probably revealed, Literature is merely one of many linguistic activities in which we participate, and as students of language we hope to find them equally interesting and deserving of our attention.

We have already discovered that there are many useful ways of describing texts, and that the distinction between what is and isn't 'literary' is extremely blurred, not least because the kinds of language usually associated with 'literary' texts is almost as often to be found in non-literary use – a theme which the rest of this book will explore.

So, although each of the chapters which follow begins and ends with texts which are quite definitely works of English Literature, we can expect to find them firmly rooted in the soil of the language from which they have sprung.

1.3 Learning points

1.3.1 Key concepts

By the end of this chapter, you will have learned:

- that there is great diversity in the styles and uses of English
- that uses of language (texts) can be described using different sets of labels
- that the boundaries between literary and other texts are often blurred
- that 'literary' uses of language often occur in non-literary texts.

1.3.2 Glossary

In the course of this chapter, you have encountered the following linguistic or literary terms:

Audience the readers of/listeners to a piece of language

Canon the traditionally accepted and respected texts of English Literature

Doggerel trivial and badly written verse, usually with contrived rhyme and awkward rhythm

Fiction/non-fiction The distinction between imaginatively created and true-to-life material

Figurative language the collective term for expressive and imaginative uses of language devices such as similes and metaphors

Genre a distinct form of text with its own rules and conventions

Grammar the rules which describe how words are combined to make meaningful texts

Graphology the factors which affect the physical layout and appearance of text on a page

Lexis vocabulary

Medium the channel through which language is conveyed

Mode the distinction between whether a text is spoken or written

Narrative story-telling

Non-fluency features hesitations, slips, repetitions which occur in natural speech

Orthography the spelling and punctuation of written language

Parable a symbolic story with a message or moral

Register the style or context of language in a particular situation

Rhyming couplets pairs of lines whose final words rhyme with each other

Syntax the word-order used to combine words into phrases and sentences

Text any passage of spoken or written language

1.4 Extension activities

1.4.1 Analysis and discussion

▷ Take any one of the levels of analysis identified on page 11 (graphology, orthography, lexis, or syntax and grammar) and compare in detail the relevant aspects of any two of the extracts, bringing out the distinctive characteristics of each one.

1.4.2 Research and data-gathering

▷ Design and carry out a survey designed to discover the amount of time devoted to the reading of 'literary' texts by various groups of people – fellow students, teachers, family, workmates, etc.

▷ Gather your own selection of texts which you might encounter in a typical day. Distinguish between 'literary' and 'non-literary' texts, and for the 'non-literary' ones, identify any features of their uses of language which might be described as 'literary'. You could, for example, look for how similes, metaphors and other idioms are used in everyday speech.

You might also find it interesting to consider such texts as books for children, advertisements, epitaphs and obituaries (in the newspapers, or in churchyards!), sports reports and commentaries.

▷ Try to discover as many examples as you can of narratives written in the form of (a) diaries and (b) series of three ('there was a farmer who had three sons', etc.).

1.4.3 Original writing

▷ To develop your awareness of the ways in which different genres work, take any one of the extracts and try to rewrite it in the style of one of the others. For example:
  - how would the Gazza news report look in the style of a folk tale?
  - could you make a pop-song out of the story of the Good Samaritan?
  - or transform Shakespeare's dialogue into a narrative?

▷ When you have completed such a transformation, write an accompanying commentary in which you identify the features of the new genre which have had to adopt.

1.5 Further reading

A readable introduction both to the history of English and some of its modern varieties can be found in D. Crystal, *The English Language* (Penguin, 1990).

An interesting selection of varied written texts is to be found in J. Brown and D. Jackson, *Varieties of Writing* (Macmillan, 1984).

A more scholarly study of varieties of written English appears in R. Carter and W. Nash, *Seeing Through Language: A Guide to Styles of English Writing* (Blackwell, 1990).

Aspects of language in literature are covered in some detail by N. F. Blake in *An Introduction to the Language of Literature* (Macmillan, 1990).

Finally, you may like to try W. R. O'Donnell and Loreto Todd's *Variety in Contemporary English* (Allen and Unwin, 1980).

2 Tell us a story: narrative

2.0 Introduction

In this chapter, we will start our explorations of Language and Literature by considering the business of story-telling – and you will discover that whether we're looking at a novel written by one of the 'classic' authors, or a joke told by one of your friends, there are many different ways of looking at **narratives**. The unit will introduce you to a number of the areas for language study shown in Figure 2.1 (page 19).

2.1 Stories around us

On your A-level course, you will spend a lot of time looking at stories. You may have to study at least one novel, enjoy the opportunity of creating a piece of your own fiction, and you may even have to examine the way people tell stories as they speak.

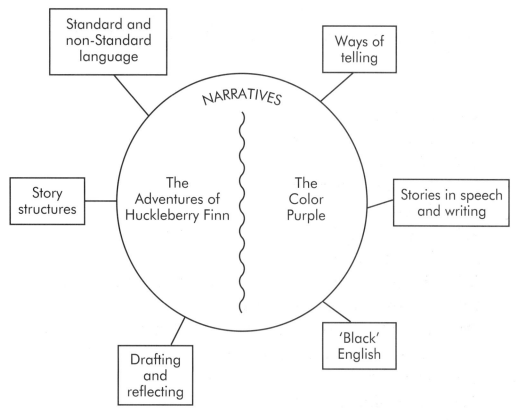

Figure 2.1

So, in this section, we will consider story-telling in a number of ways – and keep coming back to two novels which are often set at A-level – Mark Twain's *The Adventures of Huckleberry Finn* and Alice Walker's *The Color Purple*.

These novels are of particular interest for a number of reasons:

- they both tell their stories from the point of view of their main character
- the narrators are, at first, young and rather immature. They develop and grow as the stories unfold.
- they were both written in varieties of English which we do not usually find represented in written language
- they both raise issues not only about the obvious 'themes' of the stories, but about attitudes towards different varieties of language.

However, before we start to look at these novels in detail, we need to be aware of just how central to all our lives the business of telling stories actually is.

The following exercise will help you realise how many different kinds of stories, and in how many different forms, surround us.

ACTIVITY 4

Think of as many different kinds of story as you can that you are likely to encounter in the course of a day – and then log them on Table 2.1, ticking the appropriate columns for each one:

Table 2.1

Story	True	Fictitious	Spoken	Written	Serious	Humorous	Prose	Verse
e.g. Personal experience	✓		✓			✓	✓	

ACTIVITY 5   WHAT'S THE STORY?

Everyone's list will be different – but if you were to include these, which columns would you tick for:

● a news broadcast
● a joke
● a children's fairy tale ?

and would you include as 'stories' at all:

● a cartoon strip
● a live sports commentary
● making plans for a holiday
● chatting with your friends?

Some types of story may be quite rare – can you think of an example of a true, spoken and serious story in verse?

ACTIVITY 6

Perhaps, too, you're beginning to think about what we actually mean by a 'story' – try to come up with a working definition which brings out the difference between a 'story' and a simple series of statements or events. (You can check your suggestion with the one offered in Section 2.5, The structure of stories.)

COMMENTARY
Whatever answers to these questions you come up with, it does seem that we spend a surprising amount of time organising and shaping our experience into ordered sequences of events – and reading and listening to them, or writing and talking about them.

Making and taking-in stories is one the most fundamental human linguistic activities there is.

2.2 Ways of telling

You will probably have been asked to 'Write a story' in English lessons more times than you can remember. In the following series of exercises, though, we're going to stick to a well-known narrative to experiment with different ways of telling the same story. This will introduce some of the different techniques used by novelists – and also suggest some approaches you can adopt when you come to attempt your own work of fiction.

ACTIVITY 7   WRITING WORKSHOP: EXPERIMENTING WITH NARRATIVE TECHNIQUES

Perhaps you included nursery rhymes or fairy tales in your list of narratives. Choose any one of these that you are familiar with – the exercises work with any – or use the example given here (Jack and Jill).

1 Begin by speaking the story, without any preparation or rehearsal – and tape it. Then, replay the tape and write down exactly what you said – including all the awkward hesitations and slips which you may make.

Such an accurate record of spoken language is called a **transcript**.

2 Write out the story afresh as a straightforward prose narrative, aiming to summarise the main events in one short paragraph. For example:

> *One morning, two children called Jack and Jill set out from their house to fetch water from the well at the top of the hill …*

Already you will begin to notice some of the differences between spoken and written language: list the main differences between your first two versions of the story using Table 2.2 on page 22 (we'll look at the contrasts between speech and writing in some detail in Section 2.4).

3 Now begin the story in the following three ways, and compare the results:
- offer an elaborate description of the setting where the story takes place
- start with a detailed physical description – imagine a close-up camera shot – of one or more of the central characters of the story
- go straight into some dialogue spoken between the characters.

When you've tried all three, discuss the differences and suggest what each of these methods achieves.

4 Stories can be narrated either by someone standing apart from the action, observing and reporting, or by someone who was actually involved in the

Table 2.2

Spoken version	Written version

events themselves. This time we'll experiment with our simple story in four ways:

- write the story as if you were an observer, completely detached from the characters and events, who happened to know everything that happened, who the people were, what they thought and felt, and what they said to each other.

  This method – which tells the story in the **third person** – involves the use of an **omniscient narrator**. For Jack and Jill, the story might begin:

  Jack set out happily on this fine morning to collect his pail of water, keen to impress Jill as he strode energetically towards the well … etc.

- Alternatively, put yourself in the position of someone who was involved in the story, and tell the story entirely as they saw and felt it. It need not be a main character – you could tell Jack and Jill's story, for instance, as if you were a farmer in a neighbouring field!

  Reporting the story from the perspective of 'I' and 'me' is called using the **first person**. (Can you suggest what the **second person is**?) Doing it this way poses a particular challenge – capturing the character of your narrator in the words which you use to tell the story.

- Some modern writers have gone further than this and tried to capture the actual stream of thought experienced by one of the characters as the story is happening. Jack's stream of thought might go something like this:

  I can't understand why it's always down to us to get the water! It's about time they got the bloomin' pipes fixed anyway – six months we've been waiting, and besides, none of the other kids in the village have to go. What's Jill so cheerful about today? Can't stand the way she's forever chewing gum and never shares it. New T-shirt she's got on today … etc

The term '**stream of consciousness**' has been coined to describe this kind of writing.

- A fourth possibility is to combine elements of third-person narrative with that of the stream of consciousness. Here the narrative slips in and out of the feelings and perceptions of one or more of the characters, sometimes observing from the outside, sometimes reporting from within. Some writers call this an '**indirect free style**'.

Identify in this example from Jack and Jill the points where this switch happens:

> *The sun was burning brightly as the two children strode off up the hill towards the distant well. It wasn't fair. Jack always made Jill go along with him, and he never let her carry the bucket – the sexist pig! Jill watched his denim-clad hips sway as he started to ascend the steepest part of the hill …*

Once again, let's think about the advantages of each of these techniques – and how it affects the language you have used. When considering the language you have chosen, you should think about:

- the vocabulary you have used in each version
- how formal or **colloquial** (close to the language of speech) you have made your language
- whether you have you told the story as if it happened in the past, or as if it is happening now (i.e. what **tense** you have used).

Now complete Table 2.3.

Table 2.3

Narrative Technique	Advantages	Choice of language
3rd person – omniscient narrator		
First person		
Stream of consciousness		
3rd person – indirect free style		

ACTIVITY 8   MORE WRITING EXPERIMENTS

We can continue our experiments with a number of other narrative techniques.

1 Stories don't have to begin at the beginning and end at the end! Like film makers such as Quentin Tarantino, the director of the film *Pulp Fiction*, you can use flashbacks and other techniques to change the sequence in which the story's events are narrated. So – try starting with Jack and Jill sprawled on the ground at the foot of the hill … or Jack just at the moment when he loses his balance …

2 Many story-tellers use dialogue to bring the stories to life – but there are several ways of doing so. Speech – and thought – can be reported directly, as in:

'Right!' said Jack

and

'Oh no!' Jill thought to herself

or indirectly, as in:

Jack said that it was all right.

Try selectively using **direct speech** to report the words used by Jack, but only indirect speech to report Jill's speech.

How does this affect the way a reader responds to each of the characters? (Compare this later with the extract from with Jane Austen's *Pride and Prejudice* on page 25.)

3 Whether the sentences you write are short, long, or a mixture of both can create a significantly different feel to your piece. The most obvious ploy would be to start your description of the scene using long sentences, switching to a series of shorter ones when you describe the rapid action of Jack's fall from the well. What is the result?

You could try reversing this – how would you describe the effects this time?

4 You may have already found that the view taken by the narrator of the events being described can convey a somewhat biased picture. This time, try deliberately to put a particular 'spin' on the story by adopting a particular attitude, or **stance**, towards their subject matter. For example:

● tell the story as if you are Jack or Jill, but allow your dislike of the other to influence the way you select and narrate events;

● tell the story (as Jack or Jill) as a young child might see things, perhaps not fully understanding the events you describe or the dialogue you overhear.

Many writers have told their story by using a narrator whose naïvety or eccentricity ultimately makes them untrustworthy. By choosing to tell their stories through the eyes of Huck Finn and Celie, the authors of *The Adventures of Huckleberry Finn* and *The Color Purple* use this technique. Some authors even supply us with alternative versions of events by different narrators whose accounts may conflict with each other so that the reader, like a detective presented with contradictory accounts from different witnesses, must reconstruct the 'truth' of events as best s/he can. Famously, in Agatha Christie's *The Murder of Roger Ackroyd*, the reader is surprised to discover that the murderer on this occasion turns out to be not the butler – but the narrator!

● A third-person narrator, on the other hand, may regard both Jack and Jill as extremely foolish – or admire them as tremendously heroic! Write this epic version of Jack and Jill.

● Now try to create an absolutely objective account of events entirely uncoloured by the point of view of the narrator. Exchange this version with a partner and identify in each other's work evidence of stance in the selection of narration of events.

▷ You may like to discuss the question 'Can any act of narration be an entirely neutral and objective representation of events?' – in relation to news reports and eye-witness accounts.

5 Narrators also adopt a stance towards their readers:
  - they may speak to them in a very detached and distant way, never directly addressing them as 'you' (i.e. using the second person) and remaining entirely impersonal;
  - on the other hand, they may try to form a more intimate relationship with the readers, almost as if they were confiding to them in a fireside chat;
  - then again, they may even seem to challenge and confront the readers, like the narrator of J. D. Salinger's *The Catcher in the Rye*:

    If you really want to hear about it, the first thing you'll probably want to know is where I was born, and what my lousy childhood was like, and how my parents were occupied and all before they had me, and all that David Copperfield kind of crap, but I don't feel like going into it.

    [J. D. Salinger, *The Catcher in the Rye*, 1951]

  Try telling your story in any of these styles.

6 Before leaving our troublesome water-fetchers, you should now attempt an experimental, full-length Jack-and-Jill narrative of your own, deploying a selection of the techniques we've been working with. (This will be a useful preparation for the original writing work you may have to attempt as part of your A-level English course.)

  Let's now observe how these narrative techniques are used in practice by writers – and speakers!

ACTIVITY 9   NARRATIVES IN ACTION

For each of the following extracts A–D, describe the narrative techniques being used and try to comment on the impressions each extract makes on you. Don't forget to look closely at:

- narrative point of view – who's telling?
- stance – attitude of narrator towards both his/her subjects and the readers
- reporting of speech or thought
- sentences and mood.

Extract A

It is a truth universally acknowledged that a single man in possession of a good fortune, must be in want of a wife.

However little known the feelings or views of such a man may be on his first entering a neighbourhood, this truth is so well fixed in the minds of the surrounding families that he is considered as the rightful property of some one or other of their daughters.

'My dear Mr Bennet,' said his lady to him one day, 'have you heard that Netherfield Park is let at last?'

Mr Bennet replied that he had not.

'But it is,' returned she; 'for Mrs Long has just been here, and she told me all about it.'

Mr Bennet made no answer.

Extract B

It was at my sister's wedding – she was married in 1978. She had a photographer coming to take all the photos. He came into the house – you know – and he took photographs in the house of Julie and the bridesmaids and everybody. He was – rather strange, he was very bossy and stand here, stand there, do this, do that or the other and – when we got to the chiurch, after the – service and evetrything and came outside and got all the group photographs start – taken. He was very obstreperous about people taking photographs – you know – at the same time.

Extract C
All the truth of my position came flashing on me; and its disappointments, dangers, disgraces, consequences of all kinds, rushed in in such a multitude that I was borne down by them and had to struggle for every breath I drew. 'Put it,' he resumed, 'as the employer of that lawyer whose name begun with a J, and might be Jaggers – put it as he had come over sea to Portsmouth and had landed there, and had wanted to come on to you. "However, you have found me out," you says just now. Well! however did I find you out? Why, I wrote from Portsmouth to a person in London, for particulars of your address. That person's name? Why, Wemmick.'

I could not have spoken one word, though it had been to save my life. I stood, with a hand on the chair-back and a hand on my breasl, where I seemed to be suffocating – I stood so, looking wildly at him, until I grasped at the chair, when the room began to surge and turn. He caught me, drew me to the sofa, put me up against the cushions, and bent on one knee before me: bringing the face that I now well remembered, and that I shuddered at, very near to mine. '

'Yes, Pip, dear boy, I've made a gentleman on you! It's me wot has done it!'

Extract D
Yes because he never did a thing like that before as ask to get his breakfast in bed with a couple of eggs since the City Arms hotel when he used to be pretending to be laid up with a sick voice doing his highness to make himself interesting for that old faggot Mrs O'Riordan that he thought he had a great leg of and she never left us a farthing ....

COMMENTARY
Extracts A, B and C include some prompt questions, but you can discuss passage D as you wish.

Extract A [Jane Austen, *Pride and Prejudice*, 1813]
Jane Austen's novel focuses on the affairs of the Bennet family.
   What kind of narrator is telling the story?
   What do you notice about the reporting of Mr and Mrs Bennet's speech and what effect does this have?
   What is the narrative stance towards (i) the two characters described and (ii) the reader?

Extract B [Mrs Thompson's narrative, 1996]
This is an example of oral narrative. The narrator is recalling an actual incident which took place at her sister's wedding many years earlier.
   Before we reach the comment about the photographer being 'obstreperous', how has the narrator already used language to convey his attitude towards him?
   There is some representation in the narrative of the photographer's speech. How accurate a record of his actual words do you take it to be?

Extract C [Charles Dickens, *Great Expectations*, 1861]
In this passage from the novel *Great Expectations*, the young narrator, Pip, learns

that the mysterious source of his wealth is not, as he had long supposed, the grand Miss Havisham, but the escaped convict Magwitch whom he had helped many years earlier. Magwitch has now returned, to reveal himself to Pip.

How has the writer conveyed to us the narrator's response to the revelation? (This may, or may not, take the reader of the novel by surprise at this point).

This scene would look very different if narrated either by an onlooker (in the third person) or by Magwitch, who may well expect the boy to be overwhelmed with surprise of a more pleasant kind and to show rather more gratitude! Try rewriting the scene from one of these alternative perspectives.

Extract D [James Joyce, *Ulysses*, 1922]
In this extract from James Joyce's novel *Ulysses*, one of the central characters, Molly Bloom, is drifting off to sleep and allowing a variety of thoughts to float through her head …

2.3 Two literary narratives: *The Adventures of Huckleberry Finn* and *The Color Purple*

Now let's start to look at some examples of the way novelists have constructed literary narratives. In this section, you'll apply some of the ideas you've already encountered to the way Mark Twain and Alice Walker set about telling their stories.

2.3.1 *The Adventures of Huckleberry Finn*

In Activity 10 below, the opening lines of *The Adventures of Huckleberry Finn* are reprinted. The novel was written during the 1880s by Samuel Langhorne Clemens, or Mark Twain as he is better known. It is set in the deep south of the USA along the Mississippi river, and it looks back some forty years to the period before the outbreak of the Civil War and the eventual abolition of slavery.

The story is told by Huck Finn, an ill-educated young boy who runs away to escape the influences of education and civilisation, and who meets up with Jim, a runaway slave.

ACTIVITY 10 LANGUAGE POINTS
Read the extract through a couple of times and use Table 2.4 to record your impressions of the story and the narrator telling it. Jot down any of the language from the text which supports your view.

You don't know about me, without you have read a book by the name of 'The Adventures of Tom Sawyer', but that ain't no matter. That book was made by Mr. Mark Twain, and he told the truth, mainly. There was things which he stretched, but mainly he told the truth. That is nothing. I never seen anybody but lied, one time or another, without it was Aunt Polly, or the widow, or maybe Mary. Aunt Polly – Tom's Aunt Polly, she is – and Mary, and the Widow Douglas, is all told about in that book – which is mostly a true book; with some stretchers, as I said before.

[Mark Twain, *The Adventures of Huckleberry Finn*, edited by Gerald Graff and James Phelan, 1995]

Table 2.4

Statement	✓ if you agree ✗ if you disagree	Evidence
(i) It is a carefully prepared piece of written language		
(ii) The author is not well educated		
(iii) It is lively and friendly		
(iv) The grammar of the extract is poor		
(v) It is a typical opening paragraph of a novel		
(vi) If I wrote an English assignment like this I would be criticised		
(vii) It feels as if the narrator is talking to you		

Exchange points of view before reading the Commentary

COMMENTARY
Statement (i)
Some aspects of the text certainly create the impression of spontaneity and disorganisation – Huck appears to repeat himself, get side-tracked into the question of whether anybody ever tells the truth all the time, and double backs on himself at the end: 'with some stretchers, as I said before'. In short, the piece lacks the kind of coherence we expect from written stories. However, before the book was published, it is likely that the author worked and re-worked his text until he was happy that it created precisely this impression!

Statement (ii)
It sounds as if the person telling the story is using the natural language of his speech – which includes expressions like 'ain't no matter' and 'I never seen anybody' not usually associated with 'education'. But Huck Finn is the narrator – not the author. As we've already discovered, authors can put their stories into the mouths of different narrators – and Clemens himself was a highly literate and learned man.

Statements (iii) and (vii)
Many readers find the narrative style attractively lively – and if you ticked this one you probably ticked (vii) ('It feels as if someone is talking to me') as well. In

fact, it sounds as if Huck talks to us as friends who know a certain amount about him already. The key features here include:

- addressing the reader directly as 'you' (i.e. using the second person) and repeatedly referring to himself in the first person
- repetition, digression and backtracking, creating the impression of spontaneity
- using colloquial expressions not usually found in written language
- claiming outright that he is using speech, when he uses the phrase 'as I said before'
- references to people whom we seem to be supposed to know – Aunt Polly, the widow, Mary – without proper introductions. This **context dependence** (see Table 2.6, page 34) is typical of conversations where we don't need to spell things out if everyone present knows what is being referred to.

Statements (iv) and (vi)

The novel is narrated using the characteristic vocabulary and grammar of a particular region – a nineteenth-century southern **dialect** of the USA. Most written language uses a 'standard' version of English, and attitudes towards such dialects are often a matter of great controversy since our society puts great value on the ability to use the preferred, Standard 'educated' English. Linguists agree, however, that regional dialects follow their own grammatical rules; nevertheless, because our society values the ability to use the preferred, Standard 'educated' English so much, teachers are always likely at least to draw your attention to the fact!

Statement (v)

How you've responded to this one – is it a typical opening of a novel? – will depend on what novels you've read in the past. Most novels in English are written in **Standard English** (or Standard American) – but some writers have tried to follow Mark Twain's example, and we'll look at some more examples of novels written in dialect in Section 2.6.

2.3.2 The Color Purple

Here is the opening of Alice Walker's novel *The Color Purple*. This novel is also set in the southern states of the USA, but unlike *The Adventures of Huckleberry Finn*, is written from within the black community. The book is the life story of its narrator, Celie, who relates events in the form of a series of letters to God (and, later, to her sister). She is 14 when the narrative opens but we see her maturing and ageing as the novel progresses. At first, Celie is the passive victim of the brutality of men, but grows in strength as the novel develops, especially through her close friendship with a singer, Shug Avery.

> *You better not never tell nobody but God. It'd kill your mammy.*
> *Dear God,*
> *I am fourteen years old. – I am – I have always been a good girl. Maybe you can give me a sign letting me know what is happening to me.*
> *Last spring after little Lucious come I heard them fussing. He was pulling on her arm. She say It too soon, Fonso, I ain't well. Finally he leave her alone. A week go by, he pulling on her arm again. She say Naw, I ain't gonna. Can't you see I'm already half dead, an all these chilren.*

She went to visit her sister doctor over Macon. Left me to see after the others. He never had a kine word to say to me. Just say You gonna do what your mammy wouldn't. First he put his thing up gainst my hip and sort of wiggle it around. Then he grab hold my titties. Then he push his thing inside my pussy. When that hurt, I cry. He start to choke me, saying You better shut up and git used to it.

[*The Color Purple*, 1982]

In some ways, Alice Walker's approach to story-telling here is quite similar to Mark Twain's. First, she chooses to tell the story from the point of view of a young and apparently unsophisticated first-person narrator (Celie). Discuss how her choice of words conveys Celie's youthfulness and innocence.

Secondly, Walker uses a non-standard dialect in which to narrate the story. Identify the constructions and expressions which differ from Standard English.

Thirdly, Celie makes several context-bound references to other characters and circumstances with no prior explanation. Find some examples of this.

However, in other ways it is interesting to contrast the two openings.

ACTIVITY 11   COMPARING NARRATIVES

Write down your observations on the different ways in which Mark Twain and Alice Walker have chosen to

● start the narrative (scene setting? introduction to the situation or character? immediate action?)
● establish the character of the narrator and others in the story (what impressions do you receive of Huck Finn and Celie and of any other characters referred to?)
● create a distinctive mood and tone at the beginning of each novel (how much amusement, seriousness, surprise or shock is created by the language of each opening?)
● establish a narrative stance (what different attitudes do Huck Finn and Celie reveal to the events and people to whom they refer?)
● establish a relationship between narrator and reader (you may feel Huck is talking directly to you; on the other hand how is the reader's relationship to Celie and her narrative different?).

2.4 Narratives in speech and writing

You might also have suggested that another feature of these narratives is the informality of the register in each case. Both authors have put into the 'mouths' of their narrators a style of expression which often feels closer to spoken, rather than written language. This is what is meant by a colloquial style (see page 23). In the case of Huck Finn, the illusion that he is talking to us rather than writing for us is deliberate – speaking would come much more easily to Huck! Although Celie's narrative is supposed to be her written thoughts, Alice Walker clearly wants to suggest both their spontaneity and Celie's lack of educational sophistication by having her use the language of speech – though she also uses the predictable abbreviations which we associate with the form of a diary.

So just what is it about the ways these books are written that makes them seem almost spoken? To answer this question we need to look at what speakers actually do when they tell us a story orally – and how spoken and written forms of English differ.

2.4.1 Oral narratives

We'll start by comparing Huck's narrative with the transcript of an actual story told by our first real-life story-teller, Mrs Dodds. (When making a transcript, it is usual not to use the conventional punctuation marks of writing but simply to indicate pauses with (.).)

ACTIVITY 12

As you read the transcript, check it against some of the features we identified in Huck Finn's narrative. Show, by completing Table 2.5, how many of these points the two narratives have in common.

---

right I'll tell you that story about when my Auntie Ivy left me outside the er shop in the pram (.) she come round our house when I was a new baby she said oh is it all right if I take Kathleen for a walk and our mam said oh er well you can as long as you er bring her straight back you know cos she's a new baby and all that so she took me to the shop got what she wanted and come out and she just went straight home and about an hour later she goes to our mamma (.) our mam says to her where's our Kathleen (.) have you left her outside in the pram outside the house she meant and Ivy goes Oh God I've left her outside the shop (.) they ran all the way back down and there I was laid fast asleep in the pram

[Mrs Dodds's narrative]

Table 2.5

Narrative Feature	✓ if present in Huck Finn's narrative	✓ if present in Mrs Dodds's narrative
'Speaking' directly to the reader/listener (i.e. using the 2nd person)		
Use of some non-standard expressions		
Occasional digression, backtracking or clarification		
Reference to other characters with little or no introduction		
Other vague or imprecise references		

You may also have noticed some other features of Mrs Dodds's narrative:

- the natural hesitations (recorded as 'er') and other non-fluency features in her speech
- the use of present-tense forms to tell a story which actually occurred many years ago ('she goes to our mam' … etc.)
- the use of long, continuous 'sentences' frequently joined by the conjunctions 'so' and 'and'
- the use made of dialogue to make the incident dramatic ('oh god I've left her outside the shop').

ACTIVITY 13

You will also find many of these features of spoken narratives in this story recounted by Mrs Marshall. To remind yourself of how a conventional written narrative might differ from an oral account:

1 convert the story into a written version of the events described

2 write a short commentary explaining the changes you have made.

When you write your commentary, you'll need to mention:
- what changes you've made to the length and construction of the sentences
- which words and phrases you've left out completely
- which expressions you've changed because they seem too informal or colloquial for your written account
- which expressions you've changed because they belong to Mrs Marshall's regional speech or dialect.

---

there was this woman right and she had a little girl and she er took her to Flamingoland right and they walked past the penguin bit right (.) you know where you can touch the penguins and em they walked off (.) you know the mother and daughter into the aviary and em (.) the little girl wandered off on her own and her mother was worried and that cos she knew the way to the car so they told her to meet the mother at the car (.) so em the mother went back to the car she was stood at the car and the little girl cane back and the mother was like oh thank god you're OK and that and then they went home (.) so when they went home the mother ran the daughter a bath and em she said to the little girl you get in the bath and I'll go down and make the tea and I'll check on you in ten minutes or so or whatever (.) the mother came up five minutes later and she heard all this splashing and all that (.) you know a lot of splashing for a little girl (.) so the mother walked in and there was the little girl sat in the bath with a baby penguin (.) so she had ha er pinched one of the baby penguins from Flamingoland.

[Mrs Marshall's narrative]

2.4.2 Differences between spoken and written language

For us to understand fully the differences between the forms which spoken and written narratives take, we need to pause to consider the characteristics of speech and writing in general – this investigation will also help our explorations of conversation and dialogue in chapters 4 and 5.

Nowadays, many of us spend so much of our time using the written word that it is easy to forget that language begins with speech – we learn it effortlessly as infants and use it unselfconsciously as adults. We are so used to seeing language that we can forget that language is primarily to be heard, but if you find yourself listening to a speaker of a language which you do not understand, you will realise just what spoken language is really like. Unlike written language, which breaks up our words with spaces, it is usually a fairly continuous stream of sound consisting of varied combinations of a limited number of **vowel** and **consonant** sounds which linguists call **phonemes**. For most speakers of English (for there is some variation between **accents**) there are 44 phonemes.

When we combine two or more of them – taking, say, a 'd' an 'o' and a 'g' to produce 'dog' – the result is a word. The units of meaning into which they in turn are combined we call **phrases** and **sentences**. We string sequences of these together to create **text** and **discourse**.

ACTIVITY 14   TO SPEAK, OR TO WRITE … THAT IS THE QUESTION!

Speech and writing have some interestingly different characteristics – and not just from the point of view of narratives. These differences help determine the different uses or functions of speech and writing in our everyday uses of language.

Use Table 2.6 to answer the question 'When do we use speech, and when writing – and why?'

Table 2.6

	Speech	Discussion points	Writing
A	Conveyed by sounds: 44 phonemes (in the 'standard' accent known as Received Pronunciation); intonation, stress and other **prosodic features** such as pitch, tempo and timbre	1 In what ways does the English spelling system meet the challenge of representing 44 sounds with only 26 letters? 2 How can the meanings which speed, volume and tone convey in speech be captured in writing?	Conveyed by letters and symbols: 26 letters (in English) and punctuation marks
B	Accompanied by gesture, eye-contact and body language (i.e. **paralinguistic features**)	Does this make it easier, or more difficult, to use speech to lie or deceive?	Self-contained – text contains all information
C	Continuous stream of sound, separated by breath pauses	We take it for granted that we know what 'words' are. Try to define what we mean by a 'word'. As you do so, consider whether 'don't' is 1 word or 2; whether 'hat' and 'hats' are 2 separate words, and whether phrases like 'get away with' (meaning to escape without punishment) count as 1 idea or 3 words	Words separated by spaces on the page
D	Usually spontaneous	In which situations would you prefer to use writing because you can prepare your language properly?	Often carefully planned and/or drafted

Table 2.6 *(cont.)*

	Speech	Discussion points	Writing
E	Often contains slips, repetitions, hesitations and fillers (i.e. non-fluency features)	Find some examples of non-fluency features in Mrs Marshall's narrative (page 32)	Initial errors edited out in re-drafting process
F	May be loosely structured and apparently rather disorganised	Which description best fits the opening of *The Adventures of Huckleberry Finn*?	Carefully structured, with logical organisation and paragraphing
G	Short-lived – unless tape-recorded	How might this influence which it is better to use in a particular situation?	Permanent
H	May appear more grammatically simple and repetitive, containing common sentence structures joined by 'and', 'but' and 'so' (i.e. **compound sentences**)	This is an inevitable result of some of the other features listed. Which?	May show greater variation in grammatical construction, including greater complexity
I	Usually constructed by 2 or more people in conversation (i.e. **dialogic**)	Who is in control of what gets talked/written about in each case?	Usually the product of one person working alone (i.e. **monologic**)
J	Speakers seek verbal and non-verbal feedback from listeners	How do listeners show their response to speakers?	No immediate feedback available
K	Often refers closely and implicitly to the circumstances in which it is spoken (i.e. **context-dependent**)	Why are speech and writing always likely to be different in this respect?	Usually makes itself clearly explicit for readers in quite different situations (i.e. **context-free**)
L	The speaker controls speed of delivery	When do you have more control over what you are trying to communicate – as a writer, or as a speaker?	The reader controls how fast s/he consumes the text
M	Learned and produced naturally by children	Which ability do you think our society values more – writing, or speaking?	Only learned and produced with some effort

Table 2.6 (*cont.*)

	Speech	Discussion points	Writing
N	May include more colloquial and non-standard dialect features than is usual in writing	Why shouldn't we find more regional or colloquial language in written texts?	Usually in Standard English
O	Unless recorded or deliberately repeated, it cannot be re-heard by the listener, so not very efficient at conveying dense amounts of information	In what situations can speech convey information more effectively – and why?	Can be re-read – so can convey larger amounts of information
P	Typically spoken at around 150 words per minute	When can reading be a faster way of accessing information?	Reading speeds of around 200 words per minute

COMMENTARY

Sounds and spellings (Discussion point A1)

The relationship between sound and spelling in English is complex, and the subject for a whole book in itself. There are many reasons why English spelling does not correspond to the pronunciations in any uniform way:

- 44 into 26 doesn't go! There are not enough single letters in the English alphabet to allocate one letter to each of the 44 phonemes
- spellings may reflect the former pronunciation and origins of words rather than how they are currently spoken (see Chapter 5, Section 5.3).

Speech in writing (Discussion points A2, B)

Some studies have suggested that as much as 70 per cent of the communication which takes place between people is conveyed through body-language and prosodic features. This is why we often give ourselves away when attempting to lie and deceive with our words! Denied the resources of their bodies and voices, writers have had to devise other ways of conveying subtle meanings, such as:

- punctuation and use of different type-faces (italics, bold print, and other graphological devices) which can imply the volume and stress with which words might be spoken
- a variety of **verbs** to report speech, and imply the pitch, intonation, tempo and attitude of the speaker, e.g. 'Mrs Brown growled' or 'murmured Harry'
- descriptions of the physical actions which accompany speech, allowing readers to draw their own conclusions about the significance of the body language, e.g. 'As I answered each of his questions his fingers drummed mechanically on the desk, his eyes fixed on a distant spot through the window to his right'

- as we have already seen, writers can also do what speakers and listeners cannot, that is, give us direct access to the inner thoughts and feelings of a character. These may or may not be consistent with the actual words spoken, e.g. ' "I'd be happy to accompany you," said Jane, hoping that the tremble in her voice did not betray the mounting anxiety she was working hard to suppress at the thought of enduring even another minute in the company of the insufferable fool.'

▷ Take a passage from any novel which features the representation of dialogue. Identify which of these techniques the writer is using to compensate for the readers not being able to see and hear directly the physical and phonetic messages which accompany the words spoken.

▷ Now convert the passage into a play or filmscript, providing all the instructions which you think the actors would require in order to give a full performance. How much extra information regarding intonation, stress, eye-contact, movement and body language, would the actors need either to be provided with, or to supply for themselves?

Words and lexemes (Discussion point C)

Faced with three 'words' like 'run', 'runs', and 'ran' – which are clearly distinct forms but variations in a single idea – and phrases like 'over the moon' and 'get away from' which consist of several words but convey a single concept (indeed, these phrases can be paraphrased by a single word, such as 'ecstatic' and 'escape'), linguists have introduced the concept of the **lexeme** – a single unit of meaning conveyed through a word or group of words.

The spontaneity of speech (Discussion points D, E, F, G, H)

There are many situations – that vital job application, a speech to a large group of people – where we welcome the opportunity to prepare ahead, drafting and re-drafting as required. Equally, there will be times when the result of not being able to do so is 'putting our foot in it' or 'dropping a clanger' – to cite two interesting metaphors! Nervousness, hesitancy or just the struggle to find the right word can lead us to many kinds of non-fluency.

Mrs Marshall's narrative contains several 'er's and 'em's (non-verbal fillers), 'you know's (verbal fillers), and a mild stutter ('she had ha er pinched'). Nevertheless, this is actually quite a fluent passage, and other speakers may be more prone to break off mid-sentence to start again, or go back to 'self-correct' a word which they feel is not the right one.

Even where only one person is talking, speech may well not follow as clearly organised a path as writing. The illusion of Huck talking in *The Adventures of Huckleberry Finn*, is partly created by the way he has to double back on himself ('with some stretchers, as I said before') and seems to get sidetracked into a mention of 'Aunt Polly, or the widow, or maybe Mary' instead of getting on with the story. This is one of the factors that contributes towards the distinctive grammar of speech: as speech is spontaneous, and we cannot plan our sentences very far ahead, our 'sentences' may lack the tight structure and complexity of some written language, and because they consist of lots of phrases joined with the **conjunctions** 'and', 'but' and 'so', can often go on longer.

If we stumble, stutter or 'put our foot in it', our consolation is usually that it is soon forgotten. This can be a good thing – but, on the other hand, where something has to be remembered or referred to as a matter of record, writing is best. A telephone call of complaint can later be denied – a written letter cannot.

Solo and duet (Discussion points I, J)

As a writer, you have complete control over your text, and you can organise it in the way which allows you to get your message over and affect your reader's response. In conversations, it is a different matter – and it is not always clear who is leading or controlling the direction in which the talk goes. Only in some situations – like interviews – will just one of the speakers largely determine what gets talked about, and in what order. Most informal conversations are apparently more random, but there is an order in their chaos, as we will see in Chapter 4.

As we take part in talk, we seek out eye-contact, body-language that conveys interest in what we have to say, and the kinds of supportive 'Mmm!'s and 'Really?' and 'Did he?!' which some linguists call **back-channel behaviour**.

Knowing me knowing you (Discussion point K)

In talk, we almost always have some direct contact with the person we are addressing, even if it is over a telephone. This means we can decide whether or not they will understand our references to 'this' and 'that', to 'him' and 'her', or to 'that matter we discussed last week'. Although some personal writing – letters, memos, etc – are equally specific in their audience, in other forms of writing – this textbook, for instance – the writer knows very little about the reader. S/he may even be alive at a different time (the future), live in a different place and have few experiences in common with the writer. So, as I write this book, it would be of little use to you if I were to suddenly write 'That thing over there reminds me of what Jonesy was saying last week' instead of 'The unusual cylindrical object in the park near my home reminds me of the observation of Mr Jones, an old friend'.

Huck Finn's context-dependent references, without any introduction, to 'Aunt Polly' and 'the widow' are of this kind.

It comes naturally (Discussion points M, N)

Whereas learning to talk comes as naturally to most human beings as learning to walk, the craft of writing requires years of conscious learning. Even in societies in which literacy was, or is, less universal, writers have enjoyed tremendous prestige, as they are/were likely to be the most privileged members of the community. Nowadays, the written word is so important in our lives that literacy is more valued than ever. How far do your GCSE certificates reflect your speaking and listening skills? Nevertheless, we still value many oral skills, albeit in less official ways. We all envy our friends who can tell a good joke, or give an entertaining speech.

Most of our oral skills are likely to be acquired in informal situations and contexts, and it is in these that many people continue to feel most comfortable. Some speakers may feel less articulate in situations which call for more formal uses of spoken language. Equally, as written language is produced for an often anonymous but widely dispersed audience, it is less usual to find regional dialect or even **slang** on paper (but see Section 2.6). This is partly to do with comprehensibility – readers from throughout the language-community need to understand a written text, not just those individuals who happen to have been brought up in the same region as the author – and partly with prestige. The high prestige which writing has always enjoyed has led to an expectation that forms of language felt to have lower status – such as slang, regional dialect, and swear words – will not be seen in print, except with the saving grace of 'inverted commas'.

Too much information? (Discussion Points L, O, P)

As listeners, our inability to retain a great deal of information conveyed to us via speech forces us to make notes and other written records which will prompt our memory in future. On the other hand, because writing is monologic you cannot ask a piece of text to clarify or put in other words a point which you cannot understand! Devoid of eye-contact, gesture and the expressive powers of prosodic features, a writer may be less effective in assisting understanding than a human agent.

However, as a reader you can 'skim' through or ignore whole chunks of text which do not interest you until you find the information you are looking for. As a listener, we can often be trapped, thinking 'when is s/he going to get to the point', and too polite to shout out 'Come on, get on with it!'

ACTIVITY 15   MORE NARRATIVES

Read the seven extracts A–G, which are from different narratives. Only one of them is a genuine oral narrative – but some of the others incorporate a few of the features usually found in speech. Using the scale in Table 2.7 on page 39, arrange the seven pieces according to how similar to, or different from spoken narratives you consider them to be – and give your reasons.

Extract A

And the same day, when the even was come, he saith unto them, Let us pass over unto the other side. And when they had sent away the multitude, they took him even as he was in the ship. And there were also with him other little ships. And there arose a great storm of wind, and the waves beat into the ship, so that it was now full. And he was in the hinder part of the ship, asleep on a pillow: and they awake him, and say unto him, Master, carest thou not that we perish?

Extract B

It aint like your regular sort of day.
Bernie pulls me a pint and puts it in front of me. He looks at me, puzzled, with his loose, doggy face but he can tell I don't want no chit-chat. That's why I'm here, five minutes after opening, for a little silent pow-wow with a pint glass.

Extract C

So Jim went to work and told me the whole thing right through, just as it happened, only he painted it up considerable. Then he said he must start in and "terpret' it, because it was sent for a warning.

Extract D

One of my uncles started to take photographs over his shoulder and he didn't like it at all – he got into a proper paddy and he walked off and left everybody to it. So one of the groom's brothers went after him, but he wasn't having it, and he just disappeared.

Extract E

On holiday in Bournemouth, where both my grandmothers lived, and conveniently there is an away match at Southampton. So I book a coach ticket, travel along the coast and squirm through a packed Dell to the far edge of the terrace; and the next day, there I am on the bottom left of the screen every time a corner is taken.

Extract F

A chair, a table, a lamp. Above, on the white ceiling, a relief ornament in the shape of a wreath, and in the centre of it a blank space, plastered over, like the place in a face where the eye has been taken out. There must have been a chandelier, once. They've removed anything you could tie a rope to.

Extract G

Harpo mope. Wipe the counter, light a cigarette, look outdoors, walk up and down. Little Squeak run long all up under him trying to git his tension. Baby this, she say, Baby that. Harpo look through her head, blow smoke.

Table 2.7

	Extract	Reasons
(most like speech) 1		
2		
3		
4		
5		
6		
(least like speech) 7		

COMMENTARY

Extract A [St Mark's Gospel, 4: 35 – 38, Authorised Version, 1611]
Although we know this as very definitely a written text, generations of church-goers would have known their Bible narratives less as texts than as stories spoken from the pulpit – and the text does have some features reminiscent of oral

narrative. Most notable, perhaps, is the simple, repetitive compound-sentence structure indicated by the frequent use of the conjunction 'and'. In written form, it appears as if the text-writer has 'broken' the precept about sentences not beginning with 'and' – but if read aloud, it can be heard as a virtually continuous stream of narrative similar to many spoken tales.

Extract B [Graham Swift's Booker prize-winning novel, *Last Orders*, 1996]
Like Huckleberry Finn, Swift's narrator confronts the reader directly, using colloquial ('chit-chat', 'pow-wow', 'fiver') and dialectal ('It aint', 'I don't want no') language. The use of the present tense ('Bernie pulls me a pint') has the effect of giving a running commentary on events actually taking place now. However, the carefully measured sentences might alert us to its literary origins!

Extract C [Mark Twain, *The Adventures of Huckleberry Finn*]
As Huck rather condescendingly recounts his companion Jim's own account of his experiences, the phrase 'only he painted it up considerable' clearly belongs to colloquial speech. If you know the whole book, this may strike you as particularly ironic, as the 'painting up' of events in the interest of telling a good story is a characteristic of oral narratives which Huck himself demonstrates amply elsewhere!

Extract D [Transcript of a recording of Mrs Thompson, 1996]
Many familiar features of oral narratives here – the frequent use of 'and' and 'so' to string sentences together, colloquial phrases like 'proper paddy' and 'he wasn't having it' – but the fluency of this speaker's account reminds us that not all oral narratives are necessarily marred by obvious non-fluency features!

Extract E [Nick Hornby, *Fever Pitch*, 1992]
The opening sentence adopts a kind of diary shorthand (instead of 'I was on holiday' …) and so feels closer to writing – but the writer does slip into the present tense to lend immediacy to the events, as many oral storytellers are instinctively inclined to do.

Extract F [Margaret Atwood, *The Handmaid's Tale*, 1985]
Although the initial rapid series of impressions suggests the narrator's stream of thoughts, the 'you' here (meaning 'anyone') is not speaking directly to the reader and the standard form of vocabulary and expression is characteristic of written language. This is consistent with the idea that the whole of the handmaid's story is actually a written document, discovered after her death. (See the Historical Note which ends the novel.)

Extract G [Alice Walker, *The Color Purple*, 1983]
The non-standard grammar of this extract (especially the verb forms), typical of the novel as a whole, reflects the natural speech of the narrator. However, the novel is presented as a series of the narrator's diary entries. So, just as the texts of less sophisticated writers – such as young children learning to write – resemble speech, so Celie's language remains richly colloquial. On the other hand, the sequence of short, unconnected sentences is less typical of spoken language.

2.5 The structure of stories

In Section 2.1, we raised the question 'what makes a story more than just a sequence of events?' Linguists and other researchers have attempted to answer this question by trying to find a common pattern, or structure, in the stories which people tell. One of these, William Labov, taped hundreds of volunteers narrating stories and proposed the well-known structure shown in Table 2.8.

Table 2.8

Element of narrative	Function
Abstract	Summarises or previews the story to follow
Orientation	Establishes the vital context for the story – who is involved, and where and when the events are taking place
Complication	A problem causes the story to develop towards a crisis
Resolution	The problem or crisis is resolved, either happily or otherwise
Evaluation	The significance or importance of the events of the narrative is assessed

ACTIVITY 16

Labov's research was carried out by analysing monologues spoken by young African-American men. Does it accurately describe story structures produced in other contexts?

Use Table 2.9 on page 42 to put Labov's structure to the test on a number of different narratives as follows:

1 Check it against our own story of Jack and Jill.

2 See how well the model describes some of the other well-known narratives which have been passed down orally over many generations, the stories we now know as 'fairy tales' or, more properly, as 'folk-tales'.

3 Examine the following recording of Mr Brown's story, made by students in 1996. How accurately does Labov's model describe the structure of Mr Brown's narrative?

---

right OK then I'm going to tell you a story about me when I was about um probably eight (.) my dad was a joiner then so he owned a van and he took me and my sister to Flanborough docks in the van (.) when I think about it now I don't know exactly what happened (.) but um anyway my theory is my younger sister pushed me off (.) so anyway I landed on my ankles no I mean landed on my feet and straight away I heard my ankles snap and it bloody hurt (.) I mean it hurt a lot (.) so while I was kicking and screaming my dad and sister had to carry me to my dad's van (.) now I thought we should be going to hospital but my (.) dad knew best and took me home (.) a few days later I was in agony (.) my mum had had me (.) uh (.)she's had me walking round like there was nothing wrong (.) well eventually she took me to the doctors and he asked me to climb on the bed and jump off (.) so I did it then he said ha ha ha did it hurt ha ha ha (.) I sort of managed to get out a um (.) no (.) ahhh (.) so he said well there you go then there's nothing wrong with you (.) so I limped out close to tears while mum thanked the doctor for proving her right (.) well to cut a long story short five weeks later I was still in pain so we went to the hospital (.) it turned (.) it turned out I'd broken both my ankles and I had had to spend the next two weeks in plaster (.) I can't remember how long (.) it was (.) well (.) ha ha ha(.)an experience (.) I'll never forget it cos my sister felt terrible and was (.) and she was really nice to me after that (.) it's good that I can laugh about it now though (laughter).

[Transcript of Mr Brown's story]

As you examine this narrative, you may notice the frequency with which some phrases appear – 'Right OK then', 'So anyway', 'So, while I was kicking', 'Well eventually', 'Well, to cut a long story short'. What function do these seem to have in retaining the interest of the listener and underlining the structure of the story?

4 Now carry out some fieldwork of your own. Tape-record and transcribe a friend/neighbour/member of your family relating a story of their own. When you have obtained your transcript, see how well the elements of your subject's story fits into the pattern proposed by Labov. To ensure the data you collect is as authentic and natural as possible:

- do not tell your subjects you are investigating their language or story-telling techniques! Instead, suggest that you are researching local history/childhood memories/etc. for a project, and ask them to recount an incident which they remember as being particularly significant or memorable which could be taped and used.
- Always ask permission of your subject to tape, transcribe and make use of their material.

Table 2.9

	Jack and Jill	**Your chosen folk tale**	**Mr Brown's story**	**Your transcript**
Abstract				
Orientation				
Complication				
Resolution				
Evaluation				

2.5.1 Written and literary narratives

Labov's structure was based on his study of oral narratives – however, written stories may not conform so obviously to this pattern. If we return to your first written version of Jack and Jill, it is unlikely that you included an Abstract stage, as your opening probably went straight into the Orientation ('Once upon a time there were two children called Jack and Jill' etc.). Why do you think written narratives are less likely to include this kind of preview of the story to follow?

Similarly, although some written stories (such as old-fashioned children's stories, fables and, occasionally, newspaper reports) may include some explicit Evaluation, many may not. Novelists will often prefer to allow the significance of the events they are narrating to remain implicit – and as a reader, you'll have to 'read between the lines'.

It is a fair bet, though, that most stories will have elements of Complication – the various adventures and developments which make up the major part of the story – and Resolution.

ACTIVITY 17   NARRATIVE STRUCTURE IN PRACTICE: CONSEQUENCES

You may have come across the old parlour game called 'Consequences' – you can play a variation of this game based on Labov's model to demonstrate his structure in practice.

1 At the top of a sheet of paper, provide the essential elements of the Orientation of a story, i.e.:

> the name(s) of your character(s)
> a place in which they are situated
> a time when the story is set
> an action which the character(s) were carrying out.

Pass the paper on!

2 Using the circumstances described in the Orientation you now have in front of you, add to the sheet a Complication which develops the situation and sets up some kind of problem or crisis.
Pass the sheet on.

3 Now it's your task to provide the Resolution to the problem presented to you by the previous two parts of the story in front of you.
Pass the paper on once again.

4 Finally, provide an Evaluation to the story in front of you by commenting on its significance, moral, memorability, etc.

ACTIVITY 18   OTHER NARRATIVE STRUCTURES

Can we also use this kind of structure to describe the kinds of extended narrative produced in written genres? Test it with the following:

- short stories of different genres (e.g. ghost stories, romantic fiction)
- detective stories
- a newspaper report
- the novel(s) or short stories you are studying as your set texts such as *The Color Purple* and *The Adventures of Huckleberry Finn*.

Keep asking the question 'Does this oral-narrative model fit, or do I need to devise different ways of describing how these narratives are organised?'

COMMENTARY

Many love stories follow Labov's pattern – boy meets girl, boy and girl encounter problems, but in the end love conquers all etc. – though not all of them (think about *Romeo and Juliet*) necessarily end happily!

Other genres of story may also follow this pattern, though if you are studying James Joyce's collection of stories *Dubliners*, you may find that some of the Resolutions (as in the story of Eveline) disappoint because they do little more than take his characters back to their original situation, which helps to explain what Joyce described as the feeling of 'paralysis' in his characters.

Many detective stories are somewhat different in that we are often presented with the 'end' of the story (i.e. the murder of the victim) near the beginning of the narrative. The rest of the narrative involves us in trying to fill in the missing gaps – thus reconstructing the Complication stage in order to 'solve' the murder.

News reports are very different. We would soon become impatient if we had to wait until the end of the report to find out 'who dunnit'! Journalists often manage to summarise the entire story – certainly the Orientation, Complication and Resolution sections – in the first couple of sentences. In fact, the opening paragraphs of news reports may often act as an Abstract, summarising the key elements of the story that follows. How far news reporters should, or do also offer a judgement or Evaluation on the events they report is a matter for some debate.

The length and complexity of novels will, of course, entail more involved structures than our rather simple model, which can only describe in the very broadest way the design of the narrative. In the case *of The Adventures of Huckleberry Finn*, after the escape of Huck and the arrival of Jim (the Orientation), there is not so much one Complication as a whole series of them – each with its own individual resolution. Novels which follow this episodic pattern – a series of adventures, often the result of the main character's travels from place to place – are sometimes called **picaresque** novels. These were particularly popular in the eighteenth and nineteenth centuries as they often lent themselves very well to publication in several instalments – rather like modern soap operas.

If *The Color Purple* is your text, you will have noted that although it is not a true picaresque story (because the central character neither travels nor seeks the adventures which happen), the story of Celie's development, which is the central Complication phase, consists of a series of distinct elements. Nevertheless, as we can see in Table 2.10 (page 45), these tend to be much less self-contained than the episodes in Huck's narrative.

Table 2.10: **The structure of** *The Adventures of Huckleberry Finn* **and** *The Color Purple*

	Huckleberry Finn	**The Color Purple**
Abstract	None given – unless you include the 'Notice' offered by Twain: 'Persons attempting to find a motive in this narrative will be prosecuted; persons attempting to find a moral in it will be banished; persons attempting to find a plot in it will be shot'. As you read the rest of the book, though, you may decide that this is less than a reliable guide to the story which follows.	None given
Orientation	• Huck's discontent with the Widow's attempt to 'sivilize' him. • His initial adventures with Tom Sawyer: these may at first look like the start of a Complication phase, but they prove to be a false start – they are only playing! • The introduction of Jim and the return of Pap completes the preparation for the adventures which are to follow	• Celie's briefly recounted childhood, her father's abuse, and the circumstances of her marriage to Mr –. • The departure of Nettie
Complication	• Huck's abduction by his father, his escape from the cabin and his subsequent meeting with Jim on Jackson's island all establish the framework within which all the subsequent adventures take place. These episodes are often like 'sub-complications'; self-contained stories-within-a-story, which include their own orientations, complications and resolutions. Think how this might apply to the Grangerfords and Hendersons episodes in chapters 17 and 18, for example.	• The introduction into the novel of Shug Avery, and her growing influence on Celie, triggers many of the key developments in the plot and Celie's character • The development of the stories of Harpo, Sofia and Squeak – and the prolonged absence of Nettie – provide the framework for Celie's development.
Resolution	• Jim achieves his freedom – but Huck then threatens, in the final paragraph, to set a new narrative going as he sets out for the west.	• Celie is reunited with Nettie – and achieves something of the freedom and happiness which she has been seeking
Evaluation	• Mark Twain makes Huck play down any such importance, as he says, finally, that 'if I'd a knowed what a trouble it was to make a book I wouldn't a tackled it'. However, this is yet another deliberate use of the naïve narrator; the true significance of the tale is left for the readers to infer!	• Left implicit throughout – but Celie begins her final letter with a prayer of thanksgiving which suggests the significance of the events she has described: 'Dear God, dear stars, dear trees, dear sky, dear peoples. Dear Everthing. Dear God. Thank you for bringing my sister Nettie and our children home.'

2.6 Whose language – Standard or non-Standard?

Both *The Adventures of Huckleberry Finn* and *The Color Purple* present us with varieties of English which may be rather different from our own – and which are certainly different from the kinds of English we are used to seeing written down in books. Usually, the texts we read use the spelling, vocabulary and grammar which educated English-users consider to be 'acceptable' or 'good' English, a variety which we call **Standard English**. However, many speakers of the language do not use these forms exclusively – in fact, there are hundreds of variations in the language that English-speakers use.

These variations are of three main types:

- differences in pronunciation, i.e. **accent**
- differences in vocabulary, i.e. **lexis**
- differences in construction of phrases and sentences, or grammar i.e. **dialect**.

2.6.1 Pronunciation and accent

The actual sound of people's speech – how they pronounce the vowel and consonant phonemes of English, and the distinctive quality of the ups-and-downs (i.e. **intonation**), pace, and stress of their speech – is a matter of **accent**.

Accents vary enormously throughout the British Isles and, indeed, the English-speaking world. Even within a local community, the variety and 'strength' of the local accent varies considerably, and is affected by many different factors – not just where you were born, but the accents of your family, your social background, the schools you attend and the accents of your friends.

Thanks to the BBC we are also very familiar with a kind of standardised pronunciation of English which strikes our ears as neutral, educated and professional. This is the so-called **Received Pronunciation** – **RP** for short – which we hear daily from newsreaders, announcers and the voice-overs on many advertisements. However, only a very small percentage of English speakers actually sound like this – as you can easily discover by listening to the different ways in which speakers from different regions pronounce words such as 'grass', 'butter', 'down', 'car park' and 'toast'.

ACTIVITY 19   ACCENTS ON PAPER

Extracts A–F are from written narratives. Try to 'hear' in your mind's ear the kind(s) of accent(s) which you think the writer has tried to convey through his/her choice of orthography (i.e. spelling and punctuation). List these in Table 2.11 and place each on the map in Figure 2.2 (page 47).

Extract A

There was no reply to my question; and on looking round, I saw only Joseph bringing in a pail of porridge for the dogs and Mrs Heathcliff, leaning over the fire, diverting herself with burning a bundle of matches which had fallen from the chimney-piece as she restored the tea-canister to its place.

The former, when he had deposited his burden, took a critical survey of the room; and, in cracked tones, grated out:

'Aw woonder hagh yah can faishion tuh stand thear i' idleness un war, when all on 'em's goan aght! Bud yah're a nowt, and it's noa use talking – yah'll niver mend uh yer ill ways; bud, goa raight t'divil, like yer mother afore ye!'
I imagined for a moment, that this piece of eloquence was addressed to me …

Table 2.11

Extract	Orthographic features	Region
A		
B		
C		
D		
E		

Figure 2.2

Extract B

See the thing is, with respect, it doesnay matter whether ye sleep on it or no; ye're still gony have to say aye or naw; when the time comes, ye follow? That's the bottom line. Whether ye take a week to work it out, at the end of the day ye're still left with the decision. Either ye go for it or ye dont.

Extract C

'And are you going to bide in Casterbridge, sir?' she asked.
'Ah – no!' … 'I'm only passing thirrough! I am on my way to Bristol, and on frae there to foreign parts.'
'We be truly sorry to hear it,' said Solomon Longways, '… and verily, to mak' acquaintance with a man a-come from so far, from the land o' perpetual snow … 'tis a thing we can't do every day …'
'Nay, but ye mistake my country. … Eh, but you should take a summer jarreny to Edinboro' … and you would never say 'tis the land of … perpetual snow.'

Extract D

How's it goin', said Jimmy.
Howyeh, Jim, said Outspan.
Howayeh, said Derek. …
Been ridin' annythin' since I seen yis last?, Jimmy asked them.
No way, said Outspan. – We've been much too bust for tha' sort o' thing. Isn't tha' righ'?
Yeah, that's righ', said Derek.
Puttin' the finishin' touches to your album?, said Jimmy.
Puttin' the finishin' touches to our name, said Outspan.

Extract E

'Show us where you live! Pint out the place!'
I pointed to where our village lay, on the flat in-shore among the alder trees and pollards, a mile or more from the church ….
'You young dog!' …'What fat cheeks you ha' got.' … 'Darn me if I couldn't eat 'em if I han't half a mind to't!
I earnestly expressed my hope that he wouldn't, and held tighter to the tombstone on which he had put me …
'Now lookee here!' said the man. 'Where's your mother?'

Extract F

'And you are a miner!' she exclaimed in surprise.
'Yes. I went down when I was ten.'
She looked at him in wondering dismay.
'When you were ten! And wasn't it very hard?' she asked.
'You soon get used to it. You live like th' mice, an' you pop out at night to see what's going on.'
'It makes me feel blind,' she frowned.
'Like a moudiwarp!' he laughed. 'Yi, an' there's some chaps as does go round like moudiwarps.' He thrust his face forward in the blind, snout-like way of a mole,

seeming to sniff and peer for direction. …
She looked at him, with a touch of appeal in her pure humility.
'Shouldn't ter like it?' he asked tenderly. ''Appen not, it 'ud dirty thee.'
She had never been 'thee'd' and 'thou'd before.

COMMENTARY

Extract A, from Haworth, Yorkshire [Emily Brontë, *Wuthering Heights*, 1847]
This passage contrasts the speech of the servant Joseph with the 'standard'
language of the narrator, Lockwood. The novel is set in Yorkshire, on the moors
around the village of Haworth, and Bronte has attempted to represent the accent
of the region in several ways:

1 The distinctive vowel sounds of this accent are variously shown. 'Goa' and
   'noa' for go and no reflect the characteristic extended vowel sound in such
   words, and other vowel variations are shown as 'niver' and 'divil' (for never
   and devil), 'Aw' for I, 'woonder' for wonder, 'faishion' for fashion, etc.
2 Joseph's guttural consonant sounds are expressed both in the use of the
   digraph 'gh' (in words like 'aght' for out and 'raight' for right) and in the
   description of his 'cracked tones'.
3 Deviant spellings are used even when the actual pronunciation of some words
   will not, in fact, differ hugely from standard. The word 'to' will, even in RP
   speakers' mouths, sound more like 'tuh' than 'to' or /tu:/, because it is usually
   said rapidly and not given particular stress, as in a phrase such as 'going to the
   station'.

So, would Joseph's 'to' in 'fashion to stand there' really sound very different
from the narrator's in 'addressed to me'? Probably not, but Bronte attempts to
represent the reality of Joseph's speech phonetically – 'tuh' – whilst retaining the
standard spelling for Lockwood's.

Extract B, Glasgow [James Kelman, *How Late It Was, How Late*, 1994]
The most consistent feature of the Glaswegian accent represented here is the
distinctive sound of the vowel in the words which are usually spelt 'you' and 'your'.
Even English RP speakers will only rarely give the full value to the 'oo' sound in
'you', but Kelman tries to suggest the distinctly Scots sound by preferring 'ye'.
   He also represents as single words 'disnay' and 'gony', corresponding to the
Standard English 'doesn't' and 'going to', reflecting both the elision (i.e. running
together of sounds) and vowels of the local speech.

Extract C, Dorset and Scotland [Thomas Hardy, *The Mayor of Casterbridge*, 1886]
In this passage, Donald Farfrae, a young Scot who is passing through a village in
the Dorset area which Thomas Hardy called Wessex, is chatting with the locals –
the landlady of an inn, Mrs Stannidge (who speaks first) and Solomon Longways,
a labourer.
   Hardy here attempts to represent two contrasting regional varieties. The precise
whereabouts of Farfrae's Scottish home remains vague – and Hardy limits himself
to suggesting the distinctive rolled 'r' in words such as 'jarreny' for journey and
'thirrough' for through. Like Kelman, he uses 'ye' for you, and also uses a range
of interjections such as 'Nay', 'Eh,' and 'Ah'.
   The Dorset accent of Mrs Stannidge and Solomon Longways is largely
represented by using apostrophes to suggest the omission of sounds – 'o'' for 'of,'
''tis' for it is – but 'mak' for make seems also to imply a different vowel sound.

Extract D, Dublin [Roddy Doyle, *The Commitments*, 1988]
In this novel, the first of Doyle' s *Barrytown Trilogy*, he tells the story of an attempt
to create a successful rock band on a working-class Dublin estate. Here, several of
the main characters meet to discuss the vital question of the band's name.

Doyle selects a number of features of the Dublin accent for representation. Most
noticeable is the use of /n/ rather than /ng/ at the ends of words like 'goin",
'ridin" and 'finishin". This is, however, a feature of many regional accents, and
even of the rather old-fashioned aristocratic form of 'marked' RP (as in 'huntin"
and 'fishin"). More distinctly Dublin, perhaps, is the loss of the final 't' in words
like 'righ" for right and 'tha" for that. Doyle also tries to show the distinct
pronunciation of the vowel in 'yis' for you(s).

Extract E, London [Charles Dickens, *Great Expectations*, 1861]
In this passage near the beginning of Dickens's story, the young narrator, Pip,
encounters the escaping convict, Magwitch, in a churchyard near his home on the
Kent marshes.

Again, most of the devices used by Dickens to represent the London speech of
Magwitch are familar – the use of apostrophes for elided consonant sounds in
words like 'ha" for have, the "em' for them. In this extract, he only shows one
example of a regionally distinctive vowel pronunciation – 'pint' for point.

Extract F, Nottingham [D. H. Lawrence, *Sons and Lovers*, 1913]
In this extract, the narrator is relating the courtship of Walter Morel, a miner, and
Gertrude Coppard. Once again, the regional speech of one character, Walter, is
clearly contrasted with the standardised language of not only the narrator but
also his future wife, Gertrude. There are numerous dialectal and accentual
features shown here. The accent is mainly represented by the omission of letters –
'an", 'th", "appen', and "ud'. Whilst the "appen' and "ud' reflect the difference
between Nottinghamshire pronunciation and RP, even RP speakers may, in
natural fluent speech, shorten or even omit the final sounds in the words 'and'
and 'the'.

On the other hand, some very distinctive features of the regional accent, such as
the vowel sound in 'like', are not shown. So, as with *Wuthering Heights*, these
spellings are selective visual signs of an accent rather than part of a
comprehensively phonetic representation of them.

The extract might also make you ask the question 'Does the orthography of
Standard English imply a particular accent, i.e. RP?' Although Standard English
may in fact be spoken in a variety of accents, in some of these extracts we are
invited to assume that the speaker whose speech is shown in standard spelling is
also likely to speak RP. This is exploited by Lawrence here to imply a significant
difference in the social backgrounds of Walter and Gertrude (see Section 2.6.6).

So, in looking closely at this selection of extracts, perhaps you can begin to reach
some conclusions about the ways in which regional accents have been
represented in novels.

- It is very difficult to achieve convincing representations of regional accents on
  paper that remain easily intelligible. Some readers report considerable
  difficulty in working out what Emily Brontë's Joseph is actually saying at many
  points in the novel!
- As a result, writers may be very selective in the way they try to indicate just a
  small number of the distinctive features of a particular accent.

- The limited range of devices available to a writer to show different accents – short of resorting to a complete phonetic transcription, which only linguists would be able to de-cipher – means that it is especially difficult to distinguish between different regional accents.
- Where standard orthography is used – as it is by most of the narrators in the novels we have looked at so far – we automatically seem to 'hear' it as a standard pronunciation or RP. This is usually the 'voice' of the narrator of the story.
- Writers may use unorthodox orthography, therefore, to suggest the differences between their characters and their narrators, both in terms of their geographical origins and their social class, as we tend to associate regional speech with people from different social backgrounds.

We will return to this point when we have considered the way writers represent regional lexis and grammar (dialect) as well as pronunciation (accent).

2.6.2 Lexis

The vocabulary available to English speakers is vast. Attempts to produce a figure for the total numbers of words – or lexemes – are doomed because the speed at which words appear in the language and develop new meanings will defeat even the most up-to-date dictionary. Estimates of the current extent of the vocabulary of English vary widely, but are all in excess of 500,000 words. A great many of these words may belong to highly specialised, technical or scientific registers, but a large 'core' belongs to Standard English. These are the words which are regarded as acceptable in writing and in formal and semi-formal situations.

The words which haven't made it – yet ! – into this lexical 'Premier League' may be variously described:

- **Slang** is the 'unofficial' language used by all kinds of social groups. Some kinds of slang may be limited to a particular close-knit group or sub-culture, such as dance-music enthusiasts or drug-users. In such cases it may have – or have had in the past – the deliberate function of cloaking private or illicit activity. Other kinds of slang may be almost universal throughout a language community – such as the words 'booze', 'fag', 'telly', etc.
- **Colloquialism** literally means the language of speech, and the term may sometimes be used to describe slang. However dictionary editors may use the description to imply that a word or phrase is informal, but close enough to Standard English to avoid the stigma of being branded slang!
- **Dialect** includes words and phrases which lie outside Standard English and which are limited to a particular region.
- **Vulgarisms** are terms which are not generally considered 'polite' – however widespread their use may be! The stronger 'swear' words may also be described as taboo.

This is not to overlook the fact that even within Standard English, we can still select from a wide spectrum of formality and informality – we can say 'Could you sub some cash as I'm a bit short at the moment?' or 'I wonder if you would consider making a small loan to alleviate my temporary financial embarrassment?'

ACTIVITY 20   THE FORMALITY SPECTRUM GAME

We can easily begin to explore this rich repertoire which all native speakers have at their fingertips:

1 Draw lots from slips of paper numbered 1–7 without revealing which number you have drawn.

2 Your task is to produce the level of formality/colloquiality/slang appropriate to your number, taking 1 as the most formal, and 7 as the loosest slang (see Figure 2.3). Think of the language you use as a set of clothes – 1 being a formal dinner suit or ball gown, 7 your scruffiest jeans and T-shirt!

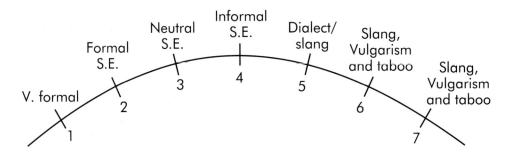

Figure 2.3

You might try this for several situations such as:
● asking someone to open a window
● complaining that you've been short-changed
● asking for a date
● report favourably on a particularly enjoyable night out.

3 As each person speaks or reads their version of the situation, the rest should try to deduce the number s/he had been allocated on the basis of the perceived degree of formality of their language.

4 As you work this out, classify the most significant words and phrases. Which would you describe as vulgarisms or slang or dialect?

Classifying lexical items in this way may throw up problems – we will return to these shortly.

We can now see that as speakers, every word or phrase we use represents a choice of style which we have to make. Just as we choose to wear whatever clothes seem to be most appropriate to different occasions, so we turn to the wardrobe of our language to supply us with the right style of expression.

If this is true in everyday situations, when we have little time to make our selections, how much more so is it true for writers of literature, whose selection of language is painstakingly deliberate?

ACTIVITY 21   CHANGING STYLES

Let's begin to explore the kinds of lexical choices made by writers, and the differences these make. We'll try to reconstruct just one sentence from a well-known novel. The story is being narrated by the guest of a landlord, whose household has just entertained him to dinner.

1   Consider some different ways of expressing the idea 'when the meal was finished', e.g.:
    - when we'd finished eating
    - after the meal
    - after we'd put away the grub
    - the business of eating being concluded
    - once we had enjoyed our repast, etc.

2   Now express the idea that there was a period of silence after the meal, e.g.:
    - nobody said nowt
    - all was silence
    - no one uttered a word
    - there was a distinct lack of conversation, etc.

3   Finally, suggest different ways of saying that the narrator went over to a window to see what the weather was like, e.g.:
    - I went ovver to 't window tuh look at weather, like
    - I conducted a meteorological inspection through the window
    - I approached a window to examine the weather, etc.

4   Now connect together the three elements of the sentence, keeping each version in a consistent style. You will produce some parallel, but very different narratives, such as:

    A   *After we'd put away the grub, nobody said nowt, so I went ovver to't window to look at weather, like.*

    and

    B   *The business of eating being concluded, and no one uttering a word of sociable conversation, I approached a window to examine the weather.*

5   What differences do you find in the impressions the two versions convey of the narrator, his character and his attitudes? Your answer will be largely influenced by the lexical choices you made.

    In fact, version B is the actual account given by Mr Lockwood of his first encounter with Heathcliff's household in *Wuthering Heights*. How does Brontë's choice of vocabulary and expression influence your response to the narrator?

ACTIVITY 22   TAKE YOUR PICK

The nature and importance of a writer's lexical choices can easily be seen if we look at the following short passage from *The Color Purple*, in which Celie, the narrator, describes how one of her new husband's children attacks her on the day of her wedding.

The account begins:

> *I spend my wedding day running from the oldest boy. He twelve. His mama died in his arms and he don't want to hear nothing bout no new one.*

The boy is about to attack Celie and cause a serious head wound by striking her with a rock. Let's consider Alice Walker's choices. She could have written:

- he grabbed a big rock

or

- he picked up a rock

or

- he seized a small boulder

or

- he lifted a large stone

and then had at least the options of writing:

- he smashed it onto my head
- he attacked me with it
- he laid my head open
- he nearly killed me with it.

Celie's style of narration, at this point in the novel, is characterised by a lack of emotional expression. Which of these possibilities would convey most effectively her unsentimental, matter-of-fact way of coping with the various kinds of cruelty and humiliation heaped upon her?

Alice Walker's narrative actually continues:

> *He pick up a rock and laid my head open. The blood run all down tween my breasts. His daddy say Don't do that! But that's all he say.*

ACTIVITY 23   DICTIONARIES

It is difficult to know how to keep track of the bewildering lexical variety of English. Usually, we expect dictionaries to be our guides – especially in cases of dispute during a game of Scrabble or the television game show 'Countdown'! But how much help are they when it comes to deciding what is Standard English, slang or dialect?

In this activity, we'll survey a range of dictionaries and the information they provide, using Table 2.12 on page 55 to record our findings.

1　Gather together at least three different dictionaries and survey a variety of common words in English which might raise some interesting questions. Some suggestions are offered in Table 2.12 – but also add your own. They might include:

- new words
- words related to technological inventions
- commonly used abbreviations
- words which you feel are on the borders of 'respectability'
- words commonly used in your region.

2　How are they classified and defined by the dictionary-writers (i.e. **lexicographers**), and how far do they agree? For each dictionary, make a note of the date of publication and for our 'test' words, record on Table 2.12 the information below:

- are the words included in the dictionary at all?
- if so, what meanings are offered?
- how, if at all, is the word classified (colloquial? informal? slang? dialect? etc.)
- is any further information provided (such as the origins, or etymology, of the words).

Some suitable dictionaries might include any of the various editions published by Oxford, Collins, Webster and Chambers – or any alternatives which you may have to hand.

Table 2.12

Word	Dict. 1	date	Dict. 2	date	Dict. 3	Date
booze						
gay						
cash						
CD-ROM						
telly						
loo						
crap						
jumbo jet						
bairn						
internet						
cool						

3 Now consider the variations you have found between the dictionaries you have included in your survey, and try to account for them. Which of the following factors – or any others – do you think explains the disagreements you have found?

- language change – some of the dictionaries are simply too old to record some of the newer words
- the primary meaning and the status – whether or not it is 'slang' or Standard English – may have changed since the dictionary was published. 'Gay' is an obvious example.
- selective censorship – some dictionaries (e.g. those designed for use in schools) choose not to include words which are considered indecent
- equally, all small- to medium-sized dictionaries will have to make a selection of some kind from the vast lexicon of English – and many will decide to exclude words which are confined to the dialect of just one region of the country
- different dictionaries use different categories – does 'colloquial' in one dictionary mean the same as 'informal' in another?
- there may be disagreement among users of the language – even among those educated academics who compile dictionaries! – at a particular time about how a word should be classified, or what is its primary meaning.

If we are finding it difficult to discover accurate and consistent information from dictionaries about the lexis of the present day, how much more of a problem do we face when turning to dictionaries for help with words which we meet when reading a novel written in a previous century?

One dictionary does try to record, comprehensively, the lexicon of English and the ways in which words change their status and meaning over time. The first complete *Oxford English Dictionary* –known as the *OED* – was completed in 1928, since when it has been updated and revised. Nowadays it is available on CD-ROM as well as in 20 very substantial volumes, and it attempts to keep track of the ever-changing landscape of English vocabulary. The enterprise has been likened both to nailing a jelly to a wall, and painting the Forth bridge! Nevertheless, the *OED* is a hugely valuable tool.

We might, for instance, be surprised to read in Jane Austen's *Mansfield Park*, that the rather prim heroine, Fanny Price, is 'fagged out' after a walk, believing the phrase to be uncharacteristically casual if not actually slang – until we consult the *OED*, which reassures us that 'fagged', with the perfectly respectable Standard English meaning of 'wearied out, excessively fatigued', occurs throughout the eighteenth and nineteenth centuries.

We shall return to some of the issues raised here – and look more closely at the *OED* – in Chapter 5, Section 5.3.

4 Try to collect as many examples of regional dialect vocabulary as you can by:
- compiling a 'dialect dictionary' to help visitors to your own region
- interviewing any friends or members of your family who have been brought up in different parts of the country
- scouring the extracts from Activity 19 and any of the narratives you may be studying (especially if they include *The Adventures of Huckleberry Finn* or one of Thomas Hardy's novels) for dialect vocabulary
- consulting a work of dialectology, such as M. F. Wakelin's *English Dialects: An Introduction* or C. Upton's *A Dialect Atlas of the British Isles*.

2.6.3 Grammatical constructions

In the previous section, we focused on the variety of English vocabulary. However, there is also considerable variation in the ways in which people combine words to construct phrases and sentences – what many people call 'grammar'.

ACTIVITY 24   GRAMMATICAL VARIATION

Let's first carry out a brief survey of some of the grammatical variations that we find in speech, both as it is represented in narratives and as we find it around us.

1 **Literary narratives**

First, if we return to the extracts in Activity 19 (pages 46–9), we can add to the accent features we noted there, and to the lexical items you will have listed as you completed Activity 21 (page 53), a number of grammatical constructions which clearly differ from Standard English (SE).

For each of the examples listed in Table 2.13, suggest what the SE equivalent would be.

Table 2.13

Source	Non-Standard construction	SE equivalent
Wuthering Heights	all on 'em	
The Mayor of Casterbridge	we be sorry to hear it	
The Commitments	been ridin' annythin' since I seen yis last?	
Sons and Lovers	there's some chaps as does go round like moudiwarps	
	shouldn't ter like it? 'Appen not, it 'ud dirty thee.	

Now, add to this list your own examples of non-Standard constructions from the following extracts in Table 2.14:

Table 2.14

Extract	Dialect construction	SE equivalent
Extract A: Charles Dickens, *Great Expectations* *When I was over yonder, t'other side of the world, I was always a looking to this side; and it come flat to be there, for all that I was a-growing rich. Everybody knowed Magwitch, and Magwitch could come, and Magwitch could go, and nobody's head would be troubled about him. They ain't so easy concerning me here, dear boy.*		
Extract B: Mark Twain, *The Adventures of Huckleberry Finn* *Tom's most well now and got his bullet around his neck on a watch-guard for a watch, and is always seeing what time it is, and so there ain't nothing more to write about, and I am rotten glad of it, because if I'd a knowed what a trouble it was to make a book I wouldn't a tackled it and ain't agoing to no more. But I reckon I got to light out for the Territory ahead of the rest, because Aunt Sally she's going to adopt me and sivilize me and I can't stand it. I been there before.*		
Extract C: Alice Walker, *The Color Purple* *Harpo girl daddy say Harpo not good enough for her. Harpo been courting the girl a while. He say he sit in the parlor with her, the daddy sit right there in the corner till everybody feel terrible. Then he go sit on the porch in front the open door where he can hear everything. Nine o'clock come, he bring Harpo his hat.*		

2 Variation around us

We can continue our survey simply by keeping our ears open, and tuned to the language we hear all around us – whether in person, in our own region, or via the media of radio and television, which can give national exposure to varieties of regional speech.

Listed in Table 2.15 are several Standard English constructions, along with a regional alternative. Where you are aware of speakers in your own area or elsewhere using a form different from either of the two forms shown below, enter it in the third column.

Table 2.15

Standard English	Dialectal variation	Your regional dialect
I was standing at the bus stop	I was stood at the bus stop	
It was he who did it	It was him what done it	
We're open from 10 'til 4	We're open from 10 while 4	
We weren't doing anything	We wasn't doing nothing	
We're going out, are we?	We're going out, is it?	
You've been badly treated	You've been badly treat (i.e. 'tret')	
What do you think of it?	What do you think on it?	
I saw him do it	I seen him do it	
They've just left	They're after leaving	

3 **Classifying variation**
Faced with this grammatical diversity, linguists attempt to group together some of the variations using different linguistic categories. Suggest which of the literary and other examples of dialect grammar you would place in each of the following categories.

- **Concord**, i.e. variations in the 'agreement' between the **subject** and the verb which follows
  e.g. I was/I were
  Other examples: ....

- **Verb tense forms**, i.e. variations in the different forms used to express different kinds of past, present and future
  e.g. I saw/I seen
  Other examples: ....

- **Prepositional usage**, i.e. variations in the use of prepositions (words such as 'in', 'on', 'of', 'for', 'until', etc.) in set phrases
  e.g. What do you think of it?/What do you think to it?
  Other examples: ....

- **Negation**, i.e. variation in the ways in which negatives are expressed
  e.g. I didn't do anything/I never did nowt
  Other examples: ....

2.6.4 Anglo-Saxon attitudes

So far, we have surveyed some of the variety of English pronunciation reflected in different accents, and some of the diversity of lexis and grammar reflected in English dialects. However, we will also encounter a wide range of attitudes towards these different forms of language – as summed up in the statements in tables 2.16 and 2.17.

ACTIVITY 25

Discuss each of the statements in tables 2.16 and 2.17 and see how far you agree.

Table 2.16 The pro's and con's of accents

Pro	Con
The variety of accents makes life interesting – it would be a boring world if everyone spoke RP!	Some accents are difficult to understand
Local accents help to identify us with our roots and are an important part of our identity and personality	Some accents are a disadvantage and simply create stereotypes
Some accents sound friendly and attractive	Some accents sound dull and off-putting

Table 2.17 The pro's and con's of dialects: lexis

Pro	Con
The variety of regional vocabulary is an important part of our heritage	Misunderstandings can easily result from using non-standard vocabulary
An area's language expresses its identity and history	The modern technologies of communication make regional variations redundant – they will die out
Dialect guides are good for tourism	Foreign learners need a standard vocabulary
It's fun to learn these words and they should be maintained	

COMMENTARY

The accent question

Although there is evidence that some rural accents are becoming rarer and more diluted, regional accents as a whole seem not to be under threat from the apparent pressures towards standardisation exerted by the pervasive RP of the radio and television media. Even among speakers of accents considered by many to be 'unfashionable' or unattractive – accents such as Birmingham and Glasgow which consistently score low in surveys of attitudes carried out by linguists – the importance of local identity and the **covert prestige** of a local accent (i.e. its association with positive values such as community, honesty, humour and warmth) often outweigh the attractions of a more prestigious accent like RP. Many professional people, even if they gradually lose some of the lexis and grammar of their regional dialect, may retain at least a trace of their local accent. Whilst it is true that some stereotypes persist and may continue to make life difficult for brain-surgeons with Birmingham accents or barristers from Liverpool, if anything, there is now wider exposure than ever of a variety of regional accents on the media and there are hopes of more enlightened attitudes.

However, some individuals consciously decide to leave their native accent behind and move towards RP in a bid for professional acceptance. Others steadfastly refuse to do so, and still others find that such a change – known as **upward convergence** – seems to happen to them willy-nilly. Meanwhile, sociolinguists such as Peter Trudgill and William Labov (see Section 2.11) have continued to find that the most pronounced regional accent features are most likely to be found in the speech of working-class males.

The lexis question

The issue of regional vocabulary seems to generate a good deal less discussion and controversy. A fair amount of such vocabulary (as with the large number of words for species of small animals and scarecrows) may well be doomed because it is associated with rural ways of life which are passing away; nevertheless, there is often some local affection for dialectal words and the conviction that such vocabulary is less 'correct' or 'proper' than the lexis of Standard English is much less pronounced than is the case for dialectal grammar – as we shall see.

ACTIVITY 26   THE GRAMMAR QUESTION

Check out your own attitudes towards the kinds of regional constructions we have considered in Activity 24 by ticking the statements from the list below that you would agree with:

(i) they are an important feature of the region's identity ☐

(ii) they are bad grammar ☐

(iii) they show speakers becoming confused or making mistakes ☐

(iv) they are attractive and interesting ☐

(v) they should be corrected in schools ☐

(vi) they are completely grammatical. ☐

COMMENTARY

Many people would tick (ii) and even (iii); some politicians would certainly tick (v), but it is unlikely that many people would tick (iv) or (vi).

However, there are very good reasons for defending such uses of language:

● when thousands of people in a region all use the same construction, we can hardly say they are all simultaneously making a 'mistake'. Usually, they are using a 'rule' which is different from Standard English, but which applies to all speakers of the dialect

● these language uses are part of a consistent grammatical system – and they often retain features of grammar (such as 'double negatives' in phrases like 'I didn't see nothing') which were previously part of accepted Standard English (see Section 5.3)

- many of the variations in dialect grammar have existed alongside the 'prestige' variety for hundreds of years. In fact, Standard English itself evolved from regional dialect – the East Midland Dialect of Middle English. Since this was the variety used in London, Oxford and Cambridge (the centres of politics, learning and the Church) from the fifteenth century onwards it came increasingly to be associated with power, authority and the printed word. By the eighteenth century, it had established itself as the prestige form of the language, and other dialects came to be seen as 'inferior' or 'incorrect'.

However, it is worth remembering that this came about not because the dialect was linguistically purer or superior, but because of social, economic, geographical and political accident. Simply put, this particular dialect 'won' the battle for prestige because it was the language of those who exercised power. Indeed, had Newcastle upon Tyne and Durham been the centres of trade and intellectual power in the fifteenth and sixteenth centuries, we might now regard the variety we know as 'Geordie' as 'correct' and 'proper' English and enjoy our Christmas Royal message being delivered in tones closer to those of Paul Gascoigne than our present Queen!

2.6.5 The status of regional varieties: the Media

Even if, linguistically, all regional varieties of English are equal, in reality, some are 'more equal than others' – to paraphrase George Orwell. Although regional accents and dialects may enjoy some covert prestige, a linguistic 'league table' of their relative status might look like Figure 2.4.

Now we can begin to see how the different values – and prestige – of linguistic varieties might be reflected in the way they are used in the Media.

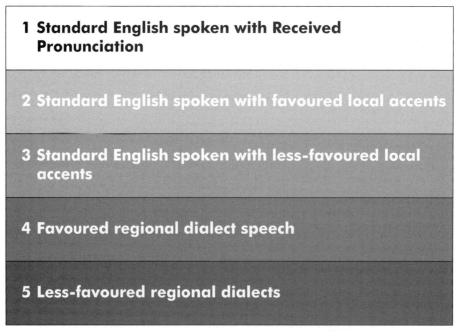

Figure 2.4 Varieties of English: league table

ACTIVITY 27

1 Record and listen closely to the varieties of English used on television and radio news broadcasts, both national and regional. How much variation do you find?
If you find that Standard English with RP – or near RP on local news – is often preferred, what do you think accounts for this?

2 Now consider the weather forecasts which either precede or follow the news. Do you find a greater variety of accents here? If so, why might this be?

3 Radio 1 has often employed DJs (such as Manchester's Mark Radcliffe) with pronounced regional accents to present its popular breakfast programme. Sample the range of presenters used by the other principal national radio stations, and compare them with local stations. What differences do you find, and what reasons might there be for these?

4 Now survey the range of accents and dialects used in a range of advertisements. Note the ways different voices are used in association with different products, and think especially about the language chosen for the 'voice over' – the unseen voice which often has the last word in an advertisement. Don't forget to note, also, the gender of the voices used. Use Table 2.18 to record your findings. Some possible products have been suggested, but also add your own.

Table 2.18 Regional varieties in advertising

Product	Voice-over (if used)				Other voices used
Beer	Male	☐	Female	☐	
	Regional	☐	RP	☐	
Bread	Male	☐	Female	☐	
	Regional	☐	RP	☐	
Fizzy drink	Male	☐	Female	☐	
	Regional	☐	RP	☐	
Car	Male	☐	Female	☐	
	Regional	☐	RP	☐	
Bank, insurance	Male	☐	Female	☐	
	Regional	☐	RP	☐	
Other	Male	☐	Female	☐	
	Regional	☐	RP	☐	

COMMENTARY

Task 1

In explaining the dominance of SE and RP in news broadcasts, your first response may well have been to stress the importance of comprehensibility. The national news, especially, needs to be clearly understood by all English speakers from Land's End to John-o'-Groats, and so Standard English with Received Pronunciation might seem the best way of ensuring this.

However, if we think about the programmes which do feature regional speech – 'Eastenders', 'Brookside', 'Coronation Street' – we find that they are usually at the top of the ratings. We therefore have to assume that most British viewers find the East London, Liverpool and Manchester speech of those programmes perfectly intelligible!

So – the answer has to do more with the status of SE and RP than with their intelligibility. Not only are they regionally neutral, but their high prestige means that the news is likely to be taken seriously and believed. This may also explain why even local news broadcasters, although they may have mild versions of their local accent, will read the news in SE and in an accent fairly close to the RP of their colleagues on the national news.

Task 2

Some television weather forecasters have, in the past, had pronounced regional accents. This has not, presumably, prevented us from understanding the information they are giving us! What it may indicate, however, is that the weather is not quite as serious or important as the news, and so we can tolerate accents which do not have quite the same high status as RP. The vocabulary and grammar of the forecast, however, is still likely to be SE.

Task 3

There may well be considerable variation from radio station to radio station. Some stations may wish to project a serious, solemn image – and so are less likely to use presenters whose accents are stereotypically associated with light-heartedness or humour! Radio 1, on the other hand, aiming for a less formal, more youthful image, may wish to exploit the values of friendliness, warmth and down-to-earth unpretentiousness traditionally associated with a Northern accent such as Mark Radcliffe's.

Task 4

Manufacturers will certainly try to exploit the stereotypical associations of different regional varieties to sell their products. The high-status RP may well be associated with up-market products, or with products whose claims need to be taken seriously (such as medicines). On the other hand, advertisements for beer, bread and crisps may need to suggest more 'down-to-earth' qualitites.

The voice-overs may differ from the other voices we hear – as with the news, which may include quotations from speakers of non-Standard varieties, the unseen voice may well be the 'voice of authority' which controls the advertisement, reinforcing the latter's message in a language which we can trust. This dominant or controlling language is sometimes called the **metalanguage** of a text.

The following television advertisement for Lucozade Low-Calorie drink is interesting in a number of ways. It features the cartoon characters Tracey and Sandra, two rather large Northern girls from the comic *Viz*:

(**Tracey** and **Sandra** enter the kitchen)
Tracey (strong northern accent): *Right. What's for afters?*
(laughter as the girls head for the fridge. As they open the fridge door, we see shelf-loads of lard. **Sandra** takes out a bottle of Lucozade Low Calorie)
Sandra (equally strong northern accent): *Tracey – what on earth's this doing in our fridge?*
(handsome, slim and bare-chested young man appears in the doorway, drinking a bottle of the product)
Young man (hint of London accent): *Actually, darling, it's mine.*
Tracey: *When we want you to move yer stuff in, we'll tell ya!*
Voice over: (Male, RP) *New Lucozade Low Calorie with Vitamins*
Tracey and Sandra (together): *Gerrit out of our fridge!*

[Transcript of advertisement, recorded from TV broadcast 1997]

This advertisement exploits the stereotypical association of Northern accents with unhealthy diets – and taps into the humour popularised among younger readers by the Newcastle-based adult comic, *Viz*. The girls' accent is synonymous with their lifestyle – and is contrasted with the sharper, more sophisticated (and more attractive!) tones of the young man's strong, confident and mildly south-eastern accent.

Yet the advertisers still feel they need the unseen voice-over of authority – the metalanguage of a male RP speaker – to underline the product name and its principal claims – 'Low Calorie, with Vitamins'.

▷ How many more advertisements can you find which use an RP voice-over metalanguage in this way?

2.6.6 Status of regional varieties: literature

It may seem a long way from Lucozade to D. H. Lawrence, but the same principles we have seen in advertisements also often apply in literary texts. From the novel extracts which we have already met, we can see that writers of narratives can represent the variety of English in two main ways:

- although the story is narrated using Standard English, when dialogue is included, this can feature other varieties. We use our linguistic understanding to draw conclusions from this about the characters' geographical, social and educational backgrounds. This is the case with the extracts from *Great Expectations* and *Sons and Lovers*.
- The story itself is told by a narrator whose own language differs from Standard English. Dialogue may include other speakers of the same dialectal variety, or speakers of quite different varieties. This is the case with *The Color Purple* and *The Adventures of Huckleberry Finn*.

Let us now return to three of the literary narratives that we have already met to see how each of these two methods works.

ACTIVITY 28

1 Identify the different varieties of English used in extracts A–C and who uses them.

2 Which variety – the standard or the regional – is being used as the metalanguage of the passage?

3 In what other ways are the differences in prestige or status of the standard and regional varieties reflected in the passage?

METHOD 1
Extract A

The business of eating being concluded, and no one uttering a word of sociable conversation, I approached a window to examine the weather.

A sorrowful sight I saw; dark night coming down prematurely, and sky and hills mingled in one bitter whirl of wind and suffocating snow.

'I don't think it possible for me to get home now, without a guide,' I could not help exclaiming. 'The roads will be buried already; and if they were bare, I could scarcely distinguish a foot in advance.'

'Hareton, drive those dozen sheep into the barn porch. They'll be covered if left in the fold all night; and put a plank before them,' said Heathcliff.

'How must I do?' I continued, with rising irritation.

There was no reply to my question; and on looking round, I saw only Joseph bringing in a pail of porridge for the dogs and Mrs Heathcliff, leaning over the fire, diverting herself with burning a bundle of matches which had fallen from the chimney-piece as she restored the tea-canister to its place.

The former, when he had deposited his burden, took a critical survey of the room; and, in cracked tones, grated out:

'Aw woonder hagh yah can faishion tuh stand thear i' idleness un war, when all on 'em's goan aght! Bud yah're a nowt, and it's noa use talking – yah'll niver mend uh yer ill ways; bud, goa raight t'divil, like yer mother afore ye!'

I imagined for a moment, that this piece of eloquence was addressed to me; and sufficiently enraged, stepped towards the aged rascal with an intention of kicking him out of the door.

[Emily Brontë, *Wuthering Heights*, 1847]

Extract B

'And you a miner!' she exclaimed in surprise.
'Yes. I went down when I was ten.'
She looked at him in wondering dismay.
'When you were ten! And wasn't it very hard?' she asked.
'You soon get used to it. You live like th' mice, an' you pop out at night to see what's going on.'
'It makes me feel blind,' she frowned.
'Like a moudiwarp!' he laughed. 'Yi, an' there's some chaps as does go round like moudiwarps.' He thrust his face forward in the blind, snout-like way of a mole, seeming to sniff and peer for direction. She looked at him, with a touch of appeal in her pure humility.
'Shouldn't ter like it?' he asked tenderly. ''Appen not, it 'ud dirty thee.'
She had never been 'thee'd' and 'thou'd before.

[D. H. Lawrence, *Sons and Lovers*, 1913]

METHOD 2
Extract C

In this extract, Huck is reunited with the runaway slave, Jim, who believes him to have drowned, and thinks he has come back to haunt him as a ghost.

He bounced up and stared at me wild. Then he drops down on both knees and puts his hands together and says:

'Doan' hurt me – don't! I hain't ever done no harm to a ghos'. I awluz liked dead people en done all I could for 'em. You go en in de river agin, whah you b'longs, en doan' do nuffn to Ole Jim 'at 'uz awluz yo' fren'.'

Well, I warn't long making him understand I warn't dead. I was ever so glad to see Jim. I warn't lonesome, now. I told him I warnt afraid of him telling the people where I was. I talked along, but he only set there and looked at me; never said nothing. Then I says:

'It's good daylight. Le's get breakfast. Make up your camp fire good.'

'What's de use er makin' up de camp fire to cook strawbries en sich truck? But you got a gun, hain't you? Den we kin git sumfn better den strawbries.'

[Mark Twain, *The Adventures of Huckleberry Finn*]

COMMENTARY

In both *Sons and Lovers* and *Wuthering Heights*, the regional varieties are contrasted with the educated, standard language of the narrator and one of the characters. Whilst the attitude of Lockwood, the narrator in *Wuthering Heights*, to Joseph's Yorkshire speech is clearly patronising and hostile, D. H. Lawrence's treatment of Walter Morel's Nottinghamshire is more sympathetic. Nevertheless, it is still of lower status than the controlling metalanguage of Standard English in which the book is written and which, just like the voice-overs of television advertisements, provides the ultimate source of authority for the reader.

The situation in *The Adventures of Huckleberry Finn* is more unusual, and helps to explain not only the controversial impact of the book when it was first published – some middle-class readers reacted with alarm to what they saw as the promotion of 'illiteracy' and 'poor English' – but also, for some, its enduring importance as the foundation-stone of American literature. The metalanguage is given to Huck, with his uneducated, colloquial Southern States dialect – and so gave, for the first time in a major work of literature, a distinct voice to the American tongue after a century of separation from Britain. As the American writer Ernest Hemingway put it, 'All modern American literature comes from one book by Mark Twain called *Huckleberry Finn*'.

Within his narrative, Huck also presents a quite different variety, the 'black' English speech of the slave, Jim. In attempting to present for the first time this distinctively different variety of English which had developed among the slave plantations of the deep South, Twain has been both praised and criticised, some readers accusing him of patronising and stereotyping black people and their speech for the amusement of his white readers. (We will consider the controversies surrounding 'black English' in Section 2.6.7.)

ACTIVITY 29

Read the article below by Melvyn Bragg. Bragg grew up in Cumbria, gaining a scholarship to Oxford University where he studied English. He has subsequently enjoyed a successful career both as a novelist and broadcaster.

In 1969 a Mrs E. R. Fieldhouse produced a survey on local dialect. She questioned 248 schoolchildren in Barrow-in-Furness. As a follow-up in 1993, a Mr J. T. Franks did a similar survey. The results make morose reading for those of us who see the dialect as the soul-speak of the old countryside, the register of a living past, the conduit of a fertile tradition.

In 1969, 44 pupils knew of and used the word swill (an oval basket woven from oak laths). In 1993, only one pupil used the word. Lonning (lane) scored 35 in 1969 and a desolate 3 in 1993. Slape (slippery) scored 50 in 1969 and 2 in 1993.

Lile (little) scored 50 in 1969 and 25 in 1993. Yam (home) scored 51 and 27; sneck (latch of a door or gate) 45 and 10.

Is the BBC the culprit, with its juggernaut standardisation for so much of this century – an accent I now recognise around part of my life and to some extent participate in, but one which I know for many reasons alienates millions? Is it the voice of power and authority which demands a clean bill of mouth before entry is allowed in influential corridors? Or is it the inevitable result of the concentration through faster and faster communications of what has become a small, compact country?

In my schooldays we had two languages, as near as dammit. When I spoke accented dialect I was – thankfully – incomprehensible to my teachers, who reacted by caning this rough beast until it did not dare give voice in the classroom. I also learnt to talk comprehensible English, albeit equally accented, as was happily pointed out to me by the young gentlemen of Oxford University in 1958. No bones broken.

In my first novel [For Want of a Nail] I represented the country people talking in the dialect which looks on the page like muddy boots on a newly fitted carpet. My editor said that it was no doubt very true but it would not travel. I kept it, and the book did travel, but his comment became an admonition and, looking back, I began to heed it. Or perhaps it was that as my life centred more and more on London, the sound and feeling of those old words began to fade.

But now the news comes from Barrow-in-Furness that we are in the death throes. Why did we not fight harder for what is so profoundly ours? We have willingly stamped out the dialect and let it go in an act of complicit vandalism. Perhaps there is no need for it in our sleek, screened, Internetted silent world. No need for babblement and blatin, no need for ahint and aslew, for douker and everly, for gawp and girt, kyne and lait, quindam and ryle, taggelt and throstle … I can't help thinking that we are much the poorer for it.

[Edited from Melvyn Bragg's article
'Why dialects are dying beyond our ken', in *The Times*, May 1997]

1   Bragg cites evidence that some dialects may be in decline. Do you agree with him that this is a bad thing?

2   Bragg also refers to some of the influences which led him to lose touch with his own native speech. What issues are there here for the attitudes which schools adopt towards the use of Standard and regional forms of English in the classroom? Draw up a suggested language policy for your own school or college.

3   Bragg also refers to the use of dialects by writers and the pressures exerted on them not to do so. Roddy Doyle (the author of *The Commitments* and *Paddy Clarke Ha Ha*) and James Kelman (*How Late It Was How Late*) are two modern novelists who have defied this trend. Identify any writers – novelists, poets or playwrights – who have given voice to the regional speech used in your area.

4   If you have access to the *OED*, check the meanings and history of some of the disappearing dialect words he mentions.

2.6.7 'Black English': *The Adventures of Huckleberry Finn* and *The Color Purple*

One of the non-Standard varieties of English which has been the focus of particular debate has been the form known as 'black English'. *The Adventures of Huckleberry Finn* presented a version of this distinctive speech to its readers – many of whom would be seeing this variety represented in print for the first time. Nearly a hundred years later, Alice Walker presented the language of 'black English' as the narrative metalanguage for the whole of her novel *The Color Purple*.

ACTIVITY 30

In this activity, we'll compare the ways in which Mark Twain and Alice Walker represent varieties of 'black English' in their novels.

Go back to the extract from *The Adventures of Huckleberry Finn* in Activity 28 (page 67), then read the extract from *The Color Purple* printed below. In this extract, the narrator, Celie, breaks the news that her step-daughter-in-law, Sofia, has been imprisoned after an assault on the wife of the mayor. (Harpo is Sofia's husband, and Squeak his recently acquired girlfriend. Mr— is Celie's husband.)

For both extracts, identify the features of 'black English' which the author has represented, using Table 2.19 to record your findings.

Table 2.19

	Jim's language	Celie's language	'Standard' equivalent
Accent features			
Dialect features – lexis			
Dialect features – grammar			

Extract from *The Color Purple*
Harpo mope. Wipe the counter, light a cigarette, look outdoors, walk up and down. Little Squeak run long all up under him trying to git his tension. Baby this, she say, Baby that. Harpo look through her head, blow smoke.

Squeak come over to the corner where me and Mr.— at. She got two bright gold teef in the side of her mouth, generally grin all the time. Now she cry. Miss Celie, she say, What the matter with Harpo?
Sofia in jail, I say.
In jail? She look like I say Sofia on the moon.
What she in jail for? she ast.
Sassing the mayor's wife, I say.
Squeak pull up a chair. Look down my throat.
What your real name? I ast her. She say, Mary Agnes.
Make Harpo call you by your real name, I say. Then maybe he see you even when he trouble.
She look at me puzzle. I let it go. I tell her what one of Sofia sister tell me and Mr.—.

Attitudes towards 'black English'

As with any other variety of English which deviates from the official, prestige standard form, 'black English' has at times been described as 'broken English', 'ungrammatical' or 'lazy' speech.

However, just as this kind of judgement of regional varieties of English ignores the facts of their historical development (see Section 2.6.4. above), so these attitudes betray an ignorance of the origins of 'black English'. This variety can be traced back to the collision between the English of the slave-plantation owners in the Caribbean and Southern United States, and the African languages of the slaves forcibly brought to work there.

The first result of such a meeting of languages was what is known as a **pidgin** – a basic means of communication between speakers of different tongues which is limited to a small shared vocabulary and a simplified grammar.

However, when subsequent generations, brought up in slavery, used this hybrid tongue as their mother tongue, it developed a more complex grammatical system – a process known as **creolisation** – and became a distinct linguistic variety (i.e. a **creole**), retaining the hallmarks both of English and the original African languages. Present-day varieties of 'black English' – both in Britain and America – can be traced back to this development.

The 'black English' controversy

The status of 'black English' has become particularly controversial in the United States, as the following article from *The Times* shows:

Black American English has been officially recognised as a distinct language in Oakland, California, where black children who speak it are in a majority ....
The move ... makes Standard English a second language for 28,000 children and offers bonuses to teachers who learn their vernacular. ...
This week's unanimous vote by Oakland Unified School District officials gives black urban slang its own name – 'Ebonics' – and traces its roots to West Africa and slavery.
'West and Niger-Congo African language systems form the basis of a distinct language spoken by black Americans historically isolated from mainstream English by slavery and segregation,' the resolution asserted.

A Guide to Black English

English	Ebonics
He goes to work	H be goin;' to work
She will be first	She-uh be firs
You're crazy	You crazy
Six million dollars	Six million dollar
My mother's name is Mary	My mama name Mary
These are two of my friends who have just come	It's two of my friend they just come.

[from 'Black American slang wins place in classroom', *The Times*, 21 December 1996]

The issue was also taken up in *The Independent*, which revealed:

Syntactical and other patterns from [these] ancestral languages survive in ... spoken English. Examples include the omission or altered use of the verb 'to be' (as in 'He a fine fellow' and 'I be a good student') or the lack of subject-verb agreement ('She love the dog').

[Language consultant Philippe] Patry pointed out that similar forms existed in the urban speech of Britain and Ireland. ... It was usually reviled by teachers and grammarians, but he pointed out that it had been used with great success as a literary language in Ireland and Scotland – for example, by Roddy Doyle in Paddy Clarke Ha Ha Ha *and James Kelman in* How Late It Was How Late.

[from 'Triumph of Black English gives new cred to street talk', *The Independent*, 22 December 1996]

The proposal to give official status to Ebonics provoked a large number of reactions, both in favour and in protest – as shown in Table 2.20 (page 72).

ACTIVITY 31

1 Using *The Times*' 'Guide to Black English', identify which – if any – of the features listed are characteristic of the speech of Jim, in *The Adventures of Huckleberry Finn*, and Celie, in *The Color Purple*.

2 What are the arguments in favour, or against, applying a similar policy to regional varieties of English (e.g. Geordie, Cockney) where the majority of pupils in a school speak in that variety?

2.7 Drafting and reflecting

Having begun to study a range of stories and the techniques involved in telling them, you can now prepare to write your own narratives – a piece of your own original writing may well be a part of your coursework at A-level.

Table 2.20 The Ebonics debate

In favour	Against
Jim Lyons, director of the National Association for Bilingual Education – 'The school board is embarking on a policy to embrace the African-American child, nurture him and add to his linguistic repertoire.' **Cissy Lacks**, a (white) teacher suspended for allowing black students to use swear words in creative-writing assignments – 'It should be natural that teachers try to work with whatever language their students speak.' **Toni Cook**, Oakland School board member – 'In my day they would teach you to talk like white folks, but whatever we are using now is not working.' **Philippe Patry**, language consultant – 'I am delighted by this recognition and validation of forms of speech previously considered abnormal.' **Lucella Harrison**, president of the school board – 'We tried remedial classes in the 60s and 70s and they did not work. We must do something different.'	**Jesse Jackson** (black American politician) – 'an unacceptable surrender bordering on disgrace … you don't have to go to school to learn to talk garbage'. **Maya Angelou** (black American poet and novelist, author of *I Know Why the Caged Bird Sings*) – 'The very idea that African-American language is a language separate and apart is very threatening, because it can encourage young men and women not to learn standard English.' **Aaron Andrews**, 16, student – 'What's black English? You mean slang? I'm black, I speak English. What they're trying to say is we don't talk proper English. That's not true. If you got a brain in your head you can talk any way you want to.' **Jim Boulet**, American lobbyist for 'proper English' – 'It's saying in the most racist way that black kids are stupid and they can't learn English.'

[Data taken from the articles cited on pages 70–1, and from 'Boyz will be boyz', *The Times*, 29 December 1996]

2.7.1 Original writing

ACTIVITY 32

Here are some suggestions for possible original writing assignments:

1 Although most of the narratives you are likely to study for A-level are novels, it is unlikely that you will have the time or space to write at such length yourself! A more appropriate style model to follow might be the work of short-story writers.

Short stories demand much simpler story lines than novels – they may hinge on a single key incident or episode – fewer characters, and more selective use of detail. They are unlikely to have the wide scope of novels such as *The Adventures of Huckleberry Finn*, which embraces a whole series of adventures, or *The Color Purple*, which tells the story of a whole lifetime. Instead, their focus may be a surprisingly ordinary turn of events, but it may be one which changes the life and experience of the central character in some way. In James Joyce's collection of stories *Dubliners*, it may be Gabriel Conroy's evening at Miss Kate's and Miss Julia's Christmas dance (in 'The Dead'), or Eveline's inability to go away with Frank in 'Eveline'. Some short stories may try to engineer a 'twist' at the end of the tale which surprises the reader.

Try to choose your material from experience – either from things that have happened to you, or which you have observed – and don't feel it has to involve death, disaster or major dramas!

You may find the following writers of 'literary' short stories an inspiration for your own writing:

> Roald Dahl, *Tales of the Unexpected*
> Thomas Hardy, *Wessex Tales*
> James Joyce, *Dubliners*
> Frank O'Connor, *My Oedipus Complex and Other Stories*
> Katharine Mansfield, *The Garden Party and Other Stories*
> Edgar Allan Poe, *Tales of Mystery and Imagination*

2 Many short stories are written for commercial publication in particular media with a well-defined audience which has clear expectations about the kinds of story they will meet. These genres may include romantic fiction, detective or crime stories, science-fiction or fantasy writing or ghost stories.

Select a genre and a number of **style models** (i.e. examples of that genre) from current publications – and identify the distinctive ingredients which characterise them. Look at:

- the kinds of characters they feature
- the settings where the stories take place
- the storylines – are the endings 'happy' or 'sad'? Are they morally quite simple ('baddies' and 'goodies' get their just rewards and punishments?) or complex (hard to say who the 'baddies' or 'goodies' are)?
- any distinctives uses of language (e.g. in the physical description of the characters in a romantic story, or in the narrative of action sequences in a war saga, or the use of scientific jargon in a science- fiction story).

Now tailor your own story to the demands of the genre, the medium in which it is published, and your audience.

3 Try either including some dialect/accent in the speech of your characters, or producing a short narrative using the distinctive dialect of your own region. Just as Mark Twain does with his novel, try to capture the particular character of your surroundings and the way of life of its inhabitants through the use of your regional speech patterns.

You willl need to do some research first to be confident about the characteristic lexis and grammatical constructions of speakers in your area.

4 Use some of the different techniques you experimented with during our workshop on Jack and Jill (see Activities 7 and 8, pages 21–5). In particular, try telling your story through the eyes of a narrator who is either a child, naïve and lacking in understanding, or a character who is in some other way unreliable.

The following novels are interesting in their use of 'unreliable narrators':

Margaret Atwood, *The Robber Bride*
William Faulkner, *As I Lay Dying*
L. P. Hartley, *The Go Between*
K. Kesey, *One Flew Over The Cuckoo's Nest*
Henry Roth, *Call It Sleep*
J. D. Salinger, *The Catcher in the Rye*
Virginia Woolf, *The Waves*
C. Thubron, *A Cruel Madness*

2.7.2 Revising and redrafting

Whatever the narrative you decide to write, it is unlikely that you will produce the perfect story first time. All writers expect to revise and redraft their work several times before it is ready for publication – but how do you know what to revise and change, once you have completed a first draft?

ACTIVITY 33

Once you have completed your first version, you need to listen and take notice of several advisers:

1 Yourself! Put the draft to one side for a couple of days, before returning to it with as critical an eye as you can. Be prepared to be radical, and cut and change freely.

2 Your editor/teacher. S/he may have a wider experience of the genre, medium and audience you are writing for – and will make suggestions which are designed to help you achieve a more successful final product.

3 A sample of your intended readers. It's best to offer them a structured questionnaire for their response rather than just asking 'what do you think of this?' By doing so, you can pinpoint aspects of the story you feel uncertain about – the ending, the development of a character, the realism of the dialogue – with appropriate questions.

2.7.3 Writing a commentary

Some A-level syllabuses may require you to write a commentary along with any original writing you submit. Although your final commentary will reflect on the entire development of the piece, and refer to successive drafts, it's a good idea to get into the habit of writing commentaries from the start.

ACTIVITY 34

Writing a commentary involves taking a step back from your work and reflecting on what you have tried to achieve. Ask yourself the following questions – a good commentary will include the answers to many, if not all, of them:

- what were the sources for the idea and how did it develop?
- how did you gather your source material, and research the requirements of a style model/audience?
- what decisions did you make about your plot, characters, narrative techniques and use of language – and at what points in the development of the piece?

- what were the main changes you made during the re-drafting process, and the reasons for them? (Be prepared to quote some details from your own drafts to illustrate your commentary, here.)
- what advice/editorial comment/other responses did readers offer you during the writing of the piece, and how did you respond to them?
- how successful do you think the final draft is, and is there still anything that you would wish to revise if you had time?

2.8. Back to the texts: some critical controversies in *The Adventures of Huckleberry Finn*

We can now return, briefly, to one of our core texts and consider it in the light of some of the linguistic issues we have been exploring.

From its publication in 1884 up until the present day, Mark Twain's book has been the subject of intense critical debate and controversy, though as times have changed – and the attitudes of the book's readers along with them – so have the causes of dispute.

2.8.1 Huck and his dialect

The first controversial issue which greeted the book's publication and which ultimately led to at least one American public library (Concord, Massachusetts) banning it was the question of Huck and his language. Some readers feared that his dialect – or 'bad English' as it was seen – and his disrespect for the values of 'sivilisation' were likely to have a bad influence on younger readers. Their views were summarised by a Boston newspaper:

> [The book] is couched in the language of a rough dialect, and all through its pages there is a systematic use of bad grammar and an employment of rough, coarse, inelegant expressions. The whole book is of a class that is more profitable for the slums than it is for respectable people, and it is trash of the veriest sort.
>
> [*The Adventures of Huckleberry Finn*, edited by Gerald Graff and James Phelan, p. 351, 1995]

We can now understand this reaction in terms of:

- the status of the 'prestige variety' and its association with the values of 'civilised' society
- the view that linguistic forms deviating from this were 'inferior' or 'incorrect'
- the association of dialects with a lack of education and respectability
- a preoccupation with the importance of teaching young people the prestige forms of language which persists to the present day.

However, the book also attracted plenty of defenders who ultimately guaranteed its position as a key work of American literature. We can understand this in terms of:

- the importance of the unofficial, non-Standard forms of language in expressing the identity and experience of the community which uses it.

ACTIVITY 35

1 Using your understanding of the linguistic issues raised in Sections 2.6. onwards, write a reply to the newspaper in defence of Mark Twain's novel.

2 Compare the arguments surrounding Huck Finn's language with the 'black English' issue discussed in Section 2.6.7. What similarities – and differences – do you find in the nature of the controversies?

2.8.2 Huck Finn and racism

For modern readers, the major problem in *The Adventures of Huckleberry Finn* is quite different. As we have seen, we have become used to meeting varieties of English other than the prestige standard form in literature, and our less intolerant linguistic attitudes makes it difficult for us to see what the officials of Concord Public Library were making such a fuss about.

However, modern readers do bring to the text quite a different set of values from our ancestors when it comes to racial questions – and this has led to a very different set of responses to the text from when the book was first published. On the one hand, a critic such as Justin Kaplan describes the book as a 'savage indictment of a society that accepted slavery as a way of life' (*Born to Trouble: One Hundred Years of 'Huckleberry Finn'*, pp. 348–9, 1985), whereas the writer Toni Morrison (in her introduction to the novel in Oxford University Press's complete facsimile edition of Mark Twain's works, 1997) says of her first experience of reading the text, 'it provoked a feeling I can only describe now as muffled rage, as though appreciation of the work required my complicity in and sanction of something shaming'.

This provides an excellent example of how changes in the outlooks and experiences of readers lead each generation to find new meanings in established texts.

Modern anxieties about the book's alleged racism have led to several attempts to have the book banned from the curriculum for American schools. The power of 'taboo' words of various kinds to cause offence – and the ways in which our sensitivities to these words can change over time – is the subject of Chapter 5, Section 5. 4, 'You taught me language'.

ACTIVITY 36

Would *you* consider the book an appropriate text for a modern multi-cultural classroom? Use the two extracts from the novel reprinted below to test the validity of the arguments offered on both sides of the case – and then go on to make your case either for or against the novel as a whole.

Extract A is from Chapter 16, as Huck and Jim are drifting down the river hoping to find Cairo, and Jim allows himself to dream of being reunited with his wife and two children, all of whom are still in slavery. Huck meanwhile, feels prompted by his conscience to betray Jim and hand him over to the authorities as a runaway slave:

Extract A

It most froze me to hear such talk. He wouldn't ever dared to talk such talk in his life before. Just see what a difference it made in him the minute he judged he was about free. It was according to the old saying, 'give a nigger an inch and he'll take an ell.'

Thinks I, this is what comes of my not thinking. Here was this nigger which I had as good as helped to run away, coming right out flat-footed and saying he would steal his children – children that belonged to a man I didn't even know; a man that hadn't ever done me no harm.

I was sorry to hear Jim say that, it was such a lowering of him. My conscience got to stirring me up hotter than ever, until at last I says to it, 'Let up on me – it ain't too late, yet – I'll paddle ashore at the first light, and tell.' I felt easy, and happy, and light as a feather, right off. All my troubles was gone. I went to looking out sharp for a light, and sort of singing to myself. By-and-by one showed. Jim sings out:

'We's safe, Huck, we's safe! Jump up and crack yo' heels, dat's de good ole' Cairo at las'! I jis knows it!'

Extract B is from Chapter 32, when Huck is inventing for Aunt Sally the tale of his having escaped from a boat involved in an accident.

Extract B
Now I struck an idea, and fetched it out:
It warn't the grounding – that didn't keep us back but a little. We blowed out a cylinder head.'
'Good gracious! Anybody hurt?'
'No'm. Killed a nigger.'
'Well it's lucky; because sometimes people do get hurt.

The main issues can be summarised as shown in Table 2.21 below:

Table 2.21 Is Huck Finn racist?

Yes	No
• The use of the word 'nigger' (used consistently throughout the book) is offensive	• The word 'nigger' was a common term at the time the book was written (the respected writer Joseph Conrad published a novel entitled *The Nigger of the 'Narcissus'* as late as 1897); to condemn it from a modern perspective is unfair
• Its use in this passage, and elsewhere, implies that the slaves were hardly human, a sub-species	
• The passage regards their suffering as insignificant	• The word is put into the mouths of several characters – including Huck Finn himself – but is not the author's
• It is part of the wider problem of Jim, his beliefs and his language being represented as a crude stereotype for the amusement of white readers (the illustrations by Edward Kemble which accompanied the original text are often grotesque caricatures)	• In fact, in this passage as elsewhere in the novel, the author is using irony to expose and criticise the inhumanity of the attitudes of his day
• The final section of the book reduces Jim to a plaything for Tom Sawyer, and his humanity is forgotten	• The representation of Jim's speech is a serious attempt to capture the nature of 'black English'

2.9 Learning points

2.9.1 Key concepts

By the end of this chapter you should have learned:

- that narratives occur in a variety of situations, literary and non-literary
- a variety of narrative techniques and points of view
- to discuss the way these are used in literary and non-literary texts
- the key differences between speech and writing as found in narratives
- how to examine the structure of narratives
- the distinction between accents and dialects, and some attitudes towards them
- the relationship of Standard and non-Standard varieties of English
- how writers make use of different varieties of English
- about the 'black English' controversy
- how to draft, re-draft and reflect on your own narrative writing
- to apply your linguistic awareness to the study of a literary text and critical controversies.

2.9.2 Glossary

Some of the literary and linguistic terms introduced in this chapter are listed below:

Accent   the distinctive pronunciation of a person, region or social group

Back-channel behaviour   the feedback given by a listener to a talker during conversation

Colloquialism   a use of language characteristic of spoken or informal styles

Concord   grammatical 'agreement' between two or more elements of a phrase

Conjunctions   the class of words whose purpose is to join phrases together within a sentence

Context dependence   the dependence of the meaning of some language (usually spoken) on its immediate circumstances

Convergence/(Divergence)   the moving of the style of a speaker's language towards (or away from) that of another person or group

Dialect   the characteristic vocabulary and grammatical constructions of a particular regional or other social group

Dialogic   involving at least two participants (*compare* monologic)

Digraphs   pairs of letters which consistently represent a single phoneme

Ebonic(s)   term coined to describe the distinctive variety of English also known as 'black English'

First (**Second** and **Third**) **person** grammatical distinction between I (or We), You and S/he (or It and Them)

Grammar   The system which allows speakers of a language to combine, create and de-cipher meaningful phrases and sentences

Graphology   The aspects of written language which affect its physical appearance and presentation

Indirect free style   a blend of external narration and internal monologue

Lexemes   a unit of meaning independent of variations in word endings

Lexis   vocabulary

Lexicon   the available vocabulary of a language

Metalanguage   the dominant or controlling language in a text

Monologic   involving only one participant (*compare* dialogic)

Narrative   a structured account of events, real or imagined

Omniscient narrator   narrative device of the storyteller who stands outside the action but knows everything

Paralinguistic features   the meaningful physical and gestural elements which accompany spoken language

Phonemes   the sounds (vowels and consonants) which are the basic building blocks of the language

Prepositions   class of words whose purpose is to define position in space or time

Prestige, overt (and **covert**)   the official (and unofficial) esteem in which varieties of English are held

Prosodic features   the vocal elements such as intonation and stress which contribute meanings to spoken language

Received Pronunciation   the regionally neutral accent associated with professional occupations and the BBC

Slang   vocabulary (other than dialect) not regarded as part of the 'standard' lexicon

Stance   the attitude taken by a writer towards the subject matter or the reader

Standard English   the accepted vocabulary and grammatical constructions of educated and written use

Stream of consciousness   narrative technique for capturing the spontaneous stream of thought passing through the mind of a character

Subject   grammatical term for the person or thing that acts on a verb (e.g. *MacDonalds* sell burgers)

Taboo   words or expressions felt to be shocking or unacceptable in polite situations

Tense   the aspect of a verb which indicates the time or duration of an action

Transcript   an accurate record of spoken language

Verbs   key class of words whose purpose is to express actions or states

Vulgarism   crude or coarse expression, which falls short of being taboo

2.10 Extension activities

We have touched on a number of linguistic and literary topics in this chapter, and you may wish to pursue some of them at greater length. Here are some suggestions to guide your further study.

2.10.1 Analysis and discussion

▷ Whatever the novels you are studying, pick out some key passages and examine closely:
  - the narrative techniques used by the writer
  - the use the writer makes of dialogue, and how far it conveys the meanings and relationships expressed in conversations
  - any use the writer makes of non-Standard speech.

▷ Pick out another episode from the novel, and rewrite it from a different point of view from the one used by the writer. What differences does this make? How has this helped you understand the writer's reasons for doing it the way s/he chose to?

2.10.2 Research and data-gathering

▷ **British and American varieties of English**

A study of any work of American literature alongside your British texts would provide a good starting-point for a more detailed study of the different varieties of English spoken on both sides of the Atlantic. Your first ports of call could well be:

> Bill Bryson, *Mother Tongue and Made in America*
> David Crystal (ed.), *Cambridge Encyclopaedia of the English Language*
> Robert McCrum *et al.*, *The Story of English*
> Albert Baugh and Thomas Cable, *A History of the English Language*

You could take your study further by taping and transcribing comparable television programmes (such as soap operas or situation comedies) from the UK and the USA. What differences in language do you find?

▷ **World English**

Equally, if you are studying a text from elsewhere in the English-speaking world, you'll find Crystal and McCrum useful guides to the development of what linguists term 'World English'.

▷ **Narratives and children**

As part of your A-level course you may be studying aspects of Language Acquisition. If so, you might like to apply our investigation of narratives in a number of ways:

● Survey the narratives which young children learn to produce – at first in speech, and then later, in writing.

● Examine the kinds of vocabulary, grammar and story structures they use, and consider how their early written stories illustrate the problems of adjusting to the differences between speech and writing.

● Examine texts produced for children of different reading ages – perhaps an abridgement of a 'classic' alongside its original – and analyse the ways in which vocabulary, grammar and meanings develop in complexity for more experienced readers.

● Extend your own original writing activities (see below) to include the production – and market testing! – of your own story for younger readers.

2.10.3 Original writing

▷ In recent years some writers have exploited the popularity of well-known novels such as *Pride and Prejudice* by writing sequels. Try writing part of your own sequel – or even a prequel (the story of what has happened before your novel begins) – to your set text, and justifying your ideas in a commentary, with reference to the original. In this way, you will demonstrate that you can put your understanding of the writer's style and techniques into practice!

2.11 Further reading

We have touched on a number of topics in this chapter; you may like to take your investigations of one or more of them further using some of the following texts:

Narrative styles and structures
Brian Abbs, *Forms of Narrative* (Cambridge University Press, 1990).

Speech and writing
There is an excellent section on this topic, as on most other aspects of language studies, in David Crystal's *Encyclopaedia of the English Language* (Cambridge University Press,1995). A more specialist text is M. A. K. Halliday, *Spoken and Written Language* (Deakin University Press, 1985).

Accents, dialects and non-standard varieties
Some useful sources include:
Peter Trudgill, *The Dialects of England* (Blackwell, 1990)
M. F. Wakelin, *English Dialects: An Introduction* (Athlone Press, 1972).

Fiction
We hope that you may have been attempted by some of the extracts used in this chapter to read the novels from which they are taken. The following list includes some of these, as well as others which you might enjoy and find interesting in the light of our discussions:

Anthony Burgess, *A Clockwork Orange*
Agatha Christie, *The Murder of Roger Ackroyd*
Charles Dickens, *Great Expectations*
Roddy Doyle, *The Commitments*, and *Paddy Clarke, Ha Ha*
L. P. Hartley, *The Go-Between*
Nick Hornby, *Fever Pitch*
D. H. Lawrence, *Sons and Lovers*
Graham Swift, *Last Orders*
Irvine Welsh, *Trainspotting*.

Seeing through verse: the language of poetry

3.0 Introduction

As part of your A-level studies you will almost certainly study at least one collection of poetry. In this chapter, we will examine the work of some of the writers (such as Seamus Heaney, Ted Hughes, William Blake and Sylvia Plath) often set at A-level and explore a number of related linguistic topics and approaches.

However, before we launch into the subject, we should pause a moment to consider what you think poetry is, what it is for, and what your feelings and attitudes towards it are.

ACTIVITY 37

With a partner, decide whether or not you would agree with the statements in Table 3.1 (page 83).

Share your thoughts with the rest of your group. At this stage, it's important to keep an open mind about all of these issues – but you should return to this exercise at at the end of the chapter and see if you have changed your mind!

Table 3.1

Statement	Agree	Disagree	Not sure
(i) Poetry is not really part of everyday life			
(ii) Everybody enjoys poetry			
(iii) I enjoyed poems as a child, but don't any more			
(iv) Poetry is just words with patterns			
(v) Poetry is to prose what whisky is to beer			
(vi) Poetry is deliberately difficult, and full of hidden meanings			
(vii) Poetry is not important			

ACTIVITY 38

Printed below is a selection of eleven texts – both spoken and written – many of which you may recognise. Your task is not to identify them, however, but to sort them into sub-groups which help answer the question, 'What do any of these texts have in common?'.

Text A

Nick Nack paddiwack give the dog a bone
This old man came rolling home

Text B

Maggie! Maggie! Maggie!
Out! Out! Out!

Text C

Between my finger and my thumb
The squat pen rests; snug as a gun.

Text D

Ooh Aah! Ooh Aah! Ooh Aah! Ooh Aah!
Ooh Aah! Cantona!

Text E

Little Lamb, who made thee?
Dost thou know who made thee?

Text F

And all the roads we have to walk are winding
And all the lights that lead us there are blinding

Text G

A million housewives every day
Pick up a can of beans and say
'Beanz meanz Heinz'

Text H

Every cloud has a silver lining

Text I

One potato two potato three potato four
Five potato six potato seven potato more

Text J

Your life was full of kindly deeds, a helping hand to all who needs,
Sincere and true in heart and mind, sweet memories you left behind

Text K

She sells sea-shells on the seashore

COMMENTARY

There are, of course, many ways in which you could classify these texts –
according to their meaning, purpose, genre, audience or age. However, you may
also have found ways of grouping them according to the ways they use sounds
and words to create patterns and structure.

Repetition

This is the basis of all patterns – whether it be a design which repeats itself as part
of a carpet or wallpaper, or a chorus which repeats itself as part of a song. This is
most obviously seen in chants such as texts B and D which consist of multiple
repetitions of a basic element.

Repetition – rhythm

You may have grouped together texts with a similar regular rhythm – such as
texts A (nursery rhyme) and F (song lyric from 'Wonderwall', by Oasis). We
notice a regular rhythm when the 'beats' of a line occur at equal intervals, creating
a repeated pattern:

Beats:	*		*		*		*		*
And	*all*	the	*roads* we		*have* to		*walk* are		*winding*
And	*all*	the	*lights* that		*lead* us		*there* are		*blinding*

(If we were looking at poetry, as opposed to lyrics designed to be sung, we
would talk about **stresses** rather than beats.)

Repetition – rhyme

Several of the texts employ rhyme – usually at the ends of lines, and in
conjunction with a regular rhythm – which is, of course, the repetition of identical
sets of phonemes within different words. So, from text F ('Wonderwall') we have
'winding'/'blinding', from text G (beans advertisement) we have 'day'/'say' as
well as 'beanz'/'meanz', and from text J (newspaper obituary notice)
'mind'/'behind'.

Repetition – near-rhyme

Some of the texts feature pairs of words that fall short of a full rhyme – so you could group together texts A ('home'/'bone'), C ('thumb'/'gun'), and text G ('meanz'/'Heinz').

Repetition – vowels and consonants (assonance and alliteration)

Some of the repeating patterns can be a little less obvious. For example, in 'Nick Nack Paddiwack', as well as the near rhyme of 'bone'/'home' you might notice that the same vowel sound is echoed in the words 'old' and 'rolling'. Similarly, in text C (from Seamus Heaney, 'Digging', *Selected Poems 1965–1975*, 1980), the vowel which occurs in 'thumb' and 'gun' is echoed in 'snug'. This repetition of vowel sounds is known as **assonance**.

You might also have observed that some of the texts feature repeated consonant sounds (i.e. **alliteration**) – most obviously, perhaps, in the well-known tongue-twister that is text K, but also in text G. Here, the unusual spelling of 'beanz' and 'meanz' draws attention, visually, to the fact which orthodox orthography disguises – the final consonant sound of all three words, is, in fact identical, and conveniently, is also the final phoneme of the company's name.

Repetition – parallelism

One final aspect of repetition which some of the texts have in common is the use of identically structured phrases. So, in text E (from William Blake's 'The Lamb' from *Songs of Innocence*) we have two lines ending in 'who made thee?', and the two lines of 'Wonderwall' follow the pattern 'And all the … are … ing'. This kind of structural repetition is sometimes called **parallelism**.

Figurative language – metaphors and similes

You may have linked together those texts which use language figuratively – i.e. the language seems to refer to meanings beyond its surface, literal ones. So, we sense that the old man in the nursery rhyme does not literally 'roll' home, but that the word humorously exaggerates the manner of his movement. The road and lights involved in the song by Oasis are the commonly metaphorical ones – life is being compared to a journey which requires a guiding light – and the sense of the common proverb that is text H ('Every cloud has a silver lining') clearly extends beyond the meteorological! When the comparison of the literal sense with something else – a cloud with a piece of bad news, or a journey along a road with our life – is implied, we usually describe it as a **metaphor**; when the comparison is made explicit, as Seamus Heaney does when he describes his 'squat pen' as being 'snug as a gun', we speak of a **simile**.

Perhaps, above all, we glimpse here the principal characteristic of the language of verse – its deliberate playing with language, its multiple meanings, and its capacity for ambiguity.

To sum up: these texts have been drawn from a variety of sources, from the school playground to the football terraces, and only two of them – the short extracts from works by Blake and Heaney – would be included in most conventional definitions of 'poetry'. However, the patterns which they display characterise a good deal of what is meant by 'poetic language' and reveal that in many different situations, we play the same kinds of linguistic games as we associate with that rarefied activity. Verse, like narrative, is all around us.

3.1 Everyday verse

Let's extend our survey of how language is used playfully and in carefully patterned ways in many everyday situations.

ACTIVITY 39 DATA-GATHERING AND ANALYSIS

1 Making reference to the different kinds of pattern outlined above, point out the techniques which contribute to the impact of the following texts:

Text A	*Patta-cake patta-cake baker's man* *Bake me a cake as quick as you can*
Text B	*Hickory Dickory Dock* *The mouse ran up the clock* *The clock struck one* *The mouse did run* *Hickory Dickory Dock*
Text C	*You can't get better than a Kwik-Fit fitter* *They're the ones to trust*
Text D	*What do we want?* *More jobs!* *When do we want them?* *Now!*
Text E	*No summer cloud is softer* *No moon has a gentler glow* *No blossom could be prettier* *No kinder breeze could blow* *No baby could be sweeter* *With tiny fingers curled* *Like a little angel holding* *All the wonder of the world*

[From a 'Keepsake to celebrate your beautiful baby' card]

2 Choose a location and brainstorm any uses of language associated with it which exhibit some of the characteristics of poetry discussed above. Some examples are offered below:

- your home
- your school/college
- a church or other place of worship
- a newspaper.

3 Choose a specific genre from the list below to investigate. Gather several examples and carry out an analysis of the distinctive ways they use linguistic patterns, or figurative language or ambiguity:
   - nursery rhymes
   - hymns – ancient and modern
   - football chants
   - the lyrics of your favourite band or songwriter
   - advertisements
   - epitaphs
   - greetings-cards messages
   - common sayings, or proverbs.

   Present your findings to the whole of your group.

4 To survey the amount of metaphorical language in everyday use, take a common metaphorical idea – the comparison of life to a journey, or the references to 'light' and 'dark' which feature in 'Wonderwall', for example – and keep a log of the expressions or **idioms** in everyday use which exploit it. (An idiom is an expression whose meaning is not logically derived from its literal sense, e.g. 'he played a blinder'.)

5 Put some of these techniques into practice – try writing your own greetings-card messages, advertising slogans, protest chants etc. for your own choice of occasion.

3.2 The right word in the right order: stylistic approaches

If you set out to create a piece of verse – whether it is a song lyric, advertising jingle or piece of serious poetry – you are involved, even more so than for other forms of writing, in a series of very deliberate choices. You will, no doubt, have a central meaning, idea, message or experience which you wish to convey to your readers, but you will face an alarming number of decisions about how you will do so.

For some writers, some of the choices may not always be conscious ones – you may hit upon a phrase or line which 'sounds right' without deliberately having opted for a line which corresponds to a particular rhythmic pattern or consciously thought, 'Now then, let's try a touch of alliteration here'!

However, as readers and students of language, we try to reach an understanding of what makes pieces of verse work and create the impact which advertisers, hymn-writers and greetings-cards manufacturers – not to mention poets such as Seamus Heaney, Ted Hughes, William Blake and Sylvia Plath – obviously believe it to have.

So, it may be helpful to think of the choices we face as writers on a number of different levels, as shown in Table 3.2:

Table 3.2 Take your choice – at five levels

Level 1: Sounds	We have already seen how verse depends not just on the meanings of the words, but on particular arrangements of the sounds which make them up. So – what effects can I achieve by paying attention to the vowels, consonants and rhythmic qualities of language?
Level 2: Words	This is the selection of individual words from the many possibilities in any given situation. Which words should I use – and how many? – at different points in my verse?
Level 3: Phrases and sentences	How do I combine my words into phrases? What kinds of sentences will I produce? What is the best order for me to put my words in?
Level 4: Graphology and orthography	Verse allows greater freedom than prose as far as the layout, presentation, punctuation and sometimes even spelling of text are concerned. So – how should I break up my text into lines? How shall I punctuate my verse to guide my reader's response?
Level 5: Structure, form and organisation	Like prose narratives, poems – whether or not they tell a 'story' – convey meanings in a structured way. What will that structure be? Will I use an established form of poetry (such as a sonnet) or develop my own?

Understanding the meanings and effects of texts as a result of these choices – conscious or unconscious, accidental or deliberate – at all of these levels is what **stylistic analysis** is about.

In the remainder of this chapter, we will explore our 'core' texts – principally, the poetry of Hughes and Heaney – and a variety of other verse in ways which you can apply to texts of all kinds.

3.2.1 Sounds

Words and sounds without meaning

The verse which younger children respond to often includes patterns of sounds being manipulated or repeated for their own sake and for the pleasure this gives. These may be the same sounds as make up words – phonemes – but combined to make 'nonsense' words with no literal sense.

Some of the best-known examples are to be found in the verse of the nineteenth-century writer, Edward Lear. Here is the first verse of his poem, 'Mr and Mrs Spikky Sparrow':

> *On a little piece of wood*
> *Mr. Spikky Sparrow stood;*
> *Mrs. Sparrow sat close by,*
> *A-making of an insect pie,*
> *For her little children five,*
> *In the nest and all alive,*
> *Singing with a cheerful smile*
> *To amuse them all the while,*
> *Twikky wikky wikky wee,*
> *Wikky bikky twikky tee,*
> *Spikky bikky bee!*

[Edward Lear, 'Mr and Mrs Spikky Sparrow', in I. and P. Opie (eds), *The Oxford Book of Children's Verse*, 1973]

Six subsequent verses consist of a further eight lines of 'normal' verse followed by variations on these nonsense sounds, such as:

> *Chippy wippy sikky tee*
> *Bikky wikky tikky mee*
> *Spikky chippy wee!*

and

> *Zikky wikky mikky bee,*
> *Witch witchy mitchy kee,*
> *Sikky tikky we!*

We might think we outgrow such childish linguistic pleasures – but consider these lyrics from well-known rock 'n' roll songs:

> *Be bop a lula and she's my baby*
> *Be bop a lula I don't mean maybe*

or

> *Shang a lang a ding dong*

or this refrain of a winning Eurovision song:

> *La – la la la, La la la*
> *La la la, La – la la la*
> *La la la – la*

or even this chorus from the song 'Sigh No More' in Shakespeare's *Much Ado About Nothing*:

> *Converting all your sighs of woe*
> *To Hey Nonny Nonny*

[Act 2, scene 3, lines 72–3]

ACTIVITY 40

1 Survey your CD collection for examples from song lyrics of 'adult' nonsense words

2 Try writing your own verse for children which, like Edward Lear's, uses a nonsense refrain.

Words which mean what they sound – onomatopoeia

It is a basic principle of modern linguistics that a word is not naturally connected to the object or idea to which it refers. So, although English-speakers agree to call a particular kind of animal a 'dog', we could just as easily call it a 'mouse', or a 'banana', or a 'dawble'. And of course, if we are French, we can equally well call it a 'chien'. The influential linguist Ferdinand de Saussure described this characteristic of language as **the arbitrariness of the sign**.

However, there is a small group of words which sound as if they *do* have a natural relationship with the things to which they refer, and writers of verse may find these **onomatopoeic** words particularly useful.

ACTIVITY 41

1 Some common examples of **onomatopoeia** are:

   pop
   sizzle
   quack
   hiss.

In groups, brainstorm as many more as you can add to this list.

2 Consider Seamus Heaney's 'Churning Day', which describes the traditional process of butter-making. Here is the final verse – with four words omitted. From your collection of onomatopoeic words, select four which would help to convey the sounds made as the milk is churned and the newly formed butter shaped into lumps by the wooden 'spades'.

> *The house would stink long after churning day,*
> *acrid as a sulphur mine. The empty crocks*
> *were ranged along the wall again, the butter*
> *in soft printed slabs was piled on pantry shelves.*
> *And in the house we moved with gravid ease,*
> *our brains turned crystals full of clean deal churns,*
> *the (1 ...) and (2 ...) of the sour-breathed milk,*
> *the (3 ...) and (4 ...) of small spades on wet lumps.*

> [Seamus Heaney, 'Churning Day', *Selected Poems 1965–1975*, 1980.
> All the poems by Heaney quoted in this book are from this anthology]

3 Check on page 91 for the words actually chosen by Heaney – and compare their effectiveness with the ones you used.

4 By surveying a range of advertisements on television, collect a range of examples of advertisers exploiting the onomatopoeic properties of words in their product names, slogans and jingles.

5 There are other groups of words which stop short of onomatopoeia, but whose meanings and sounds seem to be loosely associated. For example, what do some words beginning with 'sl', such as 'slip', 'slide', 'slime', 'slobber', and 'sloppy' have in common? Identify other similar groups.

6 If you are studying the poetry of Seamus Heaney, consider what use Heaney makes of onomatopoeic, or near-onomatopoeic words in the poems 'Death of a Naturalist' and 'The Wife's Tale'.

(Heaney's choice of words for 'Churning Day': 1 – 'plash'; 2 – 'gurgle'; 3 – 'pat'; 4 – 'slap'.)

The music of words

We have already looked at a number of ways in which verse plays with, and creates patterns from the material sounds of language, and identified some common features such as rhythm, rhyme, near-rhyme, alliteration, and assonance (see Section 3.1). When we look at the choices we face at our Level 3 – phrases and sentences – we'll look more closely at how we can manipulate the pace and rhythms of language. First, though, let's concentrate on what songwriters already know very well – how our choice of words is influenced not just by what they mean, but also by how they sound.

Consider, for example, the following well-known love poem. Try reading aloud only the vowel sounds – and note especially each occurrence of the longer vowel phonemes. What sort of pattern do you find, and what would you say it contributes to the mood and feel of the poem?

> *The Owl and the Pussy-cat went to sea*
> *In a beautiful pea-green boat,*
> *They took some honey and plenty of money*
> *Wrapped up in a five-pound note.*
> *The Owl looked up to the stars above,*
> *And sang to a small guitar*
> *'O lovely Pussy! O Pussy my love,*
> *What a beautiful pussy you are,*
> *You are,*
> *You are,*
> *What a beautiful Pussy you are!'*

[Edward Lear, 'The Owl and the Pussy-cat', 1871]

ACTIVITY 42

Compare these two ways of expressing the same basic idea:

> In sooth I know not why I am so sad
> I've really no idea what I'm so miserable about.

1 Read each of them aloud.

2 What differences did you find in the 'feel' of the lines?

3 Consider the words which make up each phrase. All of the words in the first version consist only of a single syllable – unlike the second. What difference does this make? (To help answer this question, try saying each of them as fast as you can.)

4 Now repeat the vowel-only reading exercise you tried above. What do you discover about the vowel sounds in each line, and how do they contribute to the poem's overall effect?

3.2.2 Words

The nature of choice

As we set about writing a piece of verse, our choice of possible words seems enormous. To understand the kinds of choices a writer faces, let's look at the following poem by Ted Hughes, in which he finds in a field full of thistles echoes of the land's history:

> *Against the rubber tongues of cows and the hoeing hands of men*
> *Thistles spike the summer air*
> *Or crackle open under a blue-black pressure.*
>
> *Every one a revengeful burst*
> *Of resurrection, a grasped fistful*
> *Of splintered weapons and Icelandic frost thrust up*
>
> *From the underground stain of a decayed Viking.*
> *They are like pale hair and the gutturals of dialects.*
> *Every one manages a plume of blood.*
>
> *Then they grow grey, like men.*
> *Mown down, it is a feud. Their sons appear,*
> *Stiff with weapons, fighting back over the same ground.*
>
> [Ted Hughes, 'Thistles' from *Selected Poems*, 1982]

Let's just focus on the opening verse. What options did Hughes have, given the ideas which he wished to convey?

In the case of some of the words, the choice is limited by the structure of phrases and the need for a certain class of word. For example, there is only a small number of alternatives to 'Against' on line 1 and 'under' on line 3:

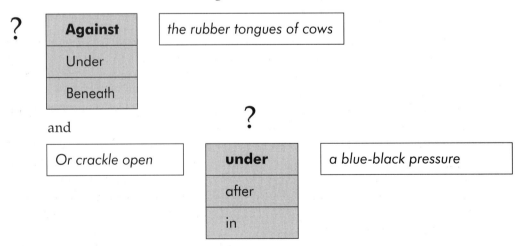

Some alternative words from the same class are grammatically possible, but would make little sense:

Onto *the rubber tongues of cows and the hoeing hands of men*

or

Or crackle open **beyond** *a blue black pressure.*

This class of words is called **prepositions** (see glossary for Chapter 2, page 79). Similarly, there are few options for filling these slots:

Against ... rubber tongues

and

under ... blue-black pressure

These might include 'the' (i.e. the **definite article**), 'a' (i.e. the **indefinite article**), 'some', 'this'/'that'/'these', or in the case of the first line, a number (e.g. *three* rubber tongues). This class of words is often called **determiners**.

However, elsewhere in these opening lines, Hughes faced more interesting choices.

ACTIVITY 43

Let's take the two phrases in the opening line:

the	rubber	tongues	of	cows
the	hoeing	hands	of	men

and

noting in passing that their structural similarity contributes something to the rhythm and balance of the line! In fact, they each use an **adjective** ('rubber','hoeing') to **pre-modify** (i.e. placed in front of) a **noun** ('tongues', 'hands'); in other words, they attribute a quality or action to an object. In addition, you will have spotted that the nouns and adjectives are connected phonetically – by the assonance (for many speakers!) of the vowel sound in 'r*u*bber t*o*ngues' and the alliteration of /h/ in '*h*oeing *h*ands'.

Your task is to suggest half-a-dozen alternatives each for the words 'rubber', 'hoeing' and 'men' – and discuss the differences they make to the lines.

COMMENTARY

'Rubber' could be replaced by other adjectives which describe more literally (as we know the cow's tongues are not actually made of rubber!) the texture of a material – 'rough', 'wet', 'crinkly' – or by more purely factual terms such as 'long', 'flat', 'pink' etc. The writer could convey an attitude towards the tongue with a word like 'nasty', 'malodorous', 'gorgeous' or 'squidgy', or remain fairly objective with terms such as 'revolving', or 'protuberant'.

'Hoeing' could be replaced by other words which describe the actions of the men's hands – verbs, in fact, moonlighting as adjectives! – such as 'digging', 'ploughing', 'clasping', or 'clutching'. Alternatively, the men need not be described as active at all; their hands could simply be 'strong', 'dirty', 'gnarled' or 'arthritic'. Hughes could pity the men – describing their hands as 'broken', 'futile', or 'bloody' – or admire them as 'noble', 'sturdy', or 'unswerving'. If the alliterative pattern is important, he could have had 'hopeless' or 'haggard'. 'Hoeing', however, implies something of the manual struggle involved in farming the kind of rough terrain associated with thistles, and simply shows the men getting on with a basic job, apparently unaware of the violent and bloody history which Hughes sees in the landscape.

At first glance, what could be more obvious than the word 'men'? Yet alternatives would include more specific occupational labels such as 'ploughmen', 'workers', or 'farmers' or 'gardeners', the less specific 'people' and 'beings', and less formal 'blokes', 'fellows' or 'chaps'.

Putting all of this together, we might have produced a first line that went:

> *Against the wonderful tongues of cows and the happy hands of blokes*
> *Thistles spike the summer air ...*

Not quite the same poem!

So, at Level 2 of our choices – Words – we can distinguish between the fairly limited word-classes whose function is mainly to act as the nuts, bolts and rivets of the sentences (prepositions, determiners, conjunctions) and the 'load-bearing' classes (verbs, nouns and adjectives – with adverbs to follow!) which offer an almost infinite choice of meaningful possibilities.

Nouns and adjectives

Nouns are the most frequent word-class and any text is likely to contain many of them. As writers, we have to decide not only which nouns we use, but also whether or not to qualify them with adjectives, and if, so, of what kind.

ACTIVITY 44

Listed in Table 3.3 are the nouns and adjectives which two poets have chosen to use in the opening lines of one of their poems.

1 In groups or pairs, classify the nouns into sub-groups in any way which seems useful or interesting.

2 On the basis of this evidence, what can you predict about each of the poems – and how would you compare the kinds of nouns used in each case?

3 Now consider the adjectives. Suggest which of the adjectives in each poem might be matched up with which of the nouns – and define the differences in the kinds of adjectives each writer has chosen to use.

Table 3.3

Poem A Nouns	Adjectives	Poem B Nouns	Adjectives
rain	heavy	season	mellow
sun	full	mists	close
week	glossy	fruitfulness	maturing
blackberries	purple	bosom-friend	mossed
clot	red	sun	
knot	green	fruit	
flesh	hard	vines	
wine	sweet	thatch-eaves	
blood	thickened	apples	
stains	summer's	cottage-trees	
tongue		fruit	
lust		ripeness	
		core	

COMMENTARY

You may notice that the nouns in Poem A are all ones in frequent everyday use, and with the exception of 'blackberries' are of one syllable. You could connect words of related meanings (in clusters of words which linguists call **semantic fields**, semantics being the aspect of language study relating to the meanings of words), grouping together 'rain'/'sun', or 'flesh'/'blood'/'clot'/'tongue', or 'stain'/'wine'/'blood' or even 'lust'/'flesh'/'tongue'. How might these groups link to the mention of blackberries? Mostly the nouns describe things that can be seen, touched, heard, tasted or smelt – these are called **concrete** nouns. Two – 'week' and 'lust' – describe concepts or feelings. These are called **abstract nouns**.

The nouns of Poem B have a certain amount in common – there are the semantic fields which link 'fruit'/'vines'/'apples'/'core' and 'sun'/'mists'. Another group of hyphenated concrete nouns includes the related 'thatch-eaves' and 'cottage-trees', as well as 'bosom-friend', which is something of an 'odd man out' as it would seem to refer to human life. However, Poem B also features two abstract nouns – 'fruitfulness' and 'ripeness' – that are semantically related to the concrete nouns 'fruit', 'vines', 'apples'.

As for adjectives, Poem A's include several which convey visual information, including colours – 'purple', 'red', 'green', 'glossy' – some of which could easily be associated with more than one of the nouns. Is it the blackberries, the wine, the blood, the stains, the tongue or even the sun, for example, that is red? Another group describes texture – 'thickened', 'heavy', 'hard' and possibly even 'full' – reinforcing the largely concrete appeal to the senses of the poem's vocabulary. Poem B uses notably fewer adjectives – but you might have noted a phonetic connection between three of them – '*m*ellow', '*m*aturing' and '*m*ossed' – and some of the nouns '*m*ossed'/'*m*ists'/ 'fruitful*ness*'/'ripe*ness*').

You will have come up with your own 'predictions' about the likely contents of each poem. However close to the originals you may be, you have learned something about the choices facing writers as far as nouns and adjectives are concerned. We can summarise these as shown in Table 3.4:

Table 3.4

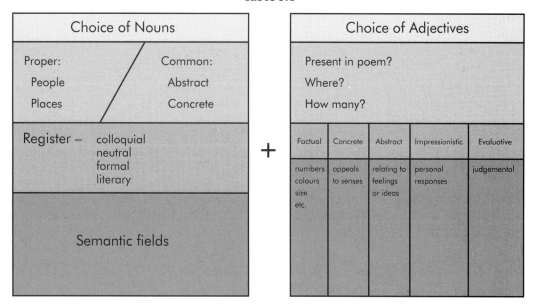

ACTIVITY 45

1 Compare the ideas you came up with in Activity 44 with the lines as they were actually written (below). How has each writer exploited the associations of the words to create surprising effects?

Poem A   *Late August, given heavy rain and sun*
               For a full week, the blackberries would ripen.
               At first, just one, a glossy purple clot
               Among others, red, green, hard as a knot.
               You ate that first one and its flesh was sweet
               Like thickened wine: summer's blood was in it
               Leaving stains upon the tongue and lust for
               Picking. ....

                                        [Seamus Heaney, 'Blackberry-Picking']

Poem B   *Season of mists and mellow fruitfulness,*
               Close bosom-friend of the maturing sun;
               Conspiring with him how to load and bless
               With fruit the vines that round the thatch-eaves run;
               To bend with apples the mossed cottage-trees,
               And fill all fruit with ripeness to the core; ...

                                        [John Keats, 'To Autumn', 1820]

2 Apply this exercise to two more poems from the collections which you are studying – try to compare two poems which are similar in subject-matter but diferent in style.

3 It may be possible to construct texts which consist only of nouns and adjectives – shopping-lists, for example. Try to produce a short piece of verse in this way – perhaps listing your impressions of a person, place or object. You could introduce into your list patterns such as:

- alliteration (possibly working through the alphabet, e.g. arching arrows, bending bows)
- pairs of opposites (words with similar numbers of syllables and stresses, e.g. summer days, winter nights)
- include in sequence items which appeal to the five senses.

Verbs and adverbs

Verbs *are* the heart of a sentence – they *define* the action or a state of affairs which *is* central to the meaning *being expressed*. Sometimes, they *appear* as a single word; at others, a writer *may have had to use* a whole sequence of words (i.e. a **verb phrase**) *to convey* the action or state. Verbs *tell* us many things about an action – not just what *happened* and when it *happened* (or *is going to happen*) but also what the speaker or writer's attitude to the action *is* and whether we *think* it *should have happened*, or *must happen*, or *didn't need to have happened*.

Sometimes, we may wish to offer more information about where, when or how something occurs – which is where **adverbs** come in. As single words they include words like 'quickly', 'here', and 'yesterday', but it is best to think of whole phrases (i.e. **adverbial phrases**) doing this job. So, if I tell you that I was running very quickly down the street the other day, I've used three adverbial phrases – one each to say something about how ('very quickly'), where ('down the street') and when ('the other day') I was running.

ACTIVITY 46   VERBS IN 'THATCHER'

To explore the possibilities this time, we'll consider a poem by Seamus Heaney which describes the long-awaited visit to a village community of the thatcher, whose skilled task is to repair the thatched roofs of cottages.

The verbs (including verb phrases) have been omitted from the text and lettered.

> (a) … for weeks, he (b) … some morning
> Unexpectedly, his bicycle (c) …
> With a light ladder and a bag of knives.
> He (d) … the old rigging, (e) … the eaves,
>
> (f) … and (g) … sheaves of lashed wheat-straw.
> Next, the bundled rods: hazel and willow
> (h) … for weight, (i) … in case they'(j) …
> It (k) … he (l) … the morning (m) …:
>
> Then (n) … the ladder, (o) … well honed blades
> And (p) … at straw and (q) … ends of rods
> That, (r) … in two, (s) … a white-pronged staple
> For (t) … his world, handful by handful.
>
> (u) … for days on sods above the rafters
> He (v) … and (w) … the butts, (x) … all together
> Into a sloped honeycomb, a stubble patch,
> And (y) … them (z) … at his Midas* touch.

> *Midas was a King in Greek mythology gifted with
> the power of turning everything he touched to gold

[Seamus Heaney, 'Thatcher']

As you see, removing the verbs leaves a lot of holes – 26 in a poem of 16 lines. However, as this is a poem describing the actions of a skilled craftsman, this should not be surprising.

1 Before we try to supply the missing pieces of 'Thatcher', carry out a numerical survey of the numbers of verbs in two other poems which you are studying. Choose one which seems to be about actions, like 'Thatcher', and one which by contrast is more descriptive and slow-paced. Note the differences you find.

   Of course, the differences may not just be a matter of the numbers of verbs you find, but the different kinds of verbs and how they are used – as we will see.

2 Returning to 'Thatcher', in pairs or groups, suggest possible verbs/verb phrases for each of the spaces (a) to (z), keeping a note not only of the ones you finally select, but also of the other possibilities which you reject.

COMMENTARY

In trying to solve this puzzle, you will have encountered choices which can teach us a lot about the way verbs work in English. You may find it useful in this commentary and in the following activity to discuss your options under some linguistic headings and using some precise terminology.

Tense

You might choose to describe the whole sequence of the thatcher's actions in the present, past or future. If, like a sports commentator, a present tense is used ('he arrives some morning', 'he checks out the old rigging,' etc.) it might give the poem immediacy. However, Heaney here prefers the **simple past** tense which is usually used for reporting completed past events ('he turned up', 'he eyed the old rigging').

Space (a): The possibilities here are various – Heaney's choice, 'bespoke', is a slightly archaic term meaning 'ordered' or 'commissioned' and survives in made-to-measure tailoring. It implies craftsmanship and a certain exclusiveness. Grammatically, it is an irregular form of the **past participle** – the part of the verb used in constructions such as 'had been ordered', or 'was received'.

Space (b): Heaney's 'turned up' is a more casual and informal choice than 'arrived' would be, and introduces us to the **phrasal verb** – consisting of a verb + preposition. There are thousands of these in English, and in general they belong to more informal styles of expression. They often carry a meaning which is different from their literal sense – the thatcher doesn't 'turn' and neither does his arrival have anything to do with 'up' – he simply arrives. As in this example, phrasal verbs often have more formal or literary single-word equivalents ('arrived').

Spaces (c) and (d): At (c), Heaney's choice – 'slung' – once again implies a degree of carelessness. Alternatives such as 'loaded with' or 'equipped with' might imply greater precision or care. By contrast, Heaney's word here at (d) – 'eyed' – suggests an expertise and precision in the thatcher's work. It is simple, monosyllabic but visually very suggestive.

Spaces (e)–(h): At (e), Heaney uses 'poked at' – another verb which almost implies random carelessness. The thatcher does know what he is doing – but to the inexpert and unskilled observer, his actions appear almost casual. At (f) and (g), the thatcher's actions are simply 'opened' and 'handled' – words from an entirely ordinary register, as it is through inexpert eyes and with non-technical vocabulary that we are viewing the work, though 'handled' begins to imply some expert assessment or checking of his materials. At (h), Heaney opts for 'hazel and willow/were flicked for weight'. In this form of the verb, whilst the person doing the flicking – the **agent** – is clearly still the thatcher, he is not named, and the object of his attentions, the hazel and willow, have become, oddly, the **subject** of the verb. This construction is known as the **passive** form of the verb – as opposed to the **active** forms which have been used elsewhere in the poem (see Activity 47, task 4 on page 103).

Spaces (i)–(m): At (i) and (j), we're back with active verbs – 'twisted' and 'they'd snap' (though the second of these applies to the bits of wood) – and (k) and (l) join together to form 'it seemed he spent'. At (m), we meet another phrasal verb. Once again, a single-word alternative such as 'preparing' would have conveyed the sense, but Heaney's choice – 'warming up' – sounds more informal, and makes the whole process seem more like an athletic performance.

Spaces (n)–(t): The third verse depicts the start of the real work, and so we are bombarded with a stream of active verbs. None of them are technical, and their one- or two-syllable simplicity is appropriate for the apparent ease of the craftsman's art. So, we have 'fixed' (n), 'laid out' – another phrasal verb – (o), 'snipped' (p), and 'sharpened' at (q); the basic 'bent' (r) and 'made' (s) and 'pinning down' at (t).

Spaces (u)–(z): The final verse, like the opening one with its 'bespoke', begins with a word which strikes us as rather archaic – 'couchant' (u), a term usually associated with heraldry, and literally, in French, 'resting' or 'lying'. Why these archaisms? Heaney's choice must be related to the ancient nature of the craft, and the semi-legendary status which he attributes to it (see also his reference to Midas in the final line). Then (v), (u) and (x) capture the rapidity of his actions with three successive, simple (again) active verbs – 'snipped', 'flushed' and 'stitched'. The last line switches the focus from the thatcher himself to the onlooking crowds – 'he left them gaping' – the single action attributed to the villagers portraying them as astonished, child-like spectators at a magical show.

We can group together the verbs in the poem in different ways which can help us understand how the poem is working. You could tabulate them as shown in Table 3.5.

Table 3.5

Agent	Verb	Tense/Form	Options	Phrasal	Active	Passive
(he)	bespoke	past participle	expected/ ordered/ commissioned/ requested/ waited for	No		✓
he	turned up	simple past	arrived	Yes	✓	
(he)	slung	past participle	loaded/packed/ equipped/ fitted up with	N		✓
he	eyed	simple past	looked at/ examined/ checked out/felt	No	✓	
(he)	poked at	simple past	looked at/ inspected/ messed about with/ played around with	Yes	✓	
(he)	opened	simple past	made/stuck in	No	✓	
(he)	handled	simple past	measured/cut	No	✓	
(he)	flicked	simple past	checked/tested	No		✓
... and so on						

Alternatively, we can collect the actions attributed to different participants as shown in Table 3.6 (page 100).

Table 3.6

THATCHER Active	Passive	VILLAGERS Active	Passive	OTHER Active	Passive
Simple, ordinary: handled opened	flicked twisted	gaping		(hazel and willow)	
Archaic, specialised: couchant				'd snap	
Implying care and skill: eyed					
Apparently casual: turned up poked at					
… and so on					

By tabulating the verbs in these ways, we can see at a glance that:
- there are many active verbs attributing actions to the thatcher
- even the passive verbs imply his actions
- some of them imply careful skill
- more of them seem to imply an apparently casual approach
- the villagers are attributed only one action – gaping.

Adverbs

Remarkably, for a poem which describes actions, 'Thatcher' employs very few adverbs ('unexpectedly') or adverbial phrases ('some morning'). This seems to be a definite choice – after all, Heaney might well have qualified each of the verbs with an appropriate adverb, e.g.: 'Opened carefully and handled with thought sheaves of lashed wheat-straw' or 'He precisely shaved and flushed the butts, stitched all together slowly'.

▷ Why do you think Heaney has not done so – and what difference has this choice made to the impact of the final poem?

Your choice of verbs

So, as you write your verse, or any text, you have a bewildering number of choices to make when it comes to verbs and adverbs, as we can see in Figure 3.1 on page 102.

ACTIVITY 47   MORE ON VERBS AND ADVERBS

1 Consider the common verb 'take'. Brainstorm as many phrasal verbs based on the verb ('take in', 'take out,' etc.) as you can along with their meanings. Some phrasal verbs may have multiple meanings – 'I can take in (i.e. understand) an idea', 'take in (i.e. accommodate) a lodger', or 'take in (i.e. deceive) someone with a lie', etc.

Here is a linguistic hypothesis: 'Phrasal verbs are always more informal or colloquial than their single-word equivalents.'

True, or false? Test the hypothesis by coming up with (i.e. proposing) a single word alternative for each of your phrasal verbs and putting them on (i.e. placing them on) a 'formality spectrum' such as we used in Activity 20 (page 52).

2 So far, we have talked only in very simple terms about verb tenses. However, it would be wrong to assume that there are just past, present and future tenses.

Take a simple sentence such as 'Giants kill trolls'. Discover how many different tenses there are in English by replacing 'kill' with variations such as 'killed', 'have killed', 'are going to kill' and 'used to kill'.

You will be able to extend your list considerably if you throw in 'will', 'shall', 'should', 'would', 'can', 'could', 'must', and 'needs' – the so-called **modal verbs**.

3 Next, the difficult part. Take two closely related tenses – for example, 'giants kill trolls' and 'giants are killing trolls', or 'giants have killed trolls' and 'giants used to kill trolls' – and try to explain to a foreign student of English when s/he should use one rather than the other.

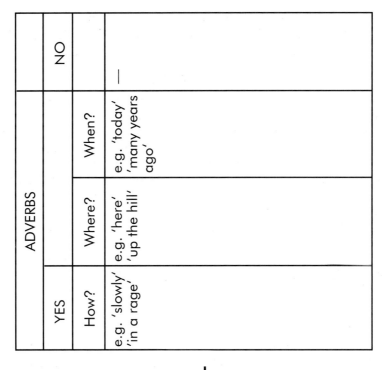

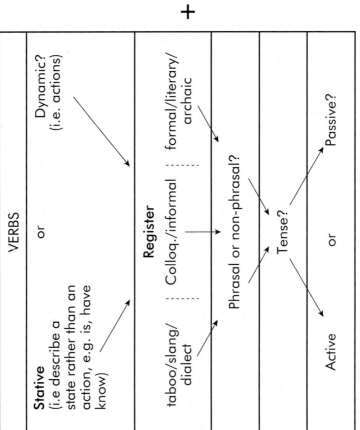

Figure 3.1 Choices: verbs and adverbs

4   Actives and passives
    Make sure you understand the difference between these forms of verbs in the
    examples in Table 3.7. In the passives, we have the option of whether or not to
    include information about the agent (shown in brackets).

Table 3.7

Actives	Passives
Giants kill trolls	Trolls are killed (by giants)
The boss sacked the workers	The workers were sacked (by the boss)
Someone totally untrustworthy informed me that the lesson was cancelled	I was informed (by someone totally untrustworthy) that the lesson was cancelled
My mate thinks the moon is made out of cheese	The moon is thought (by my mate) to be made out of cheese.

How would you describe the different impacts of these two forms, and what
reason might there be for using one rather than the other? Assist your thinking
by surveying a range of texts and noting the uses of active and passive forms.

5   Survey and analyse the uses of verbs in any two of the poems you are
    studying (or any other two pieces of verse – you could revisit some of the
    extracts we looked at, or other data you collected, in Section 3.1). What does
    this comparison reveal about the two pieces?

Semantic fields

We have already begin to see that even if we think we know what we want to say
in our verse, we still face a wide choice from within the lexicon of English – and
the choices we make will be vital for the impact of our poem on our readers. It is
sometimes said that there is no such thing in English as a pure **synonym** (i.e. one
word with exactly the same meaning as another), because even words with very
similar surface meaning (or **denotation**) will have different sets or associations, or
connotations. A thesaurus can be a very useful writing tool, as it groups words
together by semantic field and allows you to select the one which has the
connotations and impact you are looking for.

ACTIVITY 48

Let's say that like Ted Hughes, you are setting out to write a poem which begins
with an impression of some distant sounds in the evening. One of these is a dog
barking; another a metal bucket being used or allowed to fall to the ground. So,
you get as far as:

A cool small evening shrunk to a dog bark and the … of a bucket.

[Ted Hughes, 'Full Moon and Little Frieda', from *Selected Poems*, 1982]

Here are some of the associated words which your thesaurus might offer you:
'rattle', 'clatter', 'clank', 'tinkle', 'clunk', 'clink'– we might note in passing some
remarkable phonetic connections between them! (see Activity 41, task 5 on page 90).

1 Which one would you choose – and why?

2 How would you define the difference – once again, for a foreign student of English – between any two of the others? In this case, your choice is largely to do with how accurately you think each of the words captures the particular noise you have in mind (for Hughes, the choice was 'clank').

3 Sometimes, however, the choice may be more difficult – if, for example, the words imply different attitudes towards the same thing.
Suppose you had chosen to write about a city. In your poem, so far, you have:

> *Under the brown fog of a winter dawn*
> *A ... flowed over London Bridge ....*

[T. S. Eliot, 'Unreal City' from *The Waste Land*, 1922]

and you search for a collective term for the large numbers of people you meet in the streets. This is the selection from your thesaurus this time: 'crowd', 'mob', 'throng', 'multitude', 'mass'.

What are the different connotations of each, and how might this influence your choice?

In a manner of speaking – figurative and literal uses of language

One last set of choices we face at Level 2 – Words – is whether or not to choose words which actually mean what they say. As we found in the commentary to Activity 38 (under 'Figurative language', page 85), even in many non-literary contexts we use language in ways which might baffle a foreign student of English who expects to find merely the dictionary sense of the words s/he hears. Opening a dictionary of idioms at random makes the point. On a single page we have:

> *I heard it on the **grapevine***
> *It was just sour **grapes***
> *You'll have to **grasp** the nettle*
> *There is frustration at **grass** roots level*
> *He doesn't let the **grass** grow under his feet*
> *It's time to put him out to **grass***
> *She's got one foot in the **grave***
> *He'd turn in his **grave**.*

In each case the meaning is not what appears from the literal sense, but is understood to be based on some kind of comparison – to tackle a difficult situation is like getting hold of a stinging plant, etc.

ACTIVITY 49

Sometimes, we make this comparison absolutely explicit, by using words such as 'like' or 'as' and forming similes. In her poem 'Morning Song', written about her infant child, Sylvia Plath uses a number of these comparisons. Using Table 3.8, identify them, and suggest what each subject has in common with the thing with which it is being compared:

Love set you going like a fat gold watch.
The midwife slapped your footsoles, and your bald cry
Took its place among the elements

Our voices echo, magnifying your arrival. New statue.
In a drafty museum, your nakedness
Shadows our safety. We stand round blankly as walls

I'm no more your mother
Than the cloud that distils a mirror to reflect its own slow
Effacement at the wind's hand.

All night your moth breath
Flickers among the flat pink roses. I wake to listen:
A far sea moves in my ear.

One cry, and I stumble from bed, cow-heavy and floral
In my Victorian nightgown.
Your mouth opens clean as a cat's. The window square

Whitens and swallows its dull stars. And now you try
Your handful of notes;
The clear vowels rise like balloons.

[Sylvia Plath, 'Morning Song', from *Selected Poems*, 1985]

Table 3.8

Subject	Being compared to	What they have in common
Baby	Fat gold watch	
Our expressions etc.	Walls	

As you complete this exercise, you may have noticed that there are other comparisons being made which are not signalled so obviously. For example, how can a baby's cry be 'bald'? In what sense is the newly born baby a 'New statue'? We are now in the area of metaphor.

Go on to identify other similar comparisons in 'Morning Song', and suggest your own answers to these and other similar questions. As you do so, make any connections or contrasts you can between the metaphors Sylvia Plath has used.

COMMENTARY
The 'baldness' of the baby's cry – stark, unrestrained – is connected with the blankness of the walls and the observer's expression to create a highly impersonal, featureless and cold atmosphere. The detachment which this seems to imply – the child is an object for contemplation in a museum, rather than than a life to be warmly embraced – is reinforced by the complex metaphor in which Plath compares the relationship of mother and child to that between a cloud and a

pool of the rainwater it has produced which simply reflects its eventual disappearance, or death.

Two metaphors based on animal life contrast the delicate lightness of the infant's breath with the heaviness the mother feels – 'moth' and 'cow'. In suggesting the child's breath 'flickers', Plath makes an interesting comparison between two senses – the sound and touch of the baby's gentle breath is described in terms of a faint light.

ACTIVITY 50

Similes and metaphors are much favoured by songwriters as well as poets. Examine and discuss the use of similes and metaphors in this song, by the Waterboys:

> I was grounded
> while you filled the skies
> I was dumbfounded by truth
> you cut through lies
> I saw the rain dirty valley
> you saw Brigadoon
> I saw the crescent
> you saw the Whole of the Moon
>
> I spoke about wings
> you just flew
> I wondered I guessed and I tried
> you just knew
> I sighed
> … but you SWOONED!
> I saw the crescent
> you saw the Whole of the Moon

[Mike Scott, 'The Whole of the Moon',
Ⓟ Dizzy Heights Music Publ Ltd / Chrysalis Music Ltd]

Some comparisons in everyday speech are in frequent use and can be highly predictable. This is Cliché World, where we are white as a sheet, cold as ice, happy as Larry, pure as the driven snow, drunk as a skunk, or even sick as a parrot. The language of sports commentary and analysis seems to be particularly prone to such phrases, and the occasions when commentators mix their metaphors is often a source of amusement – indeed, these have gifted to the language a new term, 'Colemanballs'. See how the confused figurative language has created unwitting humour in the following examples:

Within a few hours, in Moscow, the Olympic Flame will have been put into cold storage for another four years
[attributed to Gordon Clough]

He is going up and down like a metronome
[attributed to Ron Pickering]

This man could be a black horse
[attributed to David Coleman]

Tahamata went through the air like a torpedo [attributed to Peter Jones]

I have other irons in the fire, but I'm keeping them close to my chest [attributed to John Bond]

Aston Villa began to harness the fruits of some good midfield work [attributed to Alan Towers]

[All quoted from Private Eye's *Colemanballs*, compiled and edited by Barry Fantoni, 1982]

However, speakers and writers are capable of endless creativity in coining new comparisons which amuse, surprise and shock. Ben Elton and Richard Curtis, for example, the writers of the TV 'Blackadder' series, came up with these variations:

I'm as bored as a pacifist's pistol

He might be as difficult to find as a piece of hay in a massive stack of needles

and even

She's as wet as a fish's wet bits

and …

As cunning as a fox who's just been appointed Professor of Cunning at Oxford University.

[from BBC TV's Video tape of 'Blackadder', First World War series]

It is the capacity of figurative language to surprise, and to make us see the world and our experiences in a new light – almost as if we are like aliens, seeing, hearing, touching, tasting or smelling them for the first time – which writers of verse try to exploit.

ACTIVITY 51

The poem below by Craig Raine illustrates this – he considers various aspects of human life as seen by a visiting Martian. He focuses (but not in this order!) on cars, telephones, the climate, night-time, dreaming, books and their effects on their readers, watches and clocks and even visiting the toilet.

Read it closely, identify from this list the objects and actions which his 'Martian's eye' perspective has focused on, and make clear the basis for the comparisons he has made:

Caxtons are mechanical birds with many wings
and some are treasured for their markings –

they cause the eyes to melt
or the body to shriek without pain.

I have never seen one fly, but
sometimes they perch on the hand.

Mist is when the sky is tired of flight
and rests its soft machine on the ground:

then the world is dim and bookish
like engravings under tissue paper.

Rain is when the earth is television.
It has the property of making colors darker.

Model T is a room with the lock inside –
A key is turned to free the world

for movement, so quick there is a film
to watch for anything missed.

But time is tied to the wrist
or kept in a box, ticking with impatience.

In homes, a haunted apparatus sleeps,
that snores when you pick it up.

If the ghost cries, they carry it
to their lips and soothe it to sleep

with sounds. And yet, they wake it up
deliberately, by tickling with a finger.

Only the young are allowed to suffer
openly. Adults go to a punishment room

with water but nothing to eat.
They lock the door and suffer the noises

alone. No one is exempt
and everyone's pain has a different smell.

At night, when all the colors die,
they hide in pairs

and read about themselves –
in color, with their eyelids shut.

[Craig Raine, 'A Martian Sends a Postcard Home',
in the *Norton Anthology of Poetry*, 1983]

In their book *Metaphors We Live By*, Lakoff and Johnson uncover many of the most frequent metaphors which underpin much of our everyday language and thinking – for example, 'up' generally has a positive value in phrases like 'high as a kite', 'on a high', 'over the moon', 'on the up' etc. – whereas 'down' has a negative value ('feeling down', 'down in the dumps' and, of course, 'life's ups and downs'). We think of time as if it were an object, like money, to be spent, saved or wasted, and life is frequently a journey, with its uphill struggles, backward steps, keeping on the straight and narrow, taking things one step at a time.

The American poet, Robert Frost, exploited this most familiar of comparisons to produce 'The Road Not Taken'. As you read it, trace the comparison he sustains between his own life's path, and a walk through the woods:

Two roads diverged in a yellow wood,
And sorry I could not travel both
And be one traveler, long I stood
And looked down one as far as I could
To where it bent in the undergrowth;

Then took the other, as just as fair,
And having perhaps the better claim,
Because it was grassy and wanted wear;
Though as for that, the passing there
Had worn them really about the same,

And both that morning equally lay
In leaves no step had trodden black.
Oh, I kept the first for another day!
Yet knowing how way leads on to way,
I doubted if I should ever come back.

I shall be telling this with a sigh
Somewhere ages and ages hence:
Two roads diverged in a wood, and I –
I took the one less traveled by,
And that has made all the difference.

[Robert Frost, 'The Road Not Taken', from *Collected Poems*, 1930]

ACTIVITY 52

1 Survey a collection of song lyrics and examine them for their use of figurative language. Are they guilty of cliché, or responsible for originality?

2 Similarly, carry out a survey of the different uses made of figurative language by any other poets you are currently studying. (If Ted Hughes is one of your texts, you might like to pay particular attention to 'October Dawn' and 'Wind'.)

3 Write you own 'Martian's Postcard' in which you describe your own selection of human objects and activities for your alien friends. You could, for example, include television, a sport, playing music, dancing, or snowfall.

3.2.3 Phrases and sentences

However careful we may be in selecting the individual words and expressions which we need for a text, our third Level of choice involves us in decisions about how to combine them into meaningful phrases and sentences.

To discover some of the options here, we'll take the opening lines or sentences of a range of Heaney's poems, from his *Selected Poems 1965–1975* – but you could carry out the same exercise with any other collection which you may be studying.

ACTIVITY 53

What kinds of opening sentences do you find here? Classify these examples using perhaps five or six categories.

1
    Between my finger and my thumb
    The squat pen rests

['Digging']

2
    All year the flax-dam festered in the heart
    Of the townland.

['Death of a Naturalist']

3   *Threshed corn lay piled like grit of ivory*
          Or solid as cement in two-lugged sacks.
                                                                    ['The Barn']

4   *Late August, given heavy rain and sun*
          For a full week, the blackberries would ripen.
                                                            ['Blackberry-Picking']

5   *A mechanical digger wrecks the drill,*
          Spins up a dark shower of roots and mould.
                                                            ['At a Potato Digging']

6   *Cut from the green hedge a forked hazel stick*
          That he held tight by the arms of the V:
          Circling the terrain, hunting the pluck
          Of water, nervous, but professionally

          Unfussed.
                                                                  ['The Diviner']

7   *The timeless waves, bright sifting, broken glass,*
          Came dazzling around, into the rocks,
          Came glinting, sifting from the Americas

          To possess Aran.
                                                               ['Lovers on Aran']

8   *Love, I shall perfect for you the child*
          Who diligently potters in my brain
          Digging with heavy spade till sods were piled
          Or puddling through muck in a deep drain.
                                                                        ['Poem']

9   *All I know is a door into the dark.*
                                                                   ['The Forge']

10   *When you have nothing more to say, just drive*
          For a day all round the peninsula.
                                                                ['The Peninsula']

11   *A gland agitating*
          mud two hundred miles in-
          land, a scale of water
          on water working up
          estuaries, he drifted
          into motion half-way
          across the Atlantic
          ['Beyond Sargasso', from 'A Lough Neagh Sequence']

12   *We have no prairies*
          To slice a big sun at evening –
                                                                     ['Bogland']

13   *Cloudburst and steady downpour now*
                 for days.

                                                     ['Gifts of Rain']

14   *Hide in the hollow trunk*
                 of the willow tree,
                 its listening familiar,
                 until, as usual, they
                 cuckoo your name
                 across the fields.

                                                     ['Oracle']

15   *Was it wind off the dumps*
                 or something in heat

                 dogging us, the summer gone sour,
                 a fouled nest incubating somewhere?

                                          ['Summer Home']

16   *I returned to a long strand,*
                 the hammered shod of a bay,
                 and found only the secular
                 powers of the Atlantic thundering.

                                                     ['North']

COMMENTARY

As usual, everyone will come up with their own ways of grouping together and distinguishing between different kinds of sentence. Here are some alternatives:

Who's talking to whom?

You may have grouped together sentences according to the 'voice' speaking. In some cases, this is apparently the personal voice of the poet, using the **first person singular** – as in extracts 1, 8, 9 and 15. These may, or may not, be the 'actual' voice of the poet, of course – it is just as likely that it is a **persona** adopted for the poem (just as when a pop singer sings 'I love you' we do not necessarily assume it is a personal outpouring). Then there are the sentences that are spoken using the plural 'we'/'us' – extracts 12 and 16 – which do not immediately make clear who else the speaker is referring to. Finally, there are those sentences which seem to be detached, observing or narrating from a third-person perspective – such as 2, 3, 4, 5, and others.

There is also the question of who the voice is speaking to. Usually, this is not made clear, and we assume it is us, the readers. But in some extracts, the voice is clearly addressing someone else – in extract 8 ('Love, I shall perfect for you'), 10 ('When you have nothing more to say') and even 14 ('Hide in the hollow trunk'). This device places the reader in the position of a sort of eavesdropper.

Sentence length

A crude but often significant distinction might be to consider the length of sentences, though it is difficult to say where 'short' sentences stop and 'longer ones' start! In fact, there are different ways of looking at this:

- you could make fairly arbitrary distinctions between sentences of, say, fewer than 5, 6–10, and more than 10 words

- you could distinguish between sentences that are contained entirely within the first line/2 lines, and those which run on for longer than this, even into the second stanza.

Sentence type: question? Statement. Order!

Most of these opening lines take the form of **statements** of various kinds – they describe, narrate or explain. However, you could group together the ones which don't – two commands (10, 'When you have nothing more to say, just drive', and 14, 'Hide in the hollow trunk') and a question (15, 'Was it wind off the sumps?').

This distinction between basic sentence types can be a helpful framework for beginning to consider sentences:

- statements (i.e. **declaratives**)
- questions (i.e. **interrogatives**)
- commands (i.e. **imperatives**).

(A fourth type – **exclamations** – is considered under **minor sentences**, below.)

Sentence type: simple, minor, or multiple

A more sophisticated approach is to consider the **structure** of the sentences. Those which contain a single verb are **simple**, though some may be considerably shorter than others. Simple sentences include 1 'Between my finger and my thumb the squat pen **rests**', 2 'All year the flax-dam **festered** in the heart Of the townland', and 3 'Threshed corn **lay** piled like grit of ivory Or solid as cement in two-lugged sacks'.

Some sentences – in defiance of one commonly held definition – may lack a verb at all. These are actually very common as exclamations ('What a fabulous shirt!'), titles and announcements ('And now for something completely different – The News!'). In our collection from Heaney's verse, 13 'Cloudburst and steady downpour now for days' is in this category. These are known as minor sentences.

More often – at least in our sample – Heaney's sentences consist of two or more connected verbs/actions. In two cases – extracts 15 and 16 – they are simply linked by using 'and 'and 'or', two of the basic conjunctions which produce **compound sentences**. Otherwise, the process of combination involves other conjunctions (such as 'because', ' since' and, as here in 10, and 14, 'when' and 'until') and making one or more of the actions dependent on (or **subordinate** to) the others. These are known as **complex sentences**.

Out of order: syntax

Writers of verse may also choose the order of words within a sentence with great care, often in ways that would be unusual in prose. In several cases in Heaney's opening lines, he seems to want us to wait in suspense to find out what the main point of the sentence actually is. In 'Digging', for example, he could have written 'The squat pen rests Between my finger and my thumb' but chooses instead to place the verb 'rests' at the end. Something similar happens in 4 'Blackberry-Picking'. Instead of 'The blackberries would ripen in late August, Given heavy rain and sun', Heaney opts for 'Late August, given heavy rain and sun For a full week, the blackberries would ripen'.

A more extreme example of this – making us wait for the **main clause** – is 11, 'Beyond Sargasso', where 'A gland agitating mud and a scale of water on water ...' hang in the air until we reach 'he drifted into motion'.

Repetition and parallelism

Even within a single sentence, special rhythmical effects can be achieved by the repetition of similar phrases in parallel – as in 7 'The timeless waves, bright sifting, broken glass, Came dazzling around, into the rocks, Came glinting, sifting from the Americas', and even in 11 'A gland agitating … a scale of water on water working …'.

The repetition of structures in successive sentences can be an effective pattern, as in the opening verses of this poem by William Blake:

> *Can I see another's woe*
> *And not be in sorrow too.*
> *Can I see another's grief,*
> *And not seek for kind relief.*
>
> *Can I see a falling tear,*
> *And not feel my sorrow's share,*
> *Can a father see his child,*
> *Weep, nor be with sorrow fill'd.*

['On Another's Sorrow', *Songs of Innocence*, 1789]

ACTIVITY 54   SENTENCES AND SYNTAX

1 Read the following poem by Ted Hughes. As you become familiar with the poem, what do you notice about the types of sentence chosen by Hughes in the final two verses, and what effects does this choice create?

> *I sit in the top of the wood, my eyes closed.*
> *Inaction, no falsifying dream*
> *Between my hooked head and hooked feet:*
> *Or in sleep rehearse perfect kills and eat.*
>
> *The convenience of the high trees!*
> *The air's buoyancy and the sun's ray*
> *Are of advantage to me;*
> *And the earth's face upward for my inspection.*
>
> *My feet are locked upon the rough bark.*
> *It took the whole of Creation*
> *To produce my foot, my each feather:*
> *Now I hold Creation in my foot*
>
> *Or fly up, and revolve it all slowly –*
> *I kill where I please because it is all mine.*
> *There is no sophistry*in my body:*
> *My manners are tearing off heads –*
>
> *The allotment of death.*
> *For the one path of my flight is direct*
> *Through the bones of the living.*
> *No arguments assert my right:*

The sun is behind me.
Nothing has changed since I began.
My eye has permitted no change.
I am going to keep things like this.
*sophistry: clever deception, false argument

['Hawk Roosting', in *Selected Poems*, 1982]

2   Now read these opening lines from Hughes's 'Esther's Tomcat'. Note any unusual features of his word-order in these verses and suggest how they help convey to you impressions of the cat.

Daylong this tomcat lies stretched flat
As an old rough mat, no mouth and no eyes,
Continual wars and wives are what

Have tattered his ears and battered his head.
Like a bundle of old rope and iron
Sleeps till blue dusk. Then reappear
His eyes, green as ringstones:he yawns wide red,
Fangs fine as a lady's needle and bright.

['Esther's Tomcat', in *Selected Poems*, 1982]

3   Consider the opening verses of William Blake's 'Tyger Tyger' alongside 'Twinkle Twinkle Little Star', a child's verse by Jane Taylor (1783–1824). What do they have in common, and how do they differ?

Tyger, Tyger, burning bright
In the forests of the night;
What immortal hand or eye,
Could frame thy fearful symmetry?
['Tyger, Tyger', from
Songs of Experience, 1794]

Twinkle, twinkle, little star
How I wonder what you are!
Up above the world so high,
Like a diamond in the sky?
[Jane Taylor, 'Twinkle, Twinkle
Little Star', in I. and P. Opie
(eds), *The Oxford Book of
Children's Verse*, 1973]

4   Read Ted Hughes's 'Crow and the Birds', below, and comment on the importance for the poem's impact of Hughes's use of parallel sentence structures:

When the eagle soared through a dawn distilling of emerald.
When the curlew trawled in seadusk through a chime of wineglasses
When the swallow swooped through a woman's song in a cavern
And the swift flicked through the breath of a violet

When the owl sailed clear of tomorrow's conscience
And the sparrow preened himself of yesterday's primrose
And the heron laboured clear of the Bessemer upglare
And the bluetit zipped clear of lace panties
And the woodpecker drummed clear of the rotovator and the rose-farm
And the peewit tumbled clear of the laundromat

While the bullfinch plumped in the apple bud
And the goldfinch bulbed in the sun
And the wryneck crooked in the moon
And the dipper peered from the dewball

Crow spraddled head-down on the beach-garbage, guzzling a dropped ice-cream.
[Ted Hughes, 'Crow and the Birds' in *Selected Poems*, 1982]

5 Gather and survey a range of advertisements and song lyrics, and investigate their use of sentence types, syntax and parallelism.

6 Experiment with your own writing – try producing short verses which:
   - follow the pattern: statement – question – command – statement etc.
   - consist only of simple or minor sentences
   - follow the pattern of 'Crow and the Birds', repeating a single basic sentence structure throughout until you reach a final, contrasting sentence.

3.2.4. Keeping up appearances

Just as the choices involved at the first Level, Sounds, are designed to appeal to the ear (or 'inner ear' if the poem is read silently), our fourth Level of choice – Graphology and orthography – influences the impact a verse on the page has on the eye. This is best illustrated by the work of writers who have experimented with the lay-out, punctuation and even spelling of text.

ACTIVITY 55

As you read and respond to each of the poems below, write down how the unusual presentation of the text is linked to the poem's meanings, and how it contributes to the visual impact of the verse.
   You might also consider how – or even if – such poems might be read aloud!

1 Although modern writers have been attracted to this kind of experimentation, the following poem by the seventeenth-century religious poet, George Herbert, provides an early example; here is the first of the two verses:

Lord, who createdst man in wealth and store,
Though foolishly he lost the same
Decaying more and more
Till he became
Most poor:
With thee
O let me rise
As larks, harmoniously,
And sing this day thy victories:
Then shall the fall further the delight in me.

['Easter Wings', 1633]

2 The popular British poet, Roger McGough, has often experimented in this way. Here are two of his poems, 'Watchwords' and 'Autumn Poem':

Watch the words   *all*   *over*

Watch words   *the*

the watchword   *away*

is watch

words are   *and*   *place*

sly as boots

takeyoureyesoffthemforaminute   *up*

     and   *they're*

['Watchwords', from *You at the Back, Selected Poems 1967–1987*, 1992]

litter

is

turning

brown

and

the

road

above

is

filled

with

hitch

hikers

heading

south

['Autumn Poem', from *You at the Back*, as above]

3 The American poet E. E. Cummings is also well known for his graphological experiments, as in this poem:

l(a

le
af
fa

ll

s)
one
l

iness

['l(a']

4 If you are studying the poetry of Ted Hughes, consider the effects of the lay-out and arrangement of lines (i.e. **lineation**) of 'Skylark', 'Heptonstall' and 'Crow's Last Stand'.

5 Advertisers, like poets, enjoy playing with the lay-out as well as the language of their verse. Collect some examples and present your findings to your class.

6 Commercial companies have always taken care to choose for their shop-fronts, labels and other printed materials a typeface which is instantly recognisable and associated with the values they wish to promote – think of Heinz, MacDonalds, Kelloggs, for example. With the spread of computer technology, you may even have a wide choice of fonts available on your word-processor package.

Collect or print-out a range of typefaces and discuss which one of them would be most suitable for:
- a firm of undertakers
- a legal document
- an invitation to a party
- a poster advertising a concert
- a firm selling fast food
- a school or college magazine.

3.2.5 Structure, form and organisation: made to measure, or off the peg?

Our Fifth-Level choices – Structure, form and organisation – may well be the place we actually start when composing our text. In Section 2.5 of Chapter 2, we discovered that many narratives are based on a number of basic structures. Similarly, if verse is to be coherent and meaningful and not simply a random collection of phrases, we should expect to recognise evidence of cohesion and coherence in its construction.

Just as there are several recognisable and traditional genres of narrative which follow a well-understood structure (fairy tales, jokes, love stories, news stories, ghost stories, etc.) so writers of verse can select from a large number of traditional forms – or design their own forms and structures to suit their needs.

So – welcome to the Poetry Store!

Off the peg
First, perhaps you'd like to try something from the convenient off-the-peg range? You could start with the basic Japanese **haiku** (designed to record images and impressions in three non-rhyming lines of 5, 7 and 5 syllables), as parodied by Roger McGough:

> only trouble with
> Japanese haiku is that
> you write one, and then
>
> only seventeen
> syllables later you want
> to write another.

['Two Haiku', from *You at the Back, Selected Poems 1967–1987*, 1982]

Or, if you fancy something lighter, why not try the **limerick** for size – as designed by Edward Lear:

There was an Old Man who supposed
That the street door was partially closed;
But some very large rats, ate his coats and his hats,
While that futile old gentleman dozed.

      [in I. and P. Opie (eds), *The Oxford Book of Children's Verse*, 1973]

Note the distinctive rhyme and rhythms, and the need for an effective punchline.

Moving a little upmarket, why not try a verse made from the most popular of traditional materials – the 5-stress, 10-syllable line (or **iambic pentameter**) as worn by Chaucer, Shakespeare and many others, with or without rhyme. One of our most popular styles is the **sonnet**, which comes in a number of variants, such as the Shakespearian:

Shall I compare thee to a summer's day?
Thou art more lovely and more temperate:
Rough winds do shake the darling buds of May,
And summer's lease hath all too short a date:
Sometimes too hot the eye of heaven shines,
And often is his fair complexion dimm'd;
And every fair from fair sometime declines,
By chance or nature's changing course untrimmed.
But thy eternal summer shall not fade,
Nor lose possession of that fair thou ow'st;
Nor shall death brag thou wandrest in his shade,
When in eternal lines to time thou growest:
So long as men can breathe, or eyes can see,
So long lives this, and this gives life to thee.

      [William Shakespeare, Sonnet XVIII]

ACTIVITY 56

1   Limber up for your verse-writing by completing a haiku a day. Remember – go for simple observations and impressions, rather than attempting to tell a story.

2   Use your friends as the subjects of your own limericks – but be careful!

3   It's easy to see **form** as just a matter of rhythm and rhyme – but the way you structure your meaning is important, too. So, in the case of Shakespeare's sonnet, after noticing the obvious rhyming pattern, try to define the structure of the poem as shown in Table 3.9 (page 119).

    Although the sonnet is a form with a long tradition, just like classic styles of clothing, it never goes out of fashion – and modern writers continue to return to it. So, now go on to attempt a sonnet of your own which follows this structure.

4   Of course, there are many other traditional forms available, which vary the patterns of rhyme, rhythm and length of stanza. A glance through any anthology of English poetry will enable you to collect examples of some of the more commmonly used.

Table 3.9

Section of poem	Meaning
First 4 lines (or **quatrain**)	(what is the main idea introduced at first?)
Second quatrain	(does it progress the argument, or restate what has gone before?)
Third quatrain	(starts with 'But' – what shift in the subject does this introduce?)
Final couplet	(does this add a twist, or summarise, or round off the poem?)

Made to measure?

Many writers, however, will also adapt traditional poetic forms and even create entirely new ones which seem better fitted to what they wish to communicate. In 'Otter', Ted Hughes uses a different stanza form in each of two parts; the one which he created specially for the first part of the poem is repeated in each of four verses, and combines graphological and rhythmical patterns:

> *Underwater eyes, an eel's*
> *Oil of water body, neither fish nor beast is the otter:*
> *Four-legged yet water – gifted, to outfish fish;*
> *With webbed feet and long ruddering tail*
> *And a round head like an old tomcat.*

['Otter', in *Selected Poems*, 1982]

Seamus Heaney's 'Beyond Sargasso', a description of the spawning journey of an eel, marks a significant departure from the more traditional forms of his other early poetry – here is the first half of the poem:

> *A gland agitating*
> *mud two hundred miles in-*
> *land, a scale of water*
> *on water working up*
> *estuaries, he drifted*
> *into motion half-way*
> *across the Atlantic,*
> *sure as the satellite's*
> *insinuating pull*
> *in the ocean, as true*
> *to his orbit.*

['Beyond Sargasso' from 'A Lough Neagh Sequence']

ACTIVITY 57

Try to work out the patterns which Heaney is using in 'Beyond Sargasso', and suggest why he might have considered this particular form appropriate for his subject.

Making it hang together: coherence and cohesion

Whatever form we choose for our verse, we still need to create a meaningful structure – and writers do so in a number of ways. We'll take the following poem by Heaney as an example:

> *My father worked with a horse-plough,*
> *His shoulders globed like a full sail strung*
> *Between the shafts and the furrow.*
> *The horses strained at his clicking tongue.*
>
> *An expert. He would set the wing*
> *And fit the bright steel-pointed sock.*
> *The sod rolled over without breaking.*
> *At the headrig, with a single pluck*
>
> *Of reins, the sweating team turned round*
> *And back into the land. His eye*
> *Narrowed and angled at the ground,*
> *Mapping the furrow exactly.*
>
> *I stumbled in his hob-nailed wake,*
> *Fell sometimes on the polished sod;*
> *Sometimes he rode me on his back*
> *Dipping and rising to his plod.*
>
> *I wanted to grow up and plough,*
> *To close one eye, stiffen my arm.*
> *All I ever did was follow*
> *In his broad shadow round the farm.*
>
> *I was a nuisance, tripping, falling,*
> *Yapping always. But today*
> *It is my father who keeps stumbling*
> *Behind me, and will not go away.*

['Follower']

We should not underestimate the importance of patterns of sound, as we explored in Section 3.2.1, in weaving a clear structure in the poem – this is what linguists call **phonological cohesion**. In 'Follower', this structure takes several forms: most obviously, its regular ABAB rhyme pattern; secondly, the regularity of each line's rhythm (most of them have four beats, or stresses – tap the lines out and see); thirdly, the echoing of individual sounds (phonemes) within the poem, in words like 'sh*ou*lders', 'gl*o*bed' and 'furr*ow*', then 'so*ck*', 'brea*k*ing' and 'plu*ck*'.

Equally, we can trace the development of the poem's meanings in the ways in which related words reappear throughout the poem. This is known as **lexical cohesion**. The opening phrase – 'My father' – announces the poem's primary subject, and is the phrase to which many subsequent pronouns – 'He', 'His', etc. – refer. (When pronouns refer back in this way linguists describe it as **anaphoric reference**.) The poem also works by contrast – and the references to the 'I' of the poet both refer back to the initial 'My' and contrast ('I stumbled', 'fell sometimes', 'All I ever did was follow') with the expert actions of his father. The repetition of 'stumbling' is vital to the effect of the final verse, as it reminds us of the previous reference to the young boy's clumsiness, and brings home sharply the reversal of roles which has occurred now that the poet is grown up and his father an old man.

How do we know that the major part of the poem is concerned with the habitual actions of the past? The poem's **grammatical cohesion** tells us so. The verbs in the opening verse are in the **simple past** – 'my father worked', 'the horses strained' – but in the second verse 'He would set the wing' makes it clear that the actions being described did not just happen on one occasion, but were part of a way of life over many years. Thus, we understand that every subsequent simple present – 'His eye narrowed and angled at the ground' – actually links back to 'He would set the wing', a meaning reinforced by the adverb 'ever' in the penultimate verse.

The contrast which the poem introduces in the final verse is signalled in three ways – first, the conjunction 'But' (as in 'Shall I Compare Thee', above) announces that what is to come is a contrast; secondly, the adverb 'today' contrasts with the previous 'ever' and, by implication, all those '-ed' endings (or **suffixes**) which mark the verbs as in the past; and finally, the switch to the repetitive present tense of 'keeps stumbling'.

ACTIVITY 58

1 First go to any of the non-literary verse you have been working with, and examine how each of these types of cohesion work in your chosen example.

2 Now do the same for any of the poems you are studying. If you are studying Ted Hughes, you might look, for example, at 'View of a Pig' or 'Wind'.

3.2.6. Putting it all together: stylistic analysis

Now that we have looked in some detail at five different levels of linguistic choice in verse texts, we need to put our understanding into practice – both in writing about texts and in producing our own.

Approaching a text: a Government Health Warning!

At this point, it might be worth sounding a note of caution. Responding to texts is not trainspotting – and although we have learned to identify a number of linguistic features, and that understanding helps us to see how a text works and what it is doing to us, we should always begin by taking an overview of the text and making sure we have at least some provisional answers to these key questions:

● what seems to be the main purpose of the text?
● what seems to be its basic meaning or sense?
● what responses and reactions might it provoke?

     humour?   astonishment?
     sadness?   anger?
     pity?   disbelief?

● am I typical of the kinds of readers for whom the text is/was written? If not, how might their reaction be different?

- in general terms, what have I noticed about the uses of language in the text? You could start with this kind of mental checklist:

emotive ☐ detached ☐ personal ☐ impersonal ☐ literal ☐

figurative ☐ concrete ☐ abstract ☐ simple ☐ complex ☐

formal ☐ informal ☐ narrative ☐ descriptive ☐ serious ☐

humorous ☐

- Only when you feel sure that you have gained this kind of overview should you then move on and try to understand the kinds of choices the writer has made at each of the five different levels.

ACTIVITY 59

1 Now apply this approach to any of the poems you are studying.

2 It is often revealing to compare two poems which tackle similar subject-matter but in different ways. We can, for example, return to Heaney's 'Blackberry-Picking' and compare it this time with 'In that Year, 1914 …' by Gary Snyder. When tackling a comparative study, try at every stage of your analysis of the texts to focus on aspects which they either have in common or contrast. Always take time to read and reread each poem thoroughly – at least twice – before you begin to annotate your copy and consciously think about the different levels of language.

Blackberry-Picking

Late August, given heavy rain and sun
For a full week, the blackberries would ripen.
At first, just one, a glossy purple clot
Among others, red, green, hard as a knot.
You ate that first one and its flesh was sweet.
Like thickened wine; summer's blood was in it
Leaving stains upon the tongue and lust for
Picking. The red ones inked up and that hunger
Sent us out with milk-cans, pea-tins, jam-pots
Where briars scratched and wet grass bleached our boots.
Round hayfields, cornfields and potato-drills
We trekked and picked until the cans were full,
Until the tinkling bottom had been covered
With green ones, and on top big dark blobs burned
Like a plate of eyes. Our hands were peppered
With thorn pricks, our palms sticky as Bluebeard's.
We hoarded the fresh berries in the byre.
But when the bath was filled we found a fur,
A rat-grey fungus, glutting on our cache.
The juice was stinking too. Once off the bush
The fruit fermented, the sweet flesh would turn sour.
I always felt like crying. It wasn't fair
That all the lovely canfuls smelt of rot.
Each year I hoped they'd keep, knew they would not.

'In that year, 1914 ...'

'In that year, 1914, we lived on the farm
And the relatives lived with us.
A banner year for wild blackberries
Dad was crazy about wild blackberries
No berries like that now.
You know Kitsap County was logged before
The turn of the century – it was easiest of all,
Close to water, virgin timber,
When I was a kid walking about in the
Stumpland, wherever you'd go a skidroad
Puncheon, all overgrown.
We went up one like that, fighting our way through
To its end near the top of a hill:
For some reason wild blackberries
Grew best there. We took off one morning
Right after milking: rode the horses
To a valley we'd been to once before
Hunting berries, and hitched the horses.
About a quarter mile up the old road
We found the full ripe of berrytime –
And with only two pails – so we
Went back home, got Mother and Ruth,
And filled lots of pails. Mother sent letters
To all the relatives in Seattle:
Effie, Aunt Lucy, Bill Moore,
Forrest, Edna, six or eight, they all came
Out to the farm, and we didn't take pails
Then: we took copper clothes-boilers,
Wash-tubs, buckets, and all went picking.
We were canning for three days.'

Once you have got a confident feel for the poems, and have also noted down a fair number of details, you could try to structure your responses in this way:

Paragraph 1: Overview of both poems – attitudes to subject-matter, relationship with reader, general statements about uses of language.

Paragraph 2: Compare and contrast the structure and organisation (Level 5) of each poem, and the meanings and effects this produces.

Paragraphs 3–6: Do the same for each of the remaining four Levels – Graphology and orthography, Phrases and sentences, Words, and Sounds.

Paragraph 7: If you still feel you can add something to your discussion by taking a final overview of what your analysis has revealed, do so briefly – but don't just repeat in summary what you have already said.

This is not the only way of organising a stylistic response to a text, of course – it is just as valid to organise your analysis by using non-linguistic subheadings. However, it is useful to keep these Levels in your mind as a mental checklist – try to ensure that in your discussion of texts, you have made some points at most, if not all, of them. But beware – be selective!

If you were to explain in detail every linguistic choice which a writer has taken at each of these Levels, you would, of course, end up with a comprehensive but extremely long and only occasionally interesting discussion. The knack then, is to select those aspects of the writer's use of language which are actually significant in the text.

For example, it may be that in a particular poem, a writer has used the word 'the' eight times – but it is hardly worth saying so unless there is something unusual or interesting about that fact (it might be interesting, though, if the poem itself consisted of only sixteen words altogether). Similarly, some texts may be more interesting at some of the Levels than others. If you are looking at a poem by E. E. Cummings or Roger McGough (see above) it is likely that you'll find a lot more to discuss at the level of graphology and orthography than if you are studying a poem by, say, Seamus Heaney.

3   You may wish to extend your stylistic study beyond a collection of literary texts which you are studying, and carry out an investigative project into the way other verse texts use language. In tackling any one of these, or similar projects, you should find the Levels' framework a useful structure within which to carry out your analysis. The possibilities are endless – they might include:

- comparing collections of verse written for readers of different age groups
- comparing song lyrics by a particular band or songwriters with some poetry written on a similar theme
- comparing the verse produced by a single poet or songwriter at different stages of his/her/their development (e.g. the 'early' and 'late' lyrics of Lennon and McCartney, or the verse in Heaney's first collection, 'Death of a Naturalist', compared to his later 'Station Island')
- comparing a collection of modern hymns/psalms with the more traditional ones.

3.3 Working the clay: form and content, words and ideas

So what is verse, or poetry? One way of thinking about this is to imagine the mass of language and thoughts we may first have about a subject as a large lump of clay – and to think of the work we do when we turn this raw material into a piece of verse as like the manipulation of a potter, who gradually shapes and forms the clay on his/her wheel until something emerges which has structure, serves its purpose (be it bowl, dish or plate) and feels, or looks, pleasing in some way.

Seamus Heaney finds another analogy. In his poem 'Digging' (below), he distinguishes his own trade of poetry from the hard physical labour of his immediate ancestors, but still manages to draw some parallels between the two activities:

Between my finger and my thumb
The squat pen rests; snug as a gun.

Under my window, a clean rasping sound
When the spade sinks into gravelly ground:
My father, digging. I look down

Till his straining rump among the flowerbeds
Bends low, comes up twenty years away
Stooping in rhythm through potato drills
Where he was digging.

The coarse boot nestled on the lug, the shaft
Against the inside knee was levered firmly.
He rooted out tall tops, buried the bright edge deep
To scatter new potatoes that we picked
Loving their cool hardness in our hands.

By God, the old man could handle a spade.
Just like his old man.

My grandfather cut more turf in a day
Than any other man on Toner's bog.
Once I carried him milk in a bottle
Corked sloppily with paper. He straightened up
To drink it, then fell to right away
Nicking and slicing neatly, heaving sods
Over his shoulder, going down and down
For the good turf. Digging.

The cold smell of potato mould, the squelch and slap
Of soggy peat, the curt cuts of an edge
Through living roots awaken in my head.
But I've no spade to follow men like them.

Between my finger and my thumb
The squat pen rests.
I'll dig with it.

ACTIVITY 60

1 A comparison between the action of digging (for peat, or turf – a traditional fuel in many Irish rural communities) and the writing of poetry underlies this poem. What parallels do you see between them? (If you are studying the poetry of Seamus Heaney, you might also consider how poems such as 'Personal Helicon', 'The Forge' and 'Thatcher' reflect Heaney's own views of the nature of his writing.)

2 If you are studying the poetry of Ted Hughes, compare this with the view of writing he presents in 'The Thought Fox'.

3.3.1 Moulding the dough

One thing which these poems do suggest is that the popular image of a poet being seized with 'inspiration' and effortlessly pouring out a work of genius is a long way from the truth. 'Inspiration' – i.e. the discovery of an idea or expression which is new and fresh – is more likely to happen as a result of hard work than arrive out of the blue!

So, in the next series of exercises, we'll pick up our 'lump of clay' – just about any old clay will do! – and shape and turn it on our 'poet's wheel'.

ACTIVITY 61 GETTING STARTED

1 Writing from experience
    The work of most poets is rooted deeply in their own experience – so this is always the place to start. Survey the collection(s) of verse you are studying to discover the most popular sources of 'raw clumps of clay' for your poet(s). Record them on Table 3.10 (some additional possibilities are also suggested).

Table 3.10

Source	Examples from set text	Other possibilities
an incident		a meeting; a surprise; a discovery; bad/good news; a day-out/visit
a person		relative; friend; neighbour; craftsman/woman; sportsman/woman
an object		photo (dig out an old album); antique; tool
a place		a street; beach; school; house; museum; club
an animal		cat; dog; bird
other		

2 Whatever the subject you choose to write about, brainstorm onto paper your first thoughts and ideas – concentrate on concrete impressions which appeal to each of the senses. Write these out as you think of them, spontaneously and in prose. This is your raw material – your 'lump of clay'.

3 Submit your 'clay' to a number of different exercises which force you to shape it in different ways:
    ● reduce it to a haiku (see Section 3.2.5, page 117)
    ● rephrase it into rhyming couplets
    ● write a possible title for the poem vertically on the page, so that each letter of the title becomes the initial letter of successive lines (such a device is called an **acrostic**). Combine this with a rhythmical and rhyming pattern for added refinement!

- write it without using any abstract nouns
- introduce a 'random' element by opening a dictionary three times and selecting the first word you see. Incorporate these words somewhere into your poem.
- write it using entirely words of one syllable
- write it using lots of alliteration
- write it so that each successive noun (or verb, or adjective) begins with successive letters of the alphabet
- introduce patterns with a repetitive element – you could repeat the same sentence structure throughout, or repeat a particular line or phrase every four lines
- go to a 'style model' – a sonnet, or a verse form used by one of your set poets – and submit your ideas to the same form.

Not all of these exercises will turn out to be productive – but sometimes, the search for a word which rhymes, or which fits the rhythm, or which begins with a particular letter, can release ideas which you would not otherwise have thought of.

4 Once you have begun to shape your clay in this way, go ahead and try to complete a draft of a verse. You may be able to submit a collection of your own poetry/lyrics as part of your A-level coursework. As usual, you should also write a commentary which describes the writing process and reflects on how your poem develops from draft to draft (see Activity 34, pages 74–5).

3.3.2 In other words ...

As you attempt some of these rather demanding linguistic exercises in pursuit of your verse or poem, at some stage the thought is certain to strike you – why bother?

After all, why should we go to the trouble of artificially rephrasing, shaping and redrafting our ideas? Is it simply to be clever, or to make our work as puzzling as possible so future readers can spend many a happy hour trying to decode our 'message'? Is this what verse is all about? Or does the form of words we choose actually change the 'message' or 'meaning' which our readers receive?

The answers to all of these questions will depend on what we think happens when we submit our ideas and our language to an intense rewriting, shaping and drafting process.

ACTIVITY 62 FORM AND CONTENT

1 Read the pairs of short texts below. Discuss for each pair this proposition: 'These two texts contain the same information and have identical meanings'.

Pair A

(i) *I can feel the tug of the halter at the nape of her neck, the wind on her naked front.*

(ii)

I can feel the tug
of the halter at the nape
of her neck, the wind
on her naked front.

Pair B

(i) *I don't know whether I should compare you to a day in Summer, because you are actually much nicer – you're less likely to be extreme in your nature and you're generally much lovelier!*

(ii)   *Shall I compare thee to a Summer's Day?*
                             Thou art more lovely and more temperate.

Pair C

(i) *It has been a very stormy night outside this house – the wind has been very loud, echoing around the hills and fields, and you could hear it in the trees in the woods. Everything was terribly dark and wet until daylight.*

(ii)   *This house has been far out at sea all night*
                             The woods crashing through darkness, the booming hills,
                             Winds stampeding the fields under the window
                             Floundering black astride and blinding wet

                             Til day rose;

Pair D

(i) *I don't like that*

(ii) *Do I not like that*

Pair E

(i) *It was in last year's long hot summer that the trouble started.*

(ii) *Trouble started during last year's long hot summer.*

COMMENTARY

On the face of it, the two texts in Pair A are identical – same word, same order, same sense. Some people might say, however, that even its unconventional lay-out, a lay-out we associate with poetry, gives a different status to the text, just as placing a picture frame around an image and placing it in an art gallery seems to say 'this is special – take a look at this!'

Pair B also have the same sense-content, but the casualness and redundancy of words in (i) such as 'actually' and 'really' dilutes the message. The demands of the sonnet form – the two lines have each to rhyme with the two lines which follow, and of course they both have to fit the iambic-pentameter rhythm – have forced the writer to condense the meaning, and it is this extra density that often characterises the meanings expressed in poetry.

Much the same could also be said of Pair C, with the added complication of the introduction of the 'stampeding' metaphor. Does this still 'mean' the same as simply saying 'the wind echoes loudly'? At one level it does, but with the metaphor, we suddenly start to compare the elements of the storm with living creatures, thus adding an additional layer to what is being communicated. There are many situations where this would not be appropriate – we wouldn't want a pilot and air-control official to be exchanging instructions for the landing of our plane using figurative and multi-layered language!

Pairs C and D are both examples of a change of emphasis being achieved as a result of a switch in the usual syntax of a sentence. Do they still 'mean' the same?

They clearly give us different messages about what is important in the sentence, and so make us respond differently to them. In Pair E, the second version (ii) pushes 'the trouble' to the front (a move known as **fronting**) and relegates 'in last year's long hot summer' to the back (known as **postponement**). Again, though the information content is similar, the two sentences seem to be giving us different messages about which of these elements is the most important.

So – there are some fine distinctions between these pairs, and in the process of moulding a 'pot' into its final shape, it may well be that the thought or idea which a writer starts with develops and changes.

Of course, apart from these subtle differences, the responses of readers and listeners to the verse versions is different simply because of the sheer fun and pleasure we take in the forms and shapes which writers of verse go to the trouble of creating!

[Sources: Pair B (ii), William Shakespeare, Sonnet XVIII, Pair C (ii), Ted Hughes, 'Wind', in *Selected Poems*, 1982; Pair D (ii), Graham Taylor, England football manager]

3.3.3 Language and thought: the controversy

Some thinkers have been tempted to go further than this – could it be that we actually think with language, and that the language we use limits or controls the thoughts we can have? Just what is the connection between the thoughts and ideas we have, and the language with which we convey them?

ACTIVITY 63   THOUGHT AND LANGUAGE

Consider the two 'models' offered in Table 3.11, which try to describe the relationship between the ideas we wish to convey and the words we use. Which of them do you think is the more accurate?

Table 3.11

Model 1: Language is like clothing	Model 2 Language is like clay
Our ideas come to us first; deciding what form of expression to give them is like choosing what to put on in the morning	Until we start to form our ideas into words, they are vague and shapeless
We choose our words according to what is appropriate in a particular situation	As we change the form of our words, our ideas themselves become different and take a different shape
Sometimes we choose our words to impress	We actually need to 'work the clay' to make our thoughts clear and precise; sometimes, we do not know what our ideas are until we have shaped them into language!
Whatever we wear, we are still the same person – so, even if we put an idea in other words, and call a spade a digging implement, the essential idea is still the same	People who speak different languages actually think differently, too

COMMENTARY

There is no easy answer to these questions. In fact, the relationship between thoughts and language is one of the biggest controversies, which has troubled not just linguists, but also psychologists and philosophers. At one extreme, the American linguists Sapir and Whorf proposed in the 1930s that our thoughts were shaped and limited by the ways in which our language was organised. This view implied that speakers of different languages really did think quite differently (Sapir and Whorf's ideas arose from their study of the culture and language of a tribe of native North Americans, the Hopi). In some ways, we often assume this to be true – politicians, whether it be Ronald Reagan (who named a new ultra-deadly nuclear missile the 'Peacekeeper'), or Margaret Thatcher (whose Conservative government insisted on calling their new tax a 'community charge' rather than a 'poll tax') seem to be believe that people will understand an idea differently if it is called something less threatening. The concept of 'political correctness' partly assumes that by changing the way we refer to people/things in language, we will come to change the way we think about them. This idea can be found in Literature, too; in the novel *1984*, George Orwell invented a whole language, Newspeak, which was so tightly controlled and restricted by the State, that its aim was to prevent citizens from even being able to think concepts like 'freedom' and 'democracy'.

   On the other hand, most modern linguists and psychologists reject this notion. Linguist Stephen Pinker, for example, in *The Language Instinct* suggests that thoughts exist independently of the words which we happen to have, and that we manipulate ideas inside our heads using a mental code he calls 'mentalese':

> *Knowing a language, then, is knowing how to translate mentalese into strings of words and vice versa. ...*
> *So, where does all this leave Newspeak? Here are my predictions for the year 2050. First since mental life goes on independently of particular languages, concepts of freedom and equality will be thinkable even if they are nameless. Second, since there are far more concepts than there are words, ... existing words will quickly gain new senses, ... Third, since children are not content to reproduce any old input ... but create a complex grammar that can go beyond it, they would creolize Newspeak into a natural language, possibly in a single generation.'*
>
> [*The Language Instinct*, 1994, p. 82]

3.4 Back to the texts: Seamus Heaney, language and identity

One of the questions we raised at the start of this chapter was whether verse had any importance. In one form or another, it clearly plays a significant part in our lives, even if the writing and reading of the kind of 'poetry' that ends up on English Literature syllabuses remains something of a minority activity. Creators of verse, like healers of the sick, have often enjoyed high status in society, whether it be the latest dub poets, Rap singers or poets Laureate.

We have seen, too, that the power of metaphor, as used by Craig Raine in his 'Martian' poem, or Ted Hughes in 'Wind', can make us look afresh at the world around us and startle us with the newness of its use of words. For some writers, however, there is more at stake. In Chapter 2, we saw how non-Standard varieties of English continue to prosper, even in the face of judgements that they are 'incorrect' or 'bad' English, because they express the sense of belonging and identity felt by people in a particular community. For some writers also, poetry can become the linguistic expression of the identity of a nation.

Let's return to Heaney, to consider his poem 'Traditions'. It begins:

> *Our guttural muse*
> *was bulled long ago*
> *by the alliterative tradition,*
> *her uvula* grows*
>
> *vestigial, forgotten*
> *like the coccyx**
> *or a Brigid's Cross*
> *yellowing in some outhouse*

* uvula: part of the soft palate of the mouth, used in the production of come vocal sounds
* coccyx: bone at the foot of the spinal column, thought to be a remnant of a tail from man's evolutionary past

Here, Heaney is referring to the 'triumph' of the English language over Gaelic, the native Celtic language of Ireland, which resulted in the gradual reduction in the number of Gaelic speakers over 300 years. We will see in Chapter 4 how the playwright Brian Friel portrayed the process of converting traditional Gaelic names to English ones (i.e. **Anglicisation**) during the nineteenth century. One survey in 1861 recorded 24.5 per cent of the Irish population as native Gaelic speakers; by 1911 the figure had shrunk to just 17 per cent.

However, even though the native language was supplanted by English, the form of English which developed itself assumed a distinctively Irish character, as Heaney goes on to describe:

> *We are to be proud*
> *of our Elizabethan English:*
> *'varsity', for example,*
> *is grass-roots stuff with us;*
>
> *we 'deem' or we 'allow'*
> *when we suppose*
> *and some cherished archaisms*
> *are correct Shakespearien.*

Nevertheless, you may think that the tone of the poem implies that this is little consolation for the loss of an entirely independent language, and elsewhere, Heaney makes it clear that in the decline of Gaelic as the language of his people, something has indeed gone. Where the language survives – in place names like Anahorish and Broagh – he finds in the sounds of the words themselves an intimate expression of the places' true identity:

Anahorish, soft gradient
of consonant, vowel-meadow,

after-image of lamps
swung through the yards
on winter evenings.

[from 'Anahorish']

Similarly, in Broagh:

The garden mould
bruised easily, the shower
gathering in your heelmark
was the black O

in Broagh
its low tattoo
among the windy boortrees
and rhubarb-blades

ended almost
suddenly, like that last
gh the strangers found
difficult to manage.

[from 'Broagh']

ACTIVITY 64

Now look at the extract below from 'Gifts of Rain', in which Heaney describes the river Moyola. Discuss what this poem has in common with 'Traditions', 'Anahorish' and 'Broagh'. How do all three poems convey Heaney's sense of importance of the native tongue?

The tawny guttural water
spells itself: Moyola
is its own score and consort,

bedding the locale
in the utterance,
reed music, an old chanter

breathing its mists
through vowels and history.
A swollen river,

a mating call of sound
rises to pleasure me, Dives,
hoarder of common ground.

3.4.1 Language and politics

As in many situations where a country's political status or identity is a matter for dispute, in Ireland language has become a political issue. A revival in the old Gaelic tongue was part of the political movement which led to the outbreak of violence in Dublin in 1916 and the establishment of an independent Republic – and the newly established country, or 'Free State' as it was first known, adopted Gaelic as its official language.

More recently, Gaelic has seen a rise in popularity in the Republic of Ireland, with one third of the population now claiming to speak the language. Only a small number of these are true 'native speakers' i.e. those for whom it is their first and mother tongue: for the rest, learning Gaelic is very much tied up with a sense of national pride and identity, as the immediate practical benefits of using it as a means of communication are limited. So it seemed to Po Pui-Tak, a Hong Kong policeman who learnt Gaelic in preparation for a visit to Ireland only to discover that virtually no one he met spoke the language.

Said Mr Po, 'Whenever I spoke my little Irish, everyone told me no one speaks Irish any more' (*The Times*, 18 July 1977).

Nevertheless, visitors to the Republic will at least see Gaelic on everything from street signs to Guinness T-shirts and 1997 saw the launch of the first Gaelic television channel, Teilifs na Gaelige.

Elsewhere, movements for political independence are often bound up with attempts to preserve languages under threat. This is even true elsewhere in the British Isles. English itself developed from the German dialects spoken by the invading Anglo-Saxon tribes who colonised the mainland from the 5th century AD onwards. The native Britons, whom they displaced, spoke a variety of tongues which can be loosely termed 'Celtic' (see Figure 3.2), the natural descendants of which are now to be found in Irish Gaelic, Scots Gaelic, and Welsh. Less well known are the related but all-but-dead languages of Manx (spoken in the Isle of Man), Cornish and Breton, the ancient language of Brittany in northern France. All

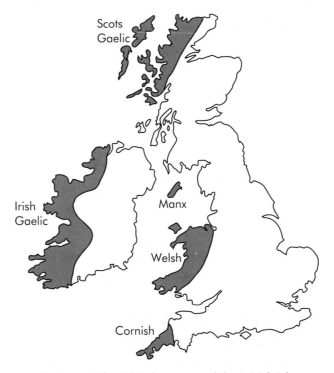

Figure 3.2 The Celtic languages of the British Isles

of these tongues are quite distinct languages, not to be confused with the distinctive varieties of English which have developed in those regions.

In the case of Cornish, efforts to revive a language considered 'dead' (the European Community have now acknowledged it as a living language) have been linked with the claims of Cornish people to be seen as distinct from England. In Scotland, where the writings of poets such as Robbie Burns and, more recently, Hugh MacDiarmid have given a distinctive voice to Scots English, there is also an increase in interest in Scots Gaelic, which is closely related to Irish Gaelic. It is, however, in Wales that the most visible and even violent language battles have been fought, to preserve and promote Welsh as a badge of the country's identity. Wales even has its own organisation – the Welsh Language Board – to help put Welsh on an equal basis to English.

Not everyone agrees this is such a good thing, however. This article by Christie Davies, Professor of Sociology at Reading University, appeared in the *Times Higher Education Supplement*:

> *The study of Welsh is compulsory in all schools in Wales. In Gwynedd all teaching is exclusively through the medium of Welsh. Yet, in my opinion, learning Welsh is of no use to anyone, since even in Wales itself the language is spoken by less than a fifth of the population …*
>
> *In the past, when Welsh was stronger, it acted as a fetter on the achievements of the Welsh people. In Cornwall, where the people were liberated from the Cornish version of Welsh in the 18th century and entered fully into the English-speaking world of science and commerce, Davy discovered sodium, Trevithick invented the steam engine and Cousin Jack went on to dominate hard-rock mining throughout the world. …*
>
> *It is not surprising that supporters of the Welsh language say that their aim is some kind of blurred bilingualism* rather than monoglot** Welshness. English speakers in Wales, as in England, would benefit more from a thorough knowledge of some other world language such as German or Spanish.*
>
> *… two libertarian principles should prevail throughout the Principality. First, all pupils should have an inalienable right to be educated through the medium of English. Second, every pupil should have the right not to study Welsh and to have access to a choice of modern languages in school.*
>
> *While the Welsh language will, should and must die out, it does not follow that the study of dead Welsh should be abandoned. On the contrary, the Welsh of the past should be made available alongside Latin and Greek for the more gifted pupils. … The traditional Welsh way of life flourishes today only in rural County Antrim [in Northern Ireland]. Shoring up a dying language will not bring back the moral culture for which it was once a vehicle.*
>
> *   ability to speak two languages fluently
> **   using only one language

['The Last Gasps of a Dead Tongue', from the *Times Higher Education Supplement*, 4 July 1997]

ACTIVITY 65
Summarise Christie Davies' arguments, and put together a letter which proposes the opposing point of view, that the Welsh language ought to be be taught and actively preserved.

3.5 Learning points

3.5.1 Key concepts

By the end of this chapter you should have learned:

- that verse is characterised by the moulding of language to patterns and form
- that the distinctive forms and patterns of verse are found in many texts and contexts
- that the linguistic choices which writers have available can be understood in terms of different levels
- how to apply this understanding to an analysis of texts
- to develop your own verse writing, and to reflect on it
- the importance poetry can have as an expression through language of a regional or nation identity.

3.5.2 Glossary

Active (*compare* passive)   the form of the verb where the agent is also the subject

Adverb/adverbial phrase   word or phrase qualifying the verb with information about where, how, or when the action takes place

Adjective   the class of words which qualify and modify nouns

Alliteration   the repetition of consonant sounds – usually at the beginnings of words

Anaphoric reference   a reference or link back to something earlier in a text

Anglicisation   the conversion of non-English words into English spelling and pronunciation

Articles (definite and **indefinite)** the words 'the' and 'a' or 'an' – part of the word-class **determiners**

Assonance   the repetition of vowel sounds

Cohesion   the aspects of a text which link and hold it together into a meaningful whole

Connotation (*compare* denotation) the implications or associations of a word/phrase beyond its surface meaning

Declarative   a sentence that is a statement

Denotation (*compare* connotation) primary meaning of a word or phrase

Determiner   class of words which accompany nouns, such as articles and numbers

Fronting (*compare* postponement)   an arrangement of the syntax of a phrase so as to bring a particular element to the beginning

Haiku   traditional syllable-based form of Japanese poetry

Iambic pentameter   traditional line of English poetry consisting of 5 pairs of stressed/unstressed syllables

Idiom   common phrase or expression whose meaning is not predictable from its literal sense

Imperative   a direct command

Limerick   traditional form of English light verse

Lineation   the arrangement of a text into lines

Interrogative   a direct question

Metaphor   an implied comparison between two things/ideas

Modal verbs   a group of verbs including might, may, shall, will, should which express a speaker/writer's attitudes and degrees of certainty towards an action

Noun (concrete, **abstract)**   the largest

class of words which refer to things (i.e. concrete, accessible to the senses) and ideas (i.e. abstract, which exist only as concepts)

Onomatopoeia   the imitation in a word or words of the sounds to which they refer

Parallelism   the repetition in sequence of phrases/sentences of similar structure

Past participle   form of the verb used in the construction of tenses such as 'I have eaten' and 'they have been sorted'

Passive (*compare* active)   the form of the verb which makes the receiver of the action the subject, and which may omit the agent of the action (e.g. 'the postman was bitten' (by the dog)).

Persona   a voice or personality created by a writer to act as the speaker of a text

Postponement (*compare* fronting)   an arrangement of the syntax of a phrase so as to place a particular element at the end

Phrasal verb   verb consisting two or more words, one of which is a preposition, and whose meaning is not predictable from its surface sense (e.g. 'I was taken in by his charm')

Pre-modification   the introduction of a qualifying word or phrase (adverbial or adjectival) before the item (verb or noun) to which it refers

Quatrain   unit of verse consisting of a group of four lines, usually following a regular rhyme pattern

Simile   an explicit comparison of two things/ideas, usually using the words 'as' or 'like'.

Sonnet   traditional form of English verse (with some variants), usually of fourteen lines

Synonyms   words or phrases of similar meaning

Semantic fields   a concept or activity which includes words of related meanings – the organising principle of a Thesaurus

Stress   the part of a word or phrase on which the natural 'beat' falls

Subject   grammatical term for the person/thing which acts on and usually comes immediately before the verb

Tense (e.g. **simple past**)   aspect of verbs which indicate the point in time and duration of an action

Verb/verb phrase   class of word/phrase which refers to an action or state

3.6 Extension Activities

3.6.1 Analysis and discussion

▷ First of all, go back to the statements which you considered at the very beginning of this chapter (Activity 37, pages 82–3). Having worked through this chapter, have you changed your mind about any of these questions?

▷ If you are studying the poetry of Seamus Heaney, read 'A New Song'. Discuss what it has to say about place-names, language and politics (this will be a useful introduction to the ideas we will discuss in relation to Brian Friel's *Translations* in Chapter 4).

▷ For whichever poet you are studying, after subjecting several poems to a close stylistic analysis, look for common factors that will allow you to begin to answer the question: 'What is distinctive and effective about the way Poet X uses language in his/her verse?'

3.6.2 Research and data-gathering

▷ Gather your own collection of chants from either the football ground or school playground, and investigate the different kinds of linguistic patterns they use.

▷ Using a handy notebook and a dictionary of idioms, take one of the areas listed below and collect as many English idioms as you can which are derived from it:
  ● the weather ('it's an ill wind', 'it's raining cats and dogs', etc.)
  ● games and sports ('an even playing field', 'moving the goal posts', etc.)
  ● money ('in for a penny', etc.)
  ● or any others you can suggest.

▷ If you have access to one of the collections of newspapers now available on CD-ROM, use the 'search' facility to gather articles which relate to the connection between language preservation and political nationalism. You could look at Scots and Irish Gaelic, Welsh, Cornish, Welsh, Breton – or more far-flung controversies such as the status of Euskera, the language of the Basques, and Canadian French and its importance for French-speaking Canadians who seek independence for the region of Quebec.

Use the material you gather to write an informative article on the political importance of languages.

3.6.3 Original writing

▷ Develop three or four of the verse-writing activities you have already attempted into a complete mini-anthology of your own verse. Collect the work of fellow-students and word-process/desk-top publish your group anthology.

3.7 Further reading

Suggestions for approaches to carrying any kind of language investigation are to be found in:

Angela Goddard, *Researching English Language* (Framework, 1993).

The most useful introduction to the role of metaphors in everyday speech, and how they influence and reflect our ways of thinking about the world, is Lakoff and Johnson's *Metaphors We Live By* (Chicago University Press, 1980).

You can find a fuller treatment of linguistic cohesion in one of the companion volumes in this series, Ian Pople's *Text and Discourse Analysis* (Stanley Thornes, 1998).

For what is now known as the 'Sapir-Whorf hypothesis' see J. B. Carroll (ed.), *Language, Thought and Reality* (M.I.T. Press, 1956) and some of the ideas raised in this chapter are discussed at length in Stephen Pinker's *The Language Instinct* (Morrow, 1994) and Jean Aitchison's *The Articulate Mammal* (Unwin Hyman, 1989].

Your own writing and reading of poetry is sure to profit from a reading of Peter Abbs's *Forms of Verse* (Cambridge University Press, 1990) or Mike Hayhoe's *Words Large as Apples* (Cambridge University Press, 1988).

4 | Talk the talk: from discourse to drama

4.0 Introduction

In this chapter we shall concentrate on the most fundamental of human activities which involves language – talk.

The acquisition of speech by young children occurs naturally and inevitably, and it is through talk – with parents, relatives and even furry toys – that children develop both their language and social skills. As we grow up, we learn to adjust the way we talk to the situations we find ourselves in, and as our command of the language itself develops, so does our ability to function in a range of circumstances. We learn to be endlessly creative and versatile, and the distinctive ways in which we behave in conversations is one of the 'fingerprints' of our individual personalities.

It is this endless variety of talk that playwrights exploit when they create their fictional characters and give them life by placing in their mouths the words which they are to speak on stage. Drama is not just about talk, of course. The Greek word 'drama' originally meant a 'thing done', rather than a 'thing said', and some forms of drama – mime, dance and slapstick – may use very little conversation. However, dialogue is likely to be central to whichever dramatic texts you are studying at A-level, and even if in many respects, the talk we find in scripts is quite different from the language of real conversations, it still reflects the same underlying principles, and this is as true of Shakespeare as it is of 'Brookside'.

It is only in recent years that serious study of natural talk has been carried out – and in analysing people's conversations, we have often drawn on the world of theatre for a vocabulary with which to describe it. For example, we will talk of 'cues' and 'roles'. However, we will concentrate first on natural talk, before moving on to look at extracts from our core text, Brian Friel's *Translations*, and other dramatic scripts.

Translations is also of interest for many other reasons. The subject of the play, set in nineteenth-century Ireland, is language itself, and its social importance to the different groups who use it. As we consider it in the later parts of this chapter, we will develop some of the ideas about language, society, politics and identity that we began to consider in Chapter 3.

However, we'll start by asking some fundamental questions about conversation.

ACTIVITY 66   WHAT IS TALK FOR?

Let's begin by thinking about the different situations in which you are likely to participate in conversations during a typical 24-hour period. What is your own role in these conversations, and what purposes do they serve? Brainstorm your ideas onto Table 4.1.

Table 4.1

Occasion/situation	Your role	Purpose(s) of talk

COMMENTARY
Your first thought might have been to describe the purposes of some your talk simply as 'communication' – but, of course, this is both too broad and too simplistic!

You could, for example, distinguish between talk which is purely functional – designed to get things done (requesting information, giving commands and instructions, passing on information, making arrangements, etc.) – and conversations whose purpose is largely social (gossip, small talk, polite chat, etc.).

The linguist M. A. K. Halliday, when trying to classify the ways in which children learned to use language, suggested some slightly more sophisticated distinctions, and proposed seven basic functions for talk (see Table 4.2, page 140) (*Explorations in the Functions of Language*, 1973). Consider these, and apply them to the situations you have listed in Table 4.1. Do the classifications help to clarify some of the different purposes in your own talk?

COMMENTARY
Questions

These will usually be followed by an appropriate answer. This may, of course, be
'I don't know'. However, we would be surprised if this was the response to 'what
is your name?' or 'what is 2 + 2?' Similarly, if we enquire 'what time is the next
train to Birmingham?' we will gladly accept 'I don't know' as a legitimate
response from a passer-by in the street, but find it baffling if it comes from an
employee of the National Rail Enquiry service! This is partly because we would
expect that the latter do (or should) know, and one assumption we make in
conversations is that people will, by and large, tell the truth. It would be
surprising if 'What's your name?' resulted in a deliberately misleading answer,
and we might interpret this as cheek ('Mickey Mouse!'), guilt ('John Smith') or
insanity ('Norman St John Polevaulter').

   Some questions may provoke challenges – 'What are you asking me for?' or '
What's it to you?' – which question our very right to ask them. Other utterances
which look like questions may actually be commands ('Would you mind opening
the window?') and produce a different range of responses (e.g.'sure').

Insults

Insults may, of course, provoke a counter-insult ('you're no Einstein yourself,
fatty!'), a challenge ('come here and say that!') or a non-verbal response (ouch)!
However, a less provocative response may also be possible – 'yes, I was rather
stupid, wasn't I?'

Invitations

Invitations may meet with an acceptance ('yeah, I'd love to') or refusal ('no
thanks') although refusals are likely to be accompanied by some excuse (and this
time we do not always expect literal truth!) and an apology – 'Sorry, I'm washing
my dog tonight'. This is an example of a **politeness strategy**, a way of avoiding
appearing brusque ('No') or offensive ('You must be joking!') (see Section 4.1.6).

Evaluation

Some kinds of response which are accepted in one situation may be totally
inappropriate elsewhere. In the classroom or quiz-show it is not unusual for an
answer to be followed by an evaluation:

   A *What's the capital of Peru?*   (Question)
   B *Lima*   (Answer)
   A *Well done!*   (Evaluation)

but if the same pattern occurred among friends we might be surprised:

   A *What's on at the cinema?*
   B *Jurassic Park*
   A *That's right – good answer!*

   Of course, it is always possible to produce an unexpected and rather
inappropriate response, or one which defies the general 'politeness principle'
which seems to underlie much of everyday discourse – but the results are likely to
be bafflement:

   Q *Where do you live?*
   A *Yes!*

offence:

> **A** *Hello, Vera!*
> **B** *Get lost!*

or amusement:

> **A** *Has the bell gone?*
> **B** *No, it was still there a few minutes ago.*

ACTIVITY 70

Now select a short extract from, a dramatic text which you are studying – perhaps Brian Friel's *Translations* – and similarly identify the patterns of exchange which occur.

4.1.3 Grice's Maxims

The linguist H. P. Grice has summarised the underlying principles of talk in what he terms four conversational **maxims**. He defines these as:

- the maxim of quantity – we will offer neither too little (silence, or a minimal response) nor too much (monopolising the floor) in any one turn
- the maxim of relevance – we will offer a contribution which relates directly to what the previous speakers have been discussing. Indeed, even if there is no explicit connection in what someone has to say, we will try to infer one
- the maxim of manner – we will tend to make our contribution clear and intelligible. Failure to do so may result in requests for clarification ('Sorry?', 'Say again')
- the maxim of quality – we will usually tend to say things which are true. As with the other maxims, this clearly can be – and is – broken, but our working assumption when we listen to someone has to be that what they are telling us is not a deliberate lie.

We can put these to the test both by applying them to any piece of conversational data – or by experimenting to see what happens when they are deliberately disregarded.

ACTIVITY 71

> **Q** *How many surrealists does it take to change a light bulb?*
> **A** *Bananas!*

Your task here is to have some fun and generate some amusement by writing and performing a short script which starts from an everyday situation but which deliberately breaks the rules of what kinds of utterance can follow, and which deliberately flouts Grice's Maxims. (We will look more closely at how humour can be generated in scripts in Section 4.5, The discourse of comedy.)

4.1.4 Whose turn is it anyway?

Our extra-terrestrial visitor may now feel guided as to what to say – but s/he/it can still be heard crying, 'But how do I know when it's my turn?', 'How long can I speak for?' and 'Who gets to decide what we talk about?'.

Well, we can start to answer this by thinking of a couple of situations where the business of **turn-taking** and the subjects under discussion is tightly controlled.

ACTIVITY 72   THREE FORMAL SITUATIONS

1 Divide into three groups, and choose which of the following formal
   conversational situations you will focus on:

   (i)   a typical classroom lesson
   (ii) a business or committee meeting
   (iii) a public meeting or open debate such as occurs on programmes such as
         'Oprah' or 'Kilroy'.

   In your groups, try to agree answers to the following questions:

   ● How is the subject for discussion determined?
   ● How do you know if it's your turn to speak?
   ● How do you know how long you can talk for?
   ● What will happen if you infringe any of the previous three rules?

2 Now come together and compare notes. What do the rules in each situation
   have in common with each other, and how far do they differ?

COMMENTARY

In these fairly formal situations it is usually fairly clear in advance what is to be
discussed – this may have been published in the form of an agenda or announced
by the chairman or teacher at the start. Responsibility for making sure the meetings
cover the **agenda** (i.e. the **topic management**) also rests with the chair or teacher.

In class, questions may be directed at named individuals, or individuals may be
selected to speak after raising their hands. Public meetings and studio debates
may have a predetermined order of speakers, or you may need to catch the eye of
the chair to 'get a turn'. Business or committee meetings may not be quite so
formal, though the chair may still select people for particular contributions.
Otherwise, it's a question of 'getting a word in edgeways' and 'seizing the floor.'

There may actually be a time-limit on how long you can speak (this is often the
case at large conferences) but more often a more informal 'rule' applies. In many
situations, brief and succinct contributions are more highly valued than rambling
speeches. On the other hand, we know that minimal contributions ('Yes', 'No'
etc.) are less than the required 'norm'.

As for rule infringement, a teacher or chair may simply interrupt speakers who
deviate from the subject, and speakers who speak out of turn are likely to be
reprimanded ('Don't interrupt! Let me/him/her finish!'). Talking for too long
may also provoke interruption, or simply restlessness and boredom!

All very well, then, for the more formal situations which our alien visitor will
face – but how about more casual conversations? Most of our social talk does not
involve a chair or an agenda, and we certainly don't have to put up hands if we
want to join in! So how do these work?

ACTIVITY 73   DATA-GATHERING

We cannot take our investigation of talk any further without collecting some
examples of the real thing.

Your task, then, is to record and transcribe a sample of natural unscripted
conversation – preferably involving more than two people.

Ideally, you should try to borrow a camcorder and make a video-recording (as
we will see, body-language and gesture is very important in turn-taking, and
conversation generally) but failing this, an audio tape will do.

COMMENTARY
Collecting good data takes time and is difficult and fraught with danger, so beware!

The easy way to start is by collecting publicly broadcast data – spontaneous studio debates, phone-ins, etc. Although the material will be limited to certain kinds of conversational situation, it avoids the pitfalls of gathering 'everyday' speech.

However, unbroadcast speech is likely to be less self-conscious and more interesting – providing you follow these guidelines:

- it is unethical, and could be illegal, not to say dangerous, to tape conversations without the participants' prior permission. So – seek consent first, explain it is for an educational project and that all names and other references which might make the source identifiable will be deleted in the transcript. You don't have to say that it is your subjects' language that you will be studying however, as this will make them doubly self-conscious. You may prefer to tell a 'white lie' and suggest you are carrying out a project into local history, experiences of work, or whatever.
- Even so, the result of this will be that some of the conversation that follows will be self-conscious and unnatural. Compensate for this by disregarding the first 20 minutes of your tape and selecting perhaps just 2 to 3 minutes towards the end of the session when you judge that the presence of the tape-recorder has, at least momentarily, been forgotten.
- You may need to allow for two or three attempts – it is difficult to guarantee the clarity of a recording without experimenting with the position of the machine.

There are many different models for transcribing spoken language. The simple method described here will not allow any sophisticated phonetic analysis of the data, but is adequate for most other kinds of discussion:

- try to tape/word process your transcription, using double-spacing
- number lines (every 5) for ease of reference
- don't use conventional punctuation. Use (.) for a brief pause, (3.0) to indicate the length of any longer pauses (i.e. 3 seconds), and ? to indicate a question.
- where two or more speakers overlap, show it with a slash line, e.g.:

    A: *I was going to tell you about the time I went to Newton (.)/ with my dog*
    B: */Oh no not that old*
      story again.

- delete or substitute names which may make the subjects identifiable
- otherwise, don't censor! If speakers hesitate, stumble or swear in the conversation, record this in your transcript
- any short passages of indecipherable material on the tape can be shown as a line of asterisks.

Meanwhile, we'll use another transcript to explore the question of turn-taking cues.

Here, Father (F) Mother (M) and their teenage son (S) are worried that they may not receive through the post some tickets for a football match which they have sent for:

    M: *Well I didn't put a stamp on because it said they were gonna send 'em back by em (4.0) by what they call it*
    S: *Still need a stamp on don't you?*
    M: *No, they were sending them back by/what they call it delivery*
    F: */registered mail*

M: /registered mail where it would cost three pound fifty (7.0) didn't they (2.0) eh
F: Awey, right, a lot of fans have failed to include (1.0) stamped addressed envelopes
S: You said you have to put a stamped addressed /envelope
F: /which causes problems
M: Yeah but it said they were gonna send it registered letter which is registered letter you're paying three (.) they were gonna stop three pound fifty off your cheques (6.0) phone'em up tomorrow (4.0)
F: Where's the piece of paper with it on? (3.0)
M: em (3.0) what night was it in Saturday night?
F: I don't know
M: Friday night's (3.0) I knew it said registered when you don't put a stamp on a registered letter (1.0) because you're paying three pound fifty for the registration.

ACTIVITY 74   CUES

1   Examine the data closely. What are the 'cues' which each of the speakers seems to follow when they 'seize the floor' in this conversation?

Be careful to distinguish between interruptions which result in a new speaker 'seizing the floor' and having a turn, and those which do not, or which are simply back-channel behaviour (see commentary to Activity 14 under 'Solo and duet', page 37). Use Table 4.4 to keep a tally.

Table 4.4

	F	M	S
previous speaker ends a sentence			
previous speaker asks a tag question (e.g. 'isn't it?', 'don't they?')			
previous speaker asks other types of question			
previous speaker pauses			
previous speaker nominates the next person to speak			
previous speaker starts to hesitate, repeat, or struggle for words			
successful interruption of previous speaker results in seizing of floor			
overlapping contribution but doesn't seize the floor			

2   Now let's consider any other features which may only be apparent on a video tape: How might the way a speaker use her/his voice as s/he speaks an utterance (i.e. the **prosodic features** of the speech) and her or his body gesture, position, posture and eye-contact (i.e. **paralinguistic features**) possibly work as turn-taking cues?

4.1.5 In general

We may take our cues from a variety of linguistic signals:

Syntactic cues: or, put more simply, we recognise when a sentence has been completed, and unless the speaker rushes straight on, we may consider this the time to take our turn.

Semantic cues: if we recognise the end of a sentence, but still feel that the speaker's meaning is incomplete, we are likely to wait for the conclusion of what s/he has to say. On the other hand, if we can confidently anticipate the speaker's full meaning without waiting for the end of his/her sentence, we may try to interrupt, offer some back-channel feedback, or even help them finish their sentence.

Phonetic cues: sentence endings may be marked by distinctive intonation patterns (though these will vary according to what kinds of sentence they are). Equally, a slowing-down or trailing-off in the voice might indicate a speaker is 'running out of steam' and we can prepare to jump in!

Pauses may naturally occur at the ends of sentence. We may tolerate brief pauses for thought mid-sentence, but these are more likely to be marked by fillers than silence, and a pause of more than a few seconds may prompt another speaker to interrupt.

Paralinguistic cues: if you have managed to videotape a conversation you may notice that people's body-language changes when they are trying to seize the floor, and when they are about to finish their turn. (Watch what happens when a contributor to a studio discussion programme such as 'Question Time' approaches the end of their turn – they may visibly relax back into their chair. Equally, observe what happens in a crowded bar as customers try to catch the server's eye and 'seize the floor' with their order!) Eye-contact is important here, too – a speaker may even use his/her eyes to select the next turn.

ACTIVITY 75   INVESTIGATING DISCOURSE

Using the data which you have gathered yourself, carry out an investigation and analysis of:
(i)   the sequence of adjacency pairs in the conversation
(ii   patterns of participation in the conversation (turn-taking, back-channel behaviour and interruption)
(iii) the observance – or not – of Grice's four Maxims.

4.1.6 Some conversational rituals – we've started, so we'll finish

In Activity 69, Conversational consequences (page 144), your fictional speakers probably began their conversation with some kind of greeting, and spent their last six turns getting around to saying their goodbyes. In fact, getting conversations underway, and bringing them to a close, can be a tricky business. It is at the beginnings and endings of talk that we can see most clearly that a strong element of ritual is involved.

So, let's try to help our alien visitor who may well be asking, 'How do I go about beginning and ending a conversation in English?'

Dear Alien Visitor,

Thank you for your letter. I hope you're feeling well, and not feeling too anxious about your visit to earth. Humans are quite friendly really and I'm sure you'll soon get the hang of things!

You ask how to get started. Well, you'll notice that when I started my letter to you I didn't just go straight into the business of our language lesson! I started instead with a bit of friendly, sociable stuff just to get warmed up. Similarly, it is common for any conversations – even relatively formal ones – to begin with some social chat which 'breaks the ice', as we say. Our human linguists call this sort of thing **phatic talk**.

For British people, the weather traditionally supplies a versatile topic of phatic conversation ('Nice day for the time of year', 'Hot enough for you?', 'Touch of Autumn in the air') whereas formal interviews may begin with some discussion of your journey ('Did you travel down by road?', 'Much traffic in the Andromeda Galaxy?' etc.) or some apparently unnecessary expressions of gratitude ('Thanks for coming'). Interviewers on chat shows will thank their guests profusely, even though they are appearing for a large fee and in order to promote a book or film!

Routine enquiries about your health ('How are you?') are just that – routine. Don't feel obliged to tell the truth, here; saying something like 'Pretty poor. I've got a shocking headache and I feel sick' is not normal, even if it is true!

If there's real business to be done – a business meeting, an interview, or whatever – the small talk may go on for a minute or so, or until people have finished their cups of tea (another important ritual!). Some informal conversations, though, may consist of little else!

Finishing a conversation is much the same, except in reverse. If you have to leave, or if you think there is nothing more to discuss, you might think you can just say, 'Right – that's it – I'm off', right?

Wrong! You may have to give some subtle signals, first, that you wish to bring the conversation to a close. Start gathering your belongings together, shift forward onto the edge of your seat, and start looking around you. Then, be prepared to 'go phatic' again – pay a compliment or two ('Well, it's been nice talking to you', ' Hope we'll meet again soon', 'I'll be in touch' – even if the truth is a long way from any of those things!. Have some excuses ready – 'Well' (a useful word, 'well'), 'I've got to fly'/'catch the bus'/'get on with the shopping' etc. It seems that we cannot bear for someone simply to say that they have had enough of our company!

Mind you, you have to be careful with the excuses you give. You can't be as truthful as to say 'Well, I'm bored with this conversation now. Bye' – but neither should you give an excuse that is too obviously ridiculous ('Well, I'd better be on my way – I've got to meet a visitor from a distant planet who's dropping in for tea')!

You may need to hang around for half a dozen turns or more even after you've said your good-bye. You may be told to 'Take care', 'Drive safely', or to 'Give my regards to the good people of the planet Zog.'

Anyway, it's been a pleasure writing to you. Hope you have a good journey and I look forward to seeing you soon.

(See what I mean?)

A well-wisher

ACTIVITY 76   OPENING AND CLOSING GAMBITS
Over a period of several days, observe a wide range of conversational encounters – formal and informal, on television and radio, and all around you.

Keep a record of the various opening and closing rituals which you observe – and make a presentation of your findings, either orally or in the form of a short article.

4.2 Co-operating and competing

Conversation has sometimes been compared to a kind of dancing – it is something two or more people agree to do, and it only works well if the participants co-operate in following agreed 'moves'. Even a heated debate, when participants are expressing extreme disagreements, must, unless it degenerates into anarchy or violence, reveal a degree of co-operation when it comes to following the 'rules' of conversation. If someone really doesn't want to take part in a conversation, s/he has only to remain silent, or offer the most minimal of responses, or, more disruptively, shout over the contributions of others. Otherwise, in whatever conversational situation we find ourselves, our tendency is to co-operate with the other participants in order to make the conversation 'work'. This is what is meant by the **co-operative principle**.

However, it is also true that in our conversations we detect and reveal the various kinds of competition and inequality which characterise our relationships and daily interactions. People with power, status and authority enjoy a degree of conversational licence denied to lesser mortals.

4.2.1. Status markers in discourse
We can see some of the ways in which this works by considering how the underlying principles of classroom discourse reflect the relative status of teacher and student.

ACTIVITY 77
Before reading on, try to define the particular 'rules of conversation' which describe the interactions and language in *your* English class.

Then go on to compare this with the commentary below.

COMMENTARY
Forms of address
Terms which are used directly when speaking to another person in a conversation are known as '**forms of address**'. For example, in most schools, teachers can choose to use their pupils' first names, or, with occasional sarcasm, their 'full' titles ('Well, Mr Johnson, you have excelled yourself, haven't you?!').The same right is not usually granted to their pupils, for whom the use of teachers' first names may be taboo. Instead, either their full title ('Mr Cassidy') or an even more respectful form ('Sir/miss') may be expected.

Turn-taking, holding and seizing the floor
Not only is it taken for granted that the high-status teacher can speak whenever (and for as long) as s/he likes, but s/he also enjoys the power of determining

who else (if anyone!) gets to take a turn. The pupils may have to signal their wish to speak by raising their hands, and any transgressions of these rules may lead to reminders like 'No talking!', 'Are you listening?' or even 'Keep Quiet!'

So, whereas a teacher may choose to seize the floor from his/her pupils at any time, the students are much less likely to attempt to interrupt him/her!

Utterance types

Even if you are allowed a reasonable number of turns, as a lower-status speaker you may not have the same freedom to choose what kind of things you can say. A teacher has the right to ask a variety of questions (the answers to many of which s/he will already know!), from 'What is the capital of France?'! to 'Why were you late this morning?', which s/he would be surprised to hear a pupil return. (See what happens when this right is challenged, in the opening of Peter Shaffer's *Equus* on page 174). Pupils are allowed, of course, to ask some kinds of question ('Sir, how do I do this?') but not others ('Did you have a row with your girlfriend last night, sir?')

Teachers also have the right to pass judgement on what their students say, a right which can be exploited as sarcasm ('So, the capital of France is Calais? Brilliant answer, Michael!'). Imagine the reaction if having been asked a question, students replied, 'Good question, sir!', or even, 'I don't think that's the best way of asking that, is it sir?'.

Agenda-setting and topic management

The teacher will certainly set the agenda for what gets talked about, and though students may delight in ambushing and sidetracking him/her from these intentions, some teachers may deliberately allow, or even encourage such diversions as 'light relief' before steering discussion back onto the intended course. Even when students are allowed to talk in small groups, they will be directed by an agenda prescribed by the teacher (via a worksheet or group-discussion task), who may police the groups in order to ensure the appropriate topics are actually being discussed.

The language of the expert

The teacher's high status may also be reflected in the languages s/he uses. It may reflect her/his status as an expert, and an assumption that the students do not share that expertise ('this is what linguists call phatic talk – you might like to make a note of that!').

Of course, in situations where this assumption is unfounded, and the speaker misjudges her/his listeners, the result may be that the latter resent being 'talked down to', or patronised – and, of course, the same teacher who has enjoyed all this conversational licence in the classroom may then have to attend a staff meeting with her/his peers and superiors in which s/he enjoys much lower status, and experiences the corresponding limits on her/his conversational rights!

(We'll see how far these characteristics are imitated by Brian Friel in a school-based passage from *Translations* in Section 4.6)

ACTIVITY 78   DISCUSSION POINTS

1   In the past, it was not unusual for male and female pupils to be addressed differently – males by surname only ('Come here, Brown!') and females by first name ('What is it, Samantha?').

Why do you think this was, and what implications did it have?

2 A wide range of forms of address is available in English, some friendly and informal, some less so. Compile your own list of these, and suggest how appropriate or not they might be in different situations. You might begin with:

son   sonny   pet   dear   darling   love   lad
mate   your highness   lover.

3 In William Golding's novel *Lord of the Flies*, a group of small boys marooned on a desert island try to maintain a degree of orderliness in their meetings by insisting that no one speaks unless they are holding a particular conch shell. You might like to try this the next time you have a class discussion, substituting a rolled-up newspaper for the conch!

In Golding's novel, the collapse of this formalised 'co-operative principle' marks the inevitable decline of the group into delinquency and violence. Why is our willingness to co-operate in conversations so vital to civilised society?

4 The status relationship between teacher and students is usually fairly obvious, and as a result, the conversational rules of the classroom are clearly established. Now try to describe the ways in which status relationships determine discourse rules in these less-structured situations:

- a family meal involving grandparents, parents, and children
- a group of small children at play (think of *Lord of the Flies* again!)
- a customer making a complaint to a shop assistant.

4.2.2 What determines conversational status?

We readily recognise that we behave quite differently in the various kinds of conversational situations we find ourselves in, not least because they seem to 'cast' us in different roles (to use the language of theatre). Sometimes we may be obliged to perform a role that is quite distant from our 'real' self.

For example, certain standards of personal behaviour and even uses of language may be required the moment we put on our 'costume' as an assistant in a burger bar, a doctor's receptionist or an air steward. At other times, our roles may seem more 'natural', but will still vary – in some company, you could be the focal point of the group, in others, merely 'one of the crowd'.

In all of these situations, it will seem that your status – the level of power and influence which you seem to enjoy – determines the kinds of things you can do and say in conversations.

So – what are the factors which determine your status in any given situation, and the conversational rights which accompany it?

ACTIVITY 79   TOP DOGS

For each of the following situations, decide who is likely to emerge as the person with the most 'clout' in the group, who the least, and how this might affect what happens in their conversations – then, write your own script of this imagined conversation to illustrate!

1 A female, 40-year-old deputy head, is stopped by a police patrol car for speeding. When the officer gets out of the car, the teacher sees that it is 21-year-old former male pupil, whom she had once punished at school for smoking behind the bikesheds.

2 A council committee is meeting to discuss how to solve the problems of environmental pollution in a town centre. It consists largely of middle-aged men with a general interest in the subject but limited scientific expertise. However, today they are joined by a female research scientist, aged 30, who is expert in this area.

3 In the Johnson family, the youngest of seven children, Brenda, has achieved fame and fortune as a television celebrity. Every Christmas, she rejoins her family – six elder brothers/sisters, her parents and a surviving grandparent.

4 A company has just appointed a lively young man, aged 29, as the manager of a retail store. The assistant manager is George, who at 46, has been with the firm for nearly twenty years, having 'worked his way up'.

5 An internationally famous and massively wealthy rock star attempts to enter an exclusive restuarant but is turned away by the uniformed doorman because he is unsuitably dressed.

COMMENTARY

There are, of course, a number of different factors involved, and in some situations the interplay of several of them can become quite complicated.

Age

In many situations, age can give you status points. It generally does in the school playground, and Granny may enjoy conversational rights (e.g. the right not to have her long stories interrupted!) denied to more junior members of the family. However, in the workplace, age and seniority are not necessarily the same thing!

Gender

Some influential recent studies – such as Jennifer Coates' *Women, Men and Language*, 1986 – have revealed that men and women do indeed use language differently, and that men may, in subtle and unconscious ways, use their quite distinct conversational behaviour to assert their own status and so gain greater control of topic management and 'air time'. In particular, men tend to interrupt more, and women give way; men are less supportive in their backchannel behaviour; they are also often more persistent, and are more likely to 'seize the floor'. These are, of course, usually the conversational rights of high status.

Profession

Some professions carry with them higher status than others in our culture – e.g. doctors and priests – but there will always be some situations when less-exalted tradesmen will come into their own. Lines of family relationships tend to be much stronger, however, and even though he may have become the managing supremo of a huge multinational corporation to whom everyone defers, a boy will always be his mother's son!

Area of expertise

If a particular activity or area of knowledge is important to and valued by a group, then anyone who excels in it is likely to enjoy high status. The talented sports player will usually enjoy high status in the playground, for instance. If the expertise is good enough, this may be enough to counteract the same individual's low-status factors.

Personal qualities or achievement

Similarly, if a person exhibits those characteristics which a particular group happens to hold dear – good looks, a sense of humour, success with the opposite sex, the ability to spit a tremendous distance, or whatever – they are likely to have high status, and the corresponding conversational privileges.

Wealth

The mere possession of wealth may, or may not guarantee high status. The rock star may find that his millions are not in themselves enough to elicit from the hotel doorman the same conversational respect which he would give a (less wealthy) member of the aristocracy.

Social position

At one extreme, the Royal Family enjoy extraordinary conversational rights. Any formalised encounter with them is surrounded by numerous codes defining what can, and cannot be said, how they ought to be addressed, which topics not to mention, etc. At the other end, even some very 'ordinary' people may feel they have the 'right' to simply ignore the requests of a beggar who approaches them in the street.

4.3 Analysing talk: a framework

We have begun to look at conversation in a number of ways, and to ask a variety of questions about it. It is sometimes helpful to think of these within a general framework, which we might be able to apply to any conversational data – or even to dramatic texts. The model in Figure 4.2 on page 158 has been adapted from a model in 'Language in the National Curriculum', a training-manual for teachers of English:

ACTIVITY 80   APPLYING THE FRAMEWORK: NATURAL SPEECH

Now let's see how helpful this framework is when we come to examine a transcript of natural speech and – later – a piece of dramatic dialogue. In the following situation, a builder calls at the home of Philip and Bronwen (a middle-aged couple) to explain how his company's property development will affect their neighbourhood (the names of the participants have been changed). Use the framework to analyse what is happening in the conversation.

> **Builder** (as he enters the house): *I saw your next door neighbour last night and urm (5.0) hello*
> **Bronwen**: *Hi*
> **Philip**: *Right*
> **Builder**: (sighs)
> **Philip**: *There's a sofa behind you*
> **Builder**: *Oh, right (.) well how it's all come about is (.) when we bought the land (.) you don't mind my knees do you?*
> **Bronwen**: *Mm*
> **Builder**: *We had your houses plotted off erm (.) an ordnance survey plot (.) and this house here (.) is it Malcolm O'Brien's?*
> **Philip** and **Bronwen**: *Yep*

1. **Turns**
   - how often, and for how long, does each speaker speak?
   - what kind of contribution does each speaker characteristically make? (question/answer/accusation/joke/agreement/etc.)
   - who gets interrupted easily? who doesn't?
   - who – if anyone – controls the turn-taking?
   - who influences the agenda and changes the topic?

2. **Relationships**
   - how do the speakers address each other (sir? Mick? mate? you silly sausage? darling?)
   - do any of the speakers rephrase or comment on the appropriateness or quality of another speaker's contribution?
   - in what ways do any of the speakers avoid being too blunt, or direct, and use 'politeness strategies' instead?
   - how much of the talk is phatic?

3. **Lexical and grammatical choices**
   - what distinguishes the style or register of the vocabulary of each of the speakers?
   - what kinds of phrase and sentence construction are typical of each speaker?

4. **Productive and paralinguistic features**
   - how is each speaker distinguished in terms of the pitch, tempo, dynamics and intonation of their utterances?
   - how are stress and intonation patterns used throughout the dialogue?
   - what role is played by pauses, hesitations, repetitions and other non-fluency features?
   - how do the speakers' gestures, movement, posture and eye-contact relate to the meanings conveyed by their language?

Figure 4.2 A framework for discourse analysis

Builder: *was out of position (.) and when we actually realised what we'd done is (.) we've actually bought within about a foot of his conservatory*
Bronwen: *Oh/*
Philip: */Aha*
Builder: *cos we've actually bought (.) you know (.) right up to the motorway*
Philip: *The parkway*
Bronwen: *Oh*
Builder: *The parkway*
Bronwen: *Oh yeah*
Builder: *and erm (2.0) so what (.) what we're proposing to do (.) is to build (.) you know here?*
Philip: *Right yeah*
Builder: *Do you?*
Bronwen: *Yes*
Builder: *Yeh (2.0) is some flats*
Philip: *Mmm*
Builder: *Now /*
Philip: */ There isn't two this side?*
Builder: *Ah yes*
Philip: *Yeh*
Builder: *Yeh (.) and I thought it would (.) I (.) two things struck us (.) we actually went to see Mr O'Brien because of his (.) conservatory*
Philip: *Yeah yeah*
Builder: *... a problem literally (.) and what we've agreed with (2.0) Mr and Mrs Bracewell is (.) they asked (.) well it was Malcolm O'Brien asked (.) if he could actually have some more land (.) instead of going up here*
Philip: *Yeah*
Builder: *we don't know (.) but (.) we're actually going to dis ...(.)we're actually going to give (.) Malcolm O'Brien and Mrs Bracewell (.) another two and a half metres of land*

COMMENTARY
As with the model for carrying out stylistic analysis of texts (see Chapter 3, page 121), you should always start by using your common-sense intuition to establish an overall understanding of what is going on.

You might easily sense, for example, that this is a rather awkward situation, and that the builder is rather hesitant – even nervous – about broaching the sensitive subject of land and the proposed development. He is, after all, on 'their territory' and, in sitting on their sofa, is their guest. Had the conversation taken place in a more neutral venue (such as an office) things might have been different. It is also immediately clear that Philip and Bronwen are doing most of the listening, and offer only limited and non-committal responses to their visitor's explanation.

1 Turns

How often, and for how long, does each speaker speak? The builder clearly has most 'floor time', though at first he only speaks a couple of sentences at a time before pausing for encouragement and feedback from Philip and Bronwen. Their responses are the very minimal ones required to signal that they are understanding the speaker and are happy for him to continue. Even when the builder appears to offer a turn-taking cue, such as a pause at the end of a sentence

– 'we've actually bought, you know, right up to the motorway(.)' – the couple only offer the briefest of responses ('the parkway').

What kind of contribution does each speaker characteristically make? Rather than coming straight to the point, the builder offers a rather rambling narrative explanation of the background to the situation. This is punctuated by occasional appeals to his listeners ('you know') and **discourse markers** such as 'what we've done is', 'what we're proposing to do is' and 'what we've agreed with Mr and Mrs Bracewell is', which mark the conversation by signalling in advance the nature of the conversation to come.

Bronwen's contributions (she speaks seven times, including once simultaneously with her husband) comprise a single-word greeting, a non-verbal response and some non-committal back-channel behaviour: 'Hi', 'Mmm', 'Yep', 'Oh' (twice), 'Oh yeh', 'Yes'.

Philip is slightly more vocal with eleven contributions, which include the unusual invitation 'There's a sofa behind you' and a request for clarification 'There isn't two this side?' along with the same kinds of non-committal minimum responses as his wife. At one point he corrects the builder, who mistakenly refers to the nearby dual-carriageway as a motorway. Is this a subtle claim for status?

Who gets interrupted easily? Who doesn't? The builder is allowed to continue with his explanation without interruption, though it would seem that he pauses frequently to allow Philip and Bronwen to 'seize the floor' if they wish.

Who – if anyone – controls the turn-taking? On the face of it, the builder is in control, but his frequent pausing suggests he is dependent on being 'allowed' to continue by his hosts.

Who influences the agenda and changes the topic? Again, the builder has come 'on business' and his presence makes the 'agenda' obvious – he has not come to discuss the weather or suggest an outing to the cinema! He is allowed to proceed with his lengthy preamble as the contributions of Philip and Bronwen are clearly not designed to change the topic – rather, they are waiting for him to get to the point!

2 Relationships

How do the speakers address each other? The participants don't address each other directly. However, the builder is careful always to refer respectfully to the neighbours, giving them their full titles ('Mr and Mrs Bracewell') or, on one occasion, their full name ('Malcolm O'Brien'). Interestingly, after briefly introducing the topic – 'I saw your next door neighbour last night' – he usually avoids the first person singular 'I' and takes shelter instead behind the corporate 'we' of his company. At one point, he actually corrects himself from 'I' to 'we':

> *And I thought it would. I (.) two things struck us. We actually went to see Mr O'Brien …*

This makes him the agent or spokesman of an organisation, rather than taking personal responsibility for the situation and the proposal, and so protects him as an individual from any attack which may follow!

Do any of the speakers rephrase or comment on the appropriateness or quality of another speaker's contribution? Not directly – but Philip does correct the builder's reference to the 'motorway'.

In what ways do any of the speakers avoid being too blunt, or direct, and use 'politeness strategies' instead? Philip and Bronwen are apparently quite civil with the builder, but their minimal utterances may come close to flouting Grice's Maxim of quantity, and thus make the builder feel uneasy. The invitation to sit down – 'there's a sofa behind you' – is less polite than the more usual 'please sit down'.

The builder builds up gradually to his point, and starts by establishing a context for the conversation ('I spoke to your neighbour last night'). There is no initial introduction to Bronwen and no hand-shaking but his 'you don't mind me knees, do you?' is an attempt at an ice-breaker. He is fairly tentative about his building plans, prefacing the detail with 'what we're proposing to do', which implies the plans are subject to the approval and agreement of Philip and Bronwen – whether or not this is actually the case!

How much of the talk is phatic? Very little indeed. There is none of the social preamble to the discussion which might have 'oiled the wheels'.

3 Lexical and grammatical choices

What distinguishes the style or register of the vocabulary of any of the speakers? Unsurprisingly, the builder's vocabulary includes some items from the register of building/planning – site, plot etc. – but for the most part, the register is not particularly technical or even topic-specific.

What kinds of phrase and sentence construction are typical of each speaker? We have already commented on the utterances of Philip and Bronwen. The builder's language includes numerous examples of 'actually': 'when we actually realised what we'd done', 'we actually went to see Mr O'Brien', 'it was Malcolm O'Brien asked if he could actually have some more land', 'we're actually going to give (.) Malcolm O'Brien and Mrs Bracewell (.) another two and a half metres of land'.

'Actually' is – actually – relatively empty of meaning here! It may be partly **idiolectal** – a feature of the builder's individually characteristic speech patterns – or a nervous linguistic 'tic' produced by the tension of the situation. You might go further and suggest that in some cases – 'we're actually going to give Malcolm O'Brien and Mrs Bracewell another two and a half metres of land' – it serves to underline the generosity of the company's actions.

The builder also struggles to produce grammatically coherent sentence constructions, and his utterances are subject to frequent revisions and self-corrections:

> *well how it's all come about is (.) when we bought the land (.) you don't mind me knees do you …We had your houses plotted*

> *when we actually realised what we'd done is (.) we've actually bought within about a foot of his conservatory*

> *a problem literally (.) and what we've agreed with (2.0) Mr and Mrs Bracewell is (.) they asked (.) well it was Malcolm O'Brien asked.*

This feature of his speech is likely to be a result of his anxiety to choose his words carefully in a tense and difficult situation.

4 Productive and paralinguistic features

Without access to a tape recording of the dialogue, we cannot, of course, comment on such matters as the intonation, stress, pitch, tempo and dynamics used by each speaker. Neither can we know how far the gestural and paralinguistic features of the conversation reflected the sensitive and awkward nature of the meeting.

However, it is clear that in addition to the grammatical non-fluency we have just noted, the builder's language is characterised by several fillers such as 'erm'.

So – the detail of your analysis of the conversation will probably have supported your first intuition: that here we have a tricky situation which none of the participants feel particularly comfortable with!

4.4 Real and scripted talk

So far we have looked at real talk – the conversations which occur spontaneously all around us in hundreds of situations every day. When scriptwriters set about creating a piece of fictional dialogue – in a television drama, film, or stage play, common sense tells us that the dialogue which they put into the mouths of their characters will be rather different. After all, just as we expect even a half-hour episode of our favourite 'soap' to be more eventful and interesting than 'real life' – a typical half hour of our own daily existence would be unlikely to fascinate millions of viewers! – so, scripted conversations are also likely to be more engaging and accessible than our ordinary talk.

However, skilled writers (and actors) who aim to create realistic dramas can often create the illusion that their talk is 'natural'. Perhaps it is in television soap operas such as 'Eastenders' and 'Brookside' that scriptwriters – and actors – work hardest to create this illusion. How successful are they – and how close to 'real' talk is the conversation which is put in the mouths of their characters? (At this point you should remind yourself of the characteristics of natural speech which we investigated in Chapter 2, Section 2.4.2, pages 32–8.)

ACTIVITY 81

1   Printed below are a transcript of a natural conversation between a hairdresser and her client (Extract A), and an extract from 'Brookside' (Extract B). Which features of natural speech have the 'Brookside' scriptwriters imitated in their dialogue, and do you think there are still any 'give-away' signs that it is, in fact, scripted and not natural?

Extract A
Client: *We eloped/ yeah we eloped*
Hairdresser: */(laughs)*
Client: *We went on to have six (.)*
Hairdresser: *Six!*
Client: *Yeah. One after the other*
Hairdresser: *Did you/ (.) You and /him(.)*
Client: */Yeah   yeah yeah*
Hairdresser: *One after the other/ Six children (.)*
Client: *Mm It's a bit weird actually (.) I think we thought we were the bloody Waltons/I'm not sure (laughs)*
Hairdresser: */(laughs)*
Client: *Yeah (.) so we did that um (.) he went off and had (.) er he was leading a double life really (.) he had another relationship while he was married to me and every time I had a baby she had one/ and we're still*

Hairdresser: /*What*
Client: *Yeah (.) that's how that ended up (.) but his mother knew about it as well his mother was living with us/she*
Hairdresser: /*His mother?*
Client: *Yeah everyone did on /his side*
Hairdresser: /*His mother was living with you?*
Client: *Yeah*
Hairdresser: *And she knew /about the woman and the kids down the road/*
Client: *Yeah she used to*   *but*
Hairdresser: *And she never said a word*
Client: *And all these things came to, light / afterwards.*
Hairdresser: (gasp)

Extract B

In this episode, the character known as Sinbad has just arrived at his friends Jimmy and Jackie Corkhill, after a row with his current girlfriend (Carmel) about her troublesome teenage son.

Here, Jackie joins him at the dining table for coffee and chat.

Jackie: (giving Sinbad a mug of coffee): *There you go.*
Sinbad: *Ah (.) ta Jack (3.0)*
Jackie: *Just like old times eh?*
Sinbad: *Yeh (.) feels like I've never been away*
Jackie: *So em (2.0) do you think you might stay here tonight then?*
Sinbad: *I dunno Jack (2.0)I suppose I'll have to if me and Carmel don't get sorted out (2.0) I mean if you don't mind like*
Jackie: *Oh no no (1.0) wouldn't see you out on the street*
Sinbad: *I dunno (1.0) what a mess eh?*
Jackie: *More trouble than it's worth?*
Sinbad: *Sometimes yeah (1.0) if it wasn't for that lad of hers(1.0)*
Jackie: *It'd be all moonlight and roses would it?*
Sinbad: *Something like that yeah*
Jackie: *Well you know there's always the extension here (.) and (.) if you can put up with Jimmy (2.0)*
Sinbad: *Move back in?*
Jackie: *If you want to yeah*
Sinbad: *Thanks for the offer Jack but (.) well I think I'll just see how things go*

['Brookside', shown during the week ending 21 September 1997]

2 Rewrite Extract A to make it suitable for inclusion for a new soap opera set partly in a hairdresser's salon.

3 Gather your own data (perhaps from a popular programme such as 'Neighbours' and a conversation between your friends) and carry out a similar investigation.

COMMENTARY

The 'Brookside' scriptwriters have clearly been skilful in incorporating many features of natural conversation. The extract includes a number of conversational clichés – the kinds of stock phrases which frequently crop up in talk, such as 'Just like old times', 'more trouble than it's worth' and 'moonlight and roses'. It even features some fillers, (e.g. 'em', 'I mean' and 'like'), mid-sentence pauses ('thanks for the offer Jack but (.) well I think'), and some sentences which are grammatically inconsistent or incomplete ('feels like I've never been away', 'there's always the extension here (.) and (.) if you can put up with Jimmy').

However, the turn-taking is very disciplined, and there is none of the overlapping between the speakers we find in the 'natural' extract when one of the speakers offers simultaneous back-channel feedback such as 'Yeah … yeah yeah'. Viewers and listeners may well find the presence of such overlapping in dramatic dialogue confusing and irritating – so, you may well have opted to 'clean up' the raw material of your transcript by removing this when converting it into a scene for a soap.

4.5 The discourse of comedy

Writers of realistic soap operas constantly strive to entertain their viewers by creating the illusion that their characters live apparently ordinary lives packed with incident and human drama. Their dialogue has to be close enough to 'real' speech to sustain the illusion that the characters are themselves 'real' (no bursting into song, as in a musical, or launching into poetic soliloquies direct to the camera, as in Shakespeare!).

However, the writers of comedy scripts have different aims and methods. They may choose to work in a setting that appears realistic (many situation comedies such as 'One Foot in the Grave' do this) or deliberately select an entirely unrealistic situation ('Red Dwarf', for example, draws on the conventions of dodgy science-fiction films).

Whatever the setting, however, the aim of the dialogue is the same – to make the viewers laugh.

Let us see if we can use our developing awareness of language and conversation to understand how some of these writers achieve their aim – of amusing us.

The following three extracts from popular humorous series illustrate a few of the ways in which comic scripts work.

4.5.1 Politeness principle – what politeness principle? From 'Fawlty Towers' to 'Blackadder'

One favoured device of comedy scriptwriters is the flagrant flouting of some the basic principles of 'normal' conversations which we have been considering. One of these is what is sometimes called the **politeness principle** – the source of much phatic talk, greeting and leave-taking rituals, and the 'softening' of language even in situations of conflict. However, many comedy series have featured a character whose conversational status is so low that the norms of politeness are ignored when he is being addressed or referred to. Think, for example, of Manuel, the Spanish waiter in John Cleese's 'Fawlty Towers', or Baldrick in the 'Blackadder' series. The treatment these characters receive could be seen as cruelty – if it wasn't for the fact that the characters involved appear neither to understand the insults or be hurt by them. Like the battered characters in a Tom and Jerry cartoon, they bounce straight back from each joke at their expense apparently unaffected.

So, Manuel is the recipient of all manner of abuse, both physical and verbal, from his eccentrically ill-tempered boss and Baldrick is apparently immune to the endless stream of insults hurled upon him.

ACTIVITY 82

The following extract is taken from an episode from the series 'Blackadder Goes Forth' which is set in the trenches of the First World War.

In this episode, Captain Blackadder (played by Rowan Atkinson) has just been insulting the pilots of the Royal Flying Corps, describing them as 'show-offs' and 'gits'. However, Baldrick and the unthinkingly patriotic George (Hugh Laurie) express great admiration for the airmen.

1 Identify the various ways in which Blackadder's breaches of the politeness principle produce humour, at Baldrick's expense.

2 Blackadder himself becomes the victim of similar abuse when he is at first mistaken for a German by the members of the Flying Corps. Identify these examples.

3 Use any other aspect of our discourse-analysis framework to identify and explain how the humour in the extract has been achieved.

***

Baldrick: *Oh, come on sir, I'd love to be a flyer, up there where the air is clear.*
Blackadder: *The chances of the air being clear anywhere near you, Baldrick, … are zero.*
Baldrick: *Aw, sir, it'd be great! Swooping and diving … brr brrr brrr*
(aircraft noises and flying gestures for several seconds)
Blackadder: *Baldrick … Baldrick … what are you doing?*
Baldrick: *I'm a Sopwith Camel, sir.*
Blackadder: *Ah, it is a Sopwith Camel – ah, right, I always get confused between the sound of a Sopwith Camel and the sound of a malodorous runt wasting everybody's time. Now, if you can do without me in the nursery for a while, I'm going to get some fresh air.*
(**Blackadder** exits to the trenches, where he is attacked by the arriving airman)
Airman: (played by Rick Mayall) *Ah! Eat knuckle, Fritz!* (He strikes **Blackadder**, who falls to the ground, where he is pinned down by the airman's boot) *How disgusting! A Bosch on the sole of my boot! I'll have to find a patch of grass to wipe it on! Probably get shunned in the officer's mess. Sorry about the pong, you fellows! Trod in a Bosch and can't get rid of the whiff!*
Blackadder: *Do you think we might dispense with hilarious doggy-doo metaphor for a moment. I'm not a Bosch; this is a British trench.*
Airman: *Is it? oh! That's a piece of luck! Thought I'd landed sausage-side!*

[from the episode 'Private Plane', 'Blackadder Goes Forth']

COMMENTARY
1

Blackadder exploits an ambiguity in 'the air is clear' – and strongly implies that Baldrick has a personal hygiene problem! In normal, 'polite' conversation, such personal references are generally considered taboo! So, we laugh not only at the ambiguity and the usual character attack on Baldrick, but also at the breaking of the politeness principle.

Equally taboo, usually, are direct insults. By using the phrase 'malodorous runt', Blackadder harks back to Baldrick's smell and compares him to a small pig – even if it is by implication when he suggests that Baldrick's impersonation of an aircraft is capable of confusion with a malodorous runt!

Blackadder also resorts to sarcasm, by describing the situation as a 'nursery' and thus suggesting that Baldrick's behaviour is infantile.

2

The airman breaks the politeness principle in several ways. First, by directly using the terms of racial abuse and stereotypes 'Bosch' and 'Fritz'; secondly, by referring to Blackadder in the third person, as if he is not even present, or as an unpleasantly insignificant object ('A Bosch on the sole of my boot!'), and thirdly, by overtly comparing him to a piece of dog excrement in which he has stepped, and sustaining this metaphor throughout his speech!

3

A variety of forms of address appear in the extract. The relative status of Blackadder and Baldrick is signalled by the fact that Baldrick is always 'Baldrick' and Blackadder 'Sir'. Part of the humour in the extract arises from the sudden reversal of Blackadder's status as he is abused by the airman and treated, in effect, with the same contempt he routinely dishes out to Baldrick. By contrast, the airman addresses his imaginary fellow-officers as 'You fellows', which places his speech in the upper-class register of military officer-speak.

4

If we look at the kinds of utterance which each character typically produces, Baldrick's declarations seem to be full of child-like enthusiasm ('Oh, come on sir,' 'I'd love to be flier', 'Aw, sir, it'd be great!'), whereas each of Blackadder's utterances is a put-down, first of Baldrick, but even of the airman. For Blackadder claims the right to evaluate the airman's utterance, and is sarcastic (in his use of the word 'hilarious') about the airman's swaggeringly patriotic but unpleasant metaphor – 'Do you think we might dispense with the hilarious doggy-doo metaphor for a moment?'. The patronising 'we' and the choice of language from a childish register ('doggy-doo') is an attempt to place the airman's antics, like those of Baldrick, on a level of immaturity below the loftily superior Blackadder!

As for Rik Mayall's airman, his speech is characterised by staccato, abbreviated minor sentences ('A Bosch on the sole of my boot!', 'Probably get shunned in the officer's mess') and the development of a single metaphor. There is no shortage of humour arising from excremental jokes in English – and here it is the relentless development of the joke in four stages (1 body on floor equals dog excrement, 2 needs wiping, 3 unpleasant reaction if this is unsuccessful, 4 a double apology which includes the nearly synonymous 'pong' and 'whiff', both faintly archaic) which generates the amusement.

4.5.2 Jokes in space – from 'A Hitchhiker's Guide to the Galaxy' to 'Red Dwarf'

If the various 'Blackadder' series have used popular versions of history as a source of linguistic humour, other comedy writers have found rich raw material in the conventions of futuristic science fiction. Programmes such as Douglas

Adams's 'The Hitchhiker's Guide to the Galaxy' and Grant and Naylor's 'Red Dwarf' have exploited our familiarity with the clichés of 'straight' science-fiction series to create series which are part **pastiche** (i.e. a faithful copy) and part **parody** (i.e. a humorous exaggeration or mockery). However, the following extract from 'Red Dwarf', although set in a distant galaxy far in the future, has a certain amount in common with 'Blackadder'.

ACTIVITY 83

1 In this episode the Admiral of the Fleet, Sir James Tranter, is offering an assignment to Ace Rimmer, the heroic space pilot. Use the discourse-analysis framework to examine the extract and comment on the humour achieved. In particular:

   (i)   how are the types and lengths of utterance of the two characters – the stereotype commander, and the absurdly heroic test pilot – typical of their roles?

   (ii) identify at least two different registers which create the bizarre cross between twentieth-century war adventure and futuristic science fiction

   (iii) what does Ace Rimmer's conversational style have in common with Blackadder's Airman, above?

Tranter: *Ever heard of a thing called the Dimension Theory of Reality?*
Ace: *Doesn't it run along the lines that there is an infinite number of parallel universes, where every possibility exists?*
Tranter: *It's along those lines. The basic tenet states that every decision that's made, the alternative decision is played out in another reality.*
Ace: *So?*
Tranter: *So, the lab boys have come up with a drive that breaks the speed of reality.*
Ace: *The boffins have hammered together a crate that can cross dimensions? When do I launch?*
Tranter: *It's a one-way ticket, Ace. There's no coming back.*
(**Ace** *looks at his watch.*)
Ace: *I'm free at fifteen hundred.*
Tranter: *You do understand – it's a prototype. There's no way of knowing if it'll even get there.*
Ace: *Where's 'there' exactly?*
Tranter: *You'll be transported to an alternative reality: a reality where there's another Arnold Rimmer. Some decision was made at some point in your lives where he went one way and you went the other. You might well find he's quite different from you.*
Ace: *Sounds like quite a caper.*
Tranter: *You'll do it?*
Ace: *I'm a test pilot in Space Corps, Bongo. It's my job to do it.*

[from the episode 'Dimension Jump', 'Red Dwarf']

2 The usual crew of 'Red Dwarf' includes a mechanoid, Kryten, a fashion-conscious pilot with an acute sense of smell, Cat, Ace Rimmer's alternative hologrammatic self, Rimmer, and the down-to-earth curry-and-lager guzzling Liverpudlian, Lister.

   Choose another extract from an episode of the show and use the discourse-analysis framework to identify ways in which the scriptwriters have conveyed the individuality of the characters and their relationships through the dialogue.

3 Some scriptwriters find their comic material in the nature of conversation itself, as in the following two extracts A and B from 'Monty Python's Flying Circus'. For each of them:

(i) explain how the sketch follows the usual 'rules' of conversations for the situation portrayed – in the case of Extract A a professional expert attending a domestic problem, and B a client visiting an office for some kind of professional service.

(ii) show how the writers have exploited our recognition of conversational 'rules' to create humour.

Extract A

A household interior. The door bell rings. A housewife (**Mrs Long Name**) opens the door to reveal a visitor, **Mr Vernon**.

Mr Vernon: *Hello, madam ... I*

Mrs Long Name: *Ah, hello ... you must have come about ...*

Mr Vernon: *Finishing the sentences, yes.*

Mrs Long Name: *Oh ... well ... perhaps you'd like to ...*

Mr Vernon: *Come through this way ... certainly...* (they go through into the sitting room) *Oh, nice place you've got here.*

Mrs Long Name: *Yes ... well ... er ... we ...*

Mr Vernon: *Like it?*

Mrs Long Name: *Yes ... yes, we certainly ...*

Mr Vernon: *Do ... Good! Now then ... when did you first start ...*

Mrs Long Name: *... finding it difficult to ...*

Mr Vernon: *Finish sentences ... yes.*

Mrs Long Name: *Well, it's not me., it's my....*

Mr Vernon: *Husband?*

Mrs Long Name: *Yes. He ...*

Mr Vernon: *Never lets you finish what you've started.*

Mrs Long Name: *Quite. I'm beginning to feel....*

Mr Vernon: *That you'll never finish a sentence again as long as you live.*

[from 'Monty Python's Flying Circus, Volume Two, Programme Forty-five, 1989]

Extract B

An office. A **man** behind a desk. Knock at the door.

Man: *Come in.*

Client: *Is this the right room for an argument?*

Man: *I've told you once.*

Client: *No you haven't.*

Man: *Yes I have.*

Client: *When?*

Man: *Just now!*

Client: *No you didn't.*

Man: *Yes I did!*

Client: *Didn't.*

Man: *Did.*

Client: *Didn't.*
Man: *I'm telling you I did.*
Client: *You did not!*
Man: *I'm sorry, is this a five-minute argument, or the full half-hour?*
Client: *Oh … Just a five-minute one.*
Man: *Fine* (makes a note) *thank you. Anyway, I did.*

[adapted from 'Monty Python's Flying Circus', Volume Two,
Programme Twenty-nine, 1989]

4.6 Applying the framework: drama

We have already begun to see how our understanding of the workings of natural conversation can help us in our response to dramatic texts. For example, even without knowing the circumstances and context of this extract from our core text, Brian Friel's *Translations*, we can deduce a lot about the participants and their situation:

Hugh: *…Vesperal salutations to you all.*
(Various responses)
Jimmy: Ave, *Hugh.*
Hugh: *James.* (He removes his hat and coat and hands them and his stick to **Manus**, as if to a footman) *Apologies for my late arrival: we were celebrating the baptism of Nellie Ruadh's baby.*
Bridget: (Innocently) *What name did she put on it, Master?*
Hugh: *Was it Eamon? Yes, it was Eamon.*
Bridget: *Eamon Donal from Tor! Cripes!*
Hugh: *And after the* caerimonia nominationis – *Maire?*
Maire: *The ritual of naming.*
Hugh: *Indeed – we then had a few libations to mark the occasion. Altogether very pleasant. The derivation of the word 'baptise' – where are my Greek scholars? Doalty?*
Doalty: *Would it be – ah – ah -*
Hugh: *Too slow. James?*
Jimmy: *'Baptizein' – to dip or immerse.*
Hugh: *Indeed – our friend Pliny Minor speaks of the* 'baptiserium' *– the cold bath.*
Doalty: *Master.*
Hugh: *Doalty?*
Doalty: *I suppose you could talk then about baptising a sheep at sheep-dipping, could you?*
(Laughter. Comments)

[Brian Friel, *Translations*, Act 1]

We can begin to understand what is going on in this extract if we refer to the prompt questions listed under each section of the framework in Figure 4.2 on page 158.

1 Turns

- There are at least six speakers present – Hugh, Jimmy, Bridget, Maire, Doalty and Manus, and their contributions are distributed as shown in Table 4.5.

Table 4.5

Participant	No. of turns	Types of utterance used
Hugh	8	• Greeting and explanation • Response to a question (from Bridget) • Several questions and prompts directed at others. These seem designed to elicit answers which he already knows, or to test the others' knowledge – like a teacher might. • Evaluations of others' utterances ('Indeed' x 2, and 'Too slow') also characteristic of classroom discourse
Jimmy	2	Jimmy and Maire each offer one (correct) response to one of Hugh's questions, and in addition it is Jimmy whose greeting of Hugh is prominent
Maire	1	
Bridget	2	Bridget initiates a question to Hugh and repeats/comments on this answer, but does not respond to any of Hugh's academic questions about language.
Doalty	3	Doalty's three turns include one request for permission to speak ('Master') and two very tentative responses, one of which is incomplete/interrupted ('Would it be ...' and 'I suppose you could talk ...')
Manus	0	

From analysing the turn-taking in this systematic way, we can already begin to make some informed observations:

- Hugh is clearly the focus of the scene, speaking as he does every other turn, whereas Manus, by contrast, remains entirely silent – a silence which invites us to ask questions about his attitude towards Hugh and his relationship with him. (From an actor's point of view, of course, Manus's silence also raises questions about what to think, and what to do. These issues may well be explored in rehearsal as the actors discuss what is known as the **sub-text** of the scene – see Section 4.7.1.)

- Most of the turns are fairly short, but Hugh alone enjoys the luxury of a turn which consists of more than one sentence when he elaborates on the baptism he has attended and diverts to the question of the word's derivation, or **etymology**.

- There is only one interruption – and this is by Hugh of Doalty. This confirms the high status which Hugh seems to enjoy, and the relatively lowly position of Doalty.

- Hugh is clearly controlling the turn-taking; he does so on four occasions by nominating the next speaker (Maire? Doalty? James? Doalty?)

- Likewise, Hugh controls the agenda and topic management. Although Maire seems interested in discussing the baptism further, Hugh shifts the topic of discussion to the more academic one of linguistic derivations as he moves abruptly from 'Altogether very pleasant' to 'The derivation of the word baptise?'.

2 Relationships
- The forms of address used in the extract are very revealing. Hugh uses the pompously Latinate (i.e. derived from Latin) 'vesperal salutations' and addresses the whole group as 'you all'. Subsequently, he addresses Jimmy as 'James' – thus insisting on the formal form of the name as if to avoid undue familiarity – and the others as 'Maire', and 'Doalty', whose full name is given elsewhere in the play as Doalty Dan Doalty. So, like teachers everywhere, Hugh exercises the right to address his pupils using his choice of name.

  Hugh's first nomination of Doalty follows his question 'where are my Greek scholars?' The evidence of Doalty's hesitation suggests he is not, in fact, a Greek scholar, and so that Hugh's attitude towards him may border on sarcasm. Manus he addresses not at all – and pointedly fails to do so as he hands him his hat, coat and stick, raising another question about the relationship of the two.

  On the other hand, Bridget addresses Hugh with the respectful 'Master', and only Jimmy presumes to use 'Hugh!', matching 'vesperal salutations' with his own piece of Latin, 'ave'. For whatever reason, it would seem that Jimmy enjoys a rather more privileged relationship with Hugh than the rest of the group.

- As noted above, Hugh comments freely on (and thus evaluates) the quality of others' utterances – 'Indeed' and 'too slow' – in a way which is typical of teachers but which generally signals higher status and greater conversational power.

- Hugh also makes no attempt to soften his criticism of Doalty's response – nothing could be blunter than 'too slow'. For his part, however, Doalty protects himself from the possibility of being wrong – he seems to expect that he might be! – by adopting tentative 'cushions' such as 'I suppose' and 'could you?' This tactic is characteristic of speakers who adopt a lower-status position in a conversation and, according to some researchers, is often more typical of female than male speakers (see Activity 79, Top dogs, page 155).

- Only a small amount of phatic talk takes place at the beginning of the extract as the baptism and the name of the child are discussed. Hugh quickly moves things along to a more academic discussion.

3 Lexical and grammatical choices
- Hugh's speech is polysyllabic, literary and Latin-based. Many of his phrases could have been more informally expressed using vocabulary not so rooted in Latin (Table 4.6, page 172). You can check the derivations of these alternatives by using a good etymological dictionary.

Table 4.6

Latinate or scholarly	Colloquial
vesperal salutations	good evening
celebrating the baptism	at a christening – or even, 'wetting the baby's head'
apologies for my late arrival	sorry I'm late
we had a few libations	we had a few drinks

Hugh's speech also includes a scholarly reference to the ancient Greek writer, Pliny Minor.

All of this suggests Hugh may be a scholarly and learned man who perhaps enjoys asserting his status by displaying his learning conspicuously in front of those who may not share it!

● Jimmy's very brief utterances are concise and scholarly, in contrast with Bridget's colloquial exclamations ('Cripes!'). Maire's one contribution is the precise definition which Hugh seeks, whereas by contrast, Doalty's brings the register of the conversation down to earth with his reference to sheep and sheep-dipping.

So – taking all of this into account, what can we deduce? It would appear that Hugh enjoys the highest status and power within this group, and is accepted as a teacher and source of knowledge. Hugh seems to make a self-conscious show of his learning and is not above making fun of one of his pupils, Doalty. Indeed, the extract displays many of the characteristic features of classroom discourse which we discussed earlier (see Section 4.2).

As the only one to address him by his first name, Jimmy seems to come closest to him in status – perhaps because he also takes his learning seriously, or perhaps because he is closest to Hugh in age? Doalty appears duly respectful of his 'superior', but the mystery is Manus. Who is he, why does Hugh treat him 'like a footman', and why do the two of them not exchange any words?

For solutions to some of these questions, we'll turn later to the full text of *Translations* in Section 4.9.

ACTIVITY 84

For each of the four extracts A–D printed below, carry out a similar analysis, using any aspect of the discourse-analysis framework to deduce as much as you can about the characters, their situation and their relationships.

Extract A

Briggs: *Now just look at that over there.*
Digga: *What?*
Briggs: *What? Can't y'see? Look, those buildings. Don't you ever bother looking at what's around you?*
Reilly: *It's only the docks, sir.*

Briggs: *You don't get buildings like that any more. Just look at the work that must have gone into that.*
Reilly: *D' you like it down here, sir?*
Briggs: *I'm often down here at weekends, taking notes, photographs. (Sharply) Are you listening, Reilly? There's a wealth of history that won't be here much longer.*
Reilly: *Me old man works down here, sir.*
Briggs: *What does he think about it?*
Reilly: *He hates it.*
Briggs: *His job or the place?*
Reilly: *The whole lot.*
Briggs: *Well, you tell him to stop and have a look at what's around him. Yes, he might see things a bit differently then.*

Extract B
Meg (rising): *I want to play a game.*
Goldberg: *A game?*
Lulu: *What game?*
Meg: *Any game*
Lulu (jumping up): *Yes, let's play a game.*
Goldberg: *What game?*
McCann: *Hide and seek.*
Lulu: *Blind man's buff.*
Meg: *Yes!*
Goldberg: *You want to play blind man's buff?*
Lulu and **Meg**: *Yes!*
Goldberg: *All right. Blind man's buff. Come on! Everyone up! (Rising)*
McCann: *Stanley – Stanley!*
Meg: *Stanley. Up.*
Goldberg: *What's the matter with him?*
Meg (Bending over him): *Stanley, we're going to play a game. Oh, come on, don't be sulky, Stan.*
Lulu: *Come on.*
Stanley rises. **McCann** rises
Goldberg: *Right! Now – who's going to be blind first?*
Lulu: *Mrs Boles.*
Meg: *Not me.*
Goldberg: *Of course you.*
Meg: *Who, me?*

Extract C
Vladimir: *So there you are again.*
Estragon: *Am I?*
Vladimir: *I'm glad to see you back. I thought you were gone for ever.*
Estragon: *Me too.*
Vladimir: *Together again at last! We'll have to celebrate this. But how? (He reflects) Get up till I embrace you.*
Estragon: (irritably) *Not now, not now.*
Vladimir: (hurt, coldly) *May one enquire where His Highness spent the night?*

Estragon: *In a ditch.*
Vladimir: (admiringly) *A ditch? Where?*
Estragon (without gesture) *Over there.*
Vladimir: *And they didn't beat you?*
Estragon: *Beat me? Certainly they beat me.*
Vladimir: *The same lot as usual?*
Estragon: *The same? I don't know.*
Vladimir: *When I think of it … all these years … but for me … where would you be …?* (Decisively) *You'd be nothing more than a little heap of bones at the present minute, no doubt about it.*

Extract D
Dysart: *Hallo. How are you this morning?*
(**Alan** stares at him)
Come on … sit down. Sorry if I gave you a start last night. I was collecting some papers from my office, and I thought I'd look in on you. Do you dream often?
Alan: *Do you?*
Dysart: *It's my job to ask the questions. Yours to answer them.*
Alan: *Says who?*
Dysart: *Says me. Do you dream often?*
Alan: *Do you?*
Dysart: *Look – Alan.*
Alan: *I'll answer if you answer. In turns.*
(Pause)
Dysart: *Very well. Only we have to speak the truth.*
Alan: (mocking) *Very well.*
Dysart: *So. Do you dream often?*
Alan: *Yes. Do you?*
Dysart: *Yes. Do you have a special dream?*
Alan: *No. Do you?*
Dysart: *Yes. What was your dream about last night?*
Alan: *Can't remember. What's yours about?*
Dysart: *I said the truth.*
Alan: *That is the truth. What's yours about? The special one?*
Dysart: *Carving up children.*

Now check your deductions against the commentary.

COMMENTARY

***Extract A**, from Willy Russell's *Our Day Out**
Here, the teacher Briggs is talking to one of the cheekier pupils, Reilly, on the coach as their class sets off through the streets of Liverpool for their school trip. The main clues are in the forms of address used throughout the extract, and the style of Briggs's speech as he evaluates and criticises the responses of his pupils, even taking it on himself to tell Reilly's father what he should do!

***Extract B**, from Harold Pinter's *The Birthday Party**
You may well have imagined these characters to be children. The brevity of the utterances, their preoccupation with children's games, and the way Stanley is addressed ('oh come on, don't be sulky!') would all lead you in this direction.

4. TALK THE TALK

In fact, they are all adults. The birthday in question is that of Meg (i.e. Mrs Boles), who receives paying-guests at her seaside house. Stanley is her long-term lodger, Lulu a friend and McCann and Goldberg are two new arrivals at the house. Even if you assumed they were children, you might have picked out the powerful position adopted by the slightly aggressive Goldberg (he has to approve the game – and then gives the commands for it to start) and the puzzle of Stanley. Why is he silent?

Extract C, from Samuel Beckett's *Waiting for Godot*
Estragon and Vladimir are the two central characters the play. All we know about them is that they live rough and each morning meet up by a tree, where they spend the day conversing and waiting for the arrival of a mysterious Mr Godot. He never arrives, but each evening a message-boy turns up to assure the two of them that he will surely be along tomorrow. They seem destined to repeat the same day, over and over with a few variations, as in the film 'Groundhog Day'. They are usually represented on stage as tramps.

From the dialogue here, you might already have begun to make deductions about the conversational dominance which Vladimir attempts to assert, and his apparent desire to engage Estragon's reponse. There are clues, however, that Estragon is not observing the co-operative principle – he doesn't really want to join in the conversational rituals which are important to Vladimir.

Extract D, extract from Peter Shaffer's *Equus*
In this extract, a psychologist (Dysart) attempts to interrogate a teenage boy (Alan) who has been accused of committing horrific acts of cruelty against horses (gouging their eyes out). Right from the start, when Alan refuses to return Dysart's greeting and just stares, there are clues that he will not accept the conversational rules which Dysart wants to play by. Dysart's response may be quite nervous – he has to create an excuse and an apology to get the conversation started. Alan continues not to accept Dysart's conversational authority, challenging and renegotiating his presumed right to ask the questions without having similar questions asked of himself. When Dysart agrees to a change in the rules, Alan's responses to Dysart's questions are absolutely minimal – 'yes', 'no' – as he is more eager to question Dysart's questions than to co-operate by giving full answers.

4.7 From page to stage

In Section 4.6 we have been dealing only with the words on the page, and so we have focused largely on the verbal aspects of the scripts, i.e. those aspects of conversation covered by the first three sections of our discourse-analysis framework. However, as we saw in Chapter 2, Section 2.4 when we looked at narratives in speech and writing, the linguistic content of an ordinary conversation only accounts for some of the communication taking place. Equally important – some would say rather more so – are the prosodic and paralinguistic elements of talk (Table 4.7 on page 176).

So, when we start to consider a dramatic script, we have to remember that it only becomes a play when it is performed – and this means 'putting back' into the

Table 4.7: Prosodic and paralinguistc elements of talk

Prosodic elements	Paralinguistic elements
Intonation – the movement up and down (or melody) of the voice over a word, phrase or sentence	Position – where we place ourselves in relation to our conversational partner(s)
Pitch – the high (soprano) or low (bass) levels at which we may speak	Posture – how we stand (upright, slouching, angled towards or away) or sit (upright, relaxed, on the edge of the seat, slumped, feet up, etc.)
Tempo – the speeds of our utterances	
Dynamics – the louds and softs in our speech	Body language – our physical behaviour (fidgeting with our hands and fingers?, arms folded or by our side?, legs crossed or not?, etc.)
Timbre – the quality and tone (harsh, rough, sweet, soft, etc.) of our voices	Eye-focus – do we seek, avoid, or maintain direct eye-contact as we talk?

dialogue all these missing elements. This is, of course, what actors and directors do when they start to prepare a play for performance. In the course of preparing and rehearsing the play, an acting company will need to make decisions about:

- the physical location of the scenes
- the physical appearance and clothing worn by the characters
- the distinctive way of speaking and moving of each character
- each character's aims, feelings, attitudes and values
- each character's feelings and attitudes towards the others
- how, at any given moment, this is expressed in terms of their paralinguistic behaviour
- how each line they speak is delivered in terms of its prosodic elements.

The process of turning the blueprint of the script into the performance of the play is rather like adding water to a 'Pot Noodle' to reconstitute the food in its original palatable form!

4.7.1 Meanings and motivation in dialogue

Perhaps the biggest problem we face when putting a script 'on its feet' is deciding what characters really mean when they speak a particular line. This is no different from the difficulties we face every day in working-out what people's 'real' feelings and intentions are behind the words they say.

We can see this problem by considering an example of some apparently trivial natural talk.

A male student (A) enters a room, sees another student (B) sitting at a desk, and approaches her. They exchange the following dialogue:

A: *Hi.*
B: *Oh, hi.*
A: *Could I borrow a pencil?*
B: *Yeah, sure.*

On the face of it, a straightforward conversational transaction! However, in many situations, we use such apparently trivial talk to negotiate more difficult issues – and it isn't always immediately clear what is going on 'beneath the surface'.

ACTIVITY 85

1 Try acting out this dialogue in these different contexts:
   - A and B are classmates, one of whom, A, simply needs to borrow a pencil from B.
   - A and B are friends who yesterday had an unpleasant quarrel. A has decided he wants to 'break the ice' and start to make up. A doesn't actually need a pencil at all.
   - A is an admirer of B, but is unsure of how to go about asking her out. His aim here is simply to make contact – again, he doesn't really need a pencil.
   - A is a tormentor and bully of B, who exploits every opportunity to intimidate and humiliate her.
   - A is a friend of B, but actually wants to borrow some money – £10 would be nice – so he can go out tonight.

2 Now repeat the exercise, but as you do so, speak aloud not just the words you actually exchange, but also the stream of thoughts and feelings which are going on in the character's head (a technique which is sometimes called **thought-tracking**).

COMMENTARY
No doubt, as you enacted each of these different scenarios, you'll have noticed how all the non-verbal aspects of the situation changed, reflecting the different streams of thought which were going on. To attempt to describe these underlying meanings behind our communication, linguists have developed an aspect of study called **pragmatics**; theatre practitioners are more likely to talk about the characters' **motivation** and the sub-text of a scene, and how this affects their performance – but they are talking about the same thing.

   Partly guided by the teachings of the early twentieth-century Russian actor and director Constantin Stanislavski, actors in rehearsal may investigate the psychology of their characters by scrutinising the whole of a play before deciding what their behaviour really means in each scene. They will need to know why a character enters, what s/he is seeking, why s/he says and does the things s/he does, and why s/he chooses to exit when they do. This is what they mean by the character's motivation or **objective**.

ACTIVITY 86

In the following extract from Anton Chekhov's *The Cherry Orchard*, the landowner Ranyevskaya and her family are about to leave their family home, which financial difficulties have forced them to sell to Lopakhin, the son of a peasant but now a wealthy businessman. Here, he is left briefly alone in a room with the cases and packed belongings, before being joined by Varya, Ranyevskaya's adopted daughter.

   There is stifled laughter and whispering outside the door. Finally **Varya** comes in.

Varya (looks round the room at some length): *That's strange. I can't find it anywhere …*

Lopakhin: *What are you looking for?*

Varya: *I packed it myself and I can't remember where.*

Pause.

Lopakhin: *Where are you off to now, then?*

Varya: *Me? To the Ragulins. I've agreed to keep an eye on the running of the house for them. Well, to be housekeeper.*

Lopakhin: *That's in Yashnevo, isn't it? What, about forty-five miles from here?*

Pause

Well, here we are, no more life in this house …

Varya (examining things): *Where is it …? Or perhaps I packed it in the trunk … No, no more life in this house. Never again.*

Lopakhin: *And I'm off to Kharkov, now… on this train, in fact. Lot of business to do. I'm leaving Yepikhodov in charge here. I've taken him on.*

Varya: *Really?*

Lopakhin: *This time last year we had snow already, if you remember. Now it's calm and sunny. The only thing is the cold. Three degrees of frost.*

Varya: *I didn't look.*

Pause

Anyway, our thermometer's broken

Pause

A Voice (from outside): *Where's Lopakhin?*

Lopakhin (as if he has been expecting this call for some time): *Coming!* (Goes rapidly out)

Varya, now sitting on the floor, lays her head on a bundle of clothing, and sobs quietly. The door opens and **Ranyevskaya** cautiously enters.

Ranyevskaya: *What?*

Pause.

We must go.

[Anton Chekhov, *The Cherry Orchard* (translated by Michael Frayn, Methuen, 1995), Act 4, p. 63]

1   Direct or enact the scene thinking only about the surface meaning of the script (i.e. Varya is looking for something, Lopakhin is waiting until it's time to leave, and they pass the time with some strained phatic talk).

2   Now subject the script to a closer study using the discourse-analysis framework. Identify the issues this throws up (e.g. why the silences? What is the true purpose behind the discussion of the weather? What is the attitude – and body language – of each character to the other?).

3   Throughout the play, there has been some talk about Lopakhin proposing marriage to Varya. However, the couple have never openly expressed their feelings to each other and find it difficult to broach the subject. What is the 'stifled laughter and whispering' behind the door? Has Varya been encouraged to go in, hoping that Lopakhin is, at last, about to propose? Was this Lopakhin's intention? Or is he embarrassed because he suspects he is expected to propose, but doesn't actually want to?

4   Now direct or enact the scene again and explore these different sub-textual possibilities.

ACTIVITY 87   FROM PRINT TO PERFORMANCE

1 Now return to one or more of the extracts we looked at in Activity 86 on page 177 and give a detailed description of what you imagine being able to see and hear happening on stage. Use the limited evidence available from the extract to construct a sub-text and motivation for your characters, and so fill in the paralinguistic and prosodic elements of their conversation. This will include:

   - a description of the set (physical surroundings, furniture, etc. on stage)
   - descriptions of the characters' physical appearances
   - detailed descriptions of how, and when the characters move about the stage and use gestures (use diagrams to illustrate)
   - line-by-line description of how the characters relate/react to each other, and how you imagine particular words/lines being spoken.

   At each stage, make sure you justify your suggestions by referring closely to what you have found in the extract.

2 Carry out a similar analysis of an extract from either *Translations* or an alternative drama text which you are studying.

4.8 A manner of speaking: styles of dialogue

So far, we have looked mainly at dramatic scripts which are fairly close to the style of natural speech. However, dramatists, like novelists and poets, can choose from a range of linguistic styles, and although some writers for theatre – and especially for television – have opted for realistic styles of dialogue, many have not.

It is to this variation of styles of dramatic script that we turn next.

ACTIVITY 88

Printed below is a selection of extracts from dramatic scripts.

1 Your task is to decide how close to the style of natural speech you find them – and arrange them in Table 4.8 (page 180), the 'realism league table', indicating some of the examples of the language which lead you to your decisions.

2 As you consider the extracts, try also to arrange them along a timeline according to your estimate of when they might have been written. They actually cover a range of over 2000 years!

Extract A
Mrs Boyle: *Isn't he come in yet?*
Mary: *No, mother.*
Mrs Boyle: *Oh, he'll come in when he likes; struttin' about the town like a paycock with Joxer, I suppose. I hear all about Mrs Tancred's son is in this mornin's paper.*
Mary: *The full details are in it this mornin'; seven wounds he had – one entherin' the neck, with an exit wound beneath the left shoulder-blade; another in the left breast penethratin' the heart, an'....*
Johnny: (springing up from the fire) *Oh, quit that readin' for God's sake! Are yous losin' all your feelin's? It'll soon be that none of you'll read anythin' that's not about butcherin'!*

Table 4.8

	Most realistic	Extract	Reasons/evidence
1.			
2.			
3.			
4.			
5.			
6.			
7.			
8.			
9.			
10.			
11.			
	Least realistic		

Extract B

Chorus: *Dead upon the tree, my Saviour,*
Let not be in vain Thy labour;
Help me, Lord in my last fear.

Dust I am, to dust am bending,
From the final doom impending
Help me, Lord, for death is near

(In the cathedral. **Thomas** and **Priests**)

Priests: *Bar the door. Bar the door*
The door is barred.
We are safe. We are safe.
They dare not break in.
They cannot break in. They have not the force.
We are safe. We are safe.

Thomas: *Unbar the doors! throw open the doors!*
I will not have the house of prayer, the church of Christ,
The sanctuary, turned into a fortress.
The Church shall protect her own, in her own way, not
As oak and stone; stone and oak decay,
Give no stay, but the Church shall endure.
The church shall be open, even to our enemies. Open the door!

Extract C

Swanney: *Are you serious?*
Renton: *Yeah. No more. I'm finished with that shite.*
Swanney: *Well, it's up to you.*
Renton: *I'm going to get it right this time. Going to get it set up and get off it for good.*
Swanney: *Sure, sure. I've heard it before.*
Renton: *The Sick Boy method.*
(They both look at Sick Boy)
Swanney: *Yeah, well, it surely worked for him.*
Renton: *He's always been lacking in moral fibre.*
Swanney: *He knows a lot about Sean Connery.*
Renton: *That's hardly a substitute.*
Swanney: *You'll need one more hit.*
Renton: *No, I don't think so.*
Swanney: *To see you through the night that lies ahead.*

Extract D

Maire: … *The best harvest in living memory, they say; but I don't want to see another like it.* (Showing **Jimmy** her hands) *Look at the blisters.*
Jimmy: Esne fatigata?
Maire: Sum fatigatissima.
Jimmy: Bene! Optime!
Maire: *That's the height of my Latin. Fit me better if I had even that much English.*
Jimmy: *English? I thought you had some English?*
Maire. *Three words. Wait – there was a spake I used to have off by heart. What's this it was?* (Her accent is strange because she is speaking a foreign language and because she doesn't understand what she is saying.) *'In Norfolk we besport ourselves around the maypoll.' What about that!*
Manus: *Maypole.*
(Again **Maire** ignores **Manus**)
Maire: *God have mercy on my Aunt Mary – she taught me that when I was about four, whatever it means. Do you know what it means, Jimmy?*
Jimmy: *Sure you know I have only Irish like yourself.*

Extract E

Angel (to Noe) *Noe! Noe! A shypp loke thou make –*
And many a chaumbyr thou shalt have therinne;
Of every kyndys best, a cowpyl thou take
With-in the shypp bord – here lyvys to wynne.
For God is sore grevyd with man for his synne
That all this wyde werd shal be dreynt with flood,
Saff thou and thi wyff shal be kept from this gynne
And also thi chylderyn, with here vertuys good.

Noe: *How shuld I have wytt, a shypp for to make?*
I am of ryght grett age, V.C. yere olde.
It is not for me this werk to undyrtake;
For feynnesse of age my leggys gyn folde.
Angel: *This dede for to do, be bothe blythe and bolde;*
God shal enforme the and rewle the ful ryght.
Of byrd and of beste take, as I the tolde,
A peyr in to the shypp, and God shal the qwyght.

Extract F

Tim: *Dang me I never felt as happy since the day I was breeched.*
Anne: *Shut thee mouth, fule!*
(First bars of the Villain's music heard in the distance. **William Corder** enters at back. He looks round and leers at **Maria**. Villain's music grows louder.)
Corder (tapping leggings with riding whip in a sinister way): *Egad, that's the pretty girl who has occupied my thoughts so much since I've been here.*
Marten: *Why it's Mister Corder! I am glad to see you here, Sir, to honour our homely festivities. I heard you had arrived in our village some days ago. Will you join our merrymaking?*
Corder: *Thanks for your kind welcome. Who is that charming girl?*
Marten: *Why, have you forgotten her. It's my daughter Maria.*

Extract G

Medea (indoors): *Do I not suffer? Am I not wronged? Should I not weep?*
Children, your mother is hated, and you are cursed:
Death take you, with your father, and perish his whole house!
Nurse: *Oh, the pity of it ! Poor Medea!*
Your children – why, what have they to do
With their father's wickedness? Why hate them?
I am sick with fear for you, children, terror
Of what may happen. The mind of a queen
Is a thing to fear. A queen is used
To giving commands, not obeying them;
And her rage once roused is hard to appease.

To have learnt to live on the common level
Is better. No grand life for me,
Just peace and quiet as I grow old.
The middle way, neither great nor mean,
Is best by far, in name and practice.
To be rich and powerful brings no blessing;
Only more utterly
Is the prosperous house destroyed, when the gods are angry.
(Enter the **Chorus** of Corinthian women)
Chorus: *I heard her voice, I heard*
That unhappy woman from Colchis
Still crying, not calm yet.

Extract H

Mrs Hardcastle: *I vow, Mr Hardcastle, you're very particular. Is there a creature in the whole country, but ourselves, that does not take a trip to town now and then, to rub off the rust a little? There's the two Miss Hoggs, and our neighbour, Mrs Grigsby, go to take a month's polishing every winter.*

Hardcastle: *Ay, and bring back vanity and affectation to last them the whole year. I wonder why London cannot keep its own fools at home. In my time, the follies of the town crept slowly among us, but now they travel faster than a stage-coach. Its fopperies come down, not only as inside passengers, but in the very basket.*

Mrs Hardcastle: *Ay, your times were fine times indeed; you have been telling us of them for many a long year. Here we live in an old rumbling mansion, that looks for all the world like an inn, but that we never see company. Our best visitors are old Mrs Oddfish, the curate's wife, and little Cripplegate, the lame dancing-master; and all our entertainment, your old stories of Prince Eugene and the Duke of Marlborough. I hate such old fashioned trumpery.*

Extract I

Caliban: *As wicked dew as e'er my mother brushed*
   With raven's feather from unwholesome fen
   Drop on you both; a south-west blow on ye,
   And blister you all o'er.

Prospero: *For this, be sure, tonight thou shalt have cramps,*
   Side-stitches that shall pen thy breath up. Urchins
   Shall, for that vast of night that they may work,
   All exercise on thee. Thou shalt be pinched
   As thick as honey-comb, each pinch more stinging
   Than bees that made 'em.

Caliban: *I must eat my dinner.*

Extract K

Restaurant. Table set for dinner with white tablecloth. Six places. **Marlene** and **Waitress**.

Marlene: *Excellent, yes, table for six. One of them's going to be late but we won't wait. I'd like a bottle of Frascati straight away if you've got one really cold.*

The **Waitress** goes

Isabella Bird arrives.

Here we are. Isabella.

Isabella: *Congratulations my dear.*

Marlene: *Well, it's a step. It makes for a party. I haven't time for a holiday. I'd like to go somewhere exotic like you but I can't get away. I don't know how you could bear to leave Hawaii. /I'd like to lie in the sun forever, except of course I*

Isabella: *I did think of settling*

Marlene: *can't bear sitting still*

ACTIVITY 89   REWRITING EXERCISES

You can develop your own dialogue and written skills by rewriting extracts originally written in a modern, realistic idiom in a more formal, artificial style – or vice versa.

1   Revisit any of the dramatic extracts we have considered in this section, and rewrite them in the style of one of the contrasting pieces. For example, you could try 'Red Dwarf' in verse, adding a Chorus (of schoolchildren?) to *Our Day Out*, or a *Murder in the Cathedral* in which all the characters speak in informal dialect!

2   Ideally, you should aim to act out your new versions, and then write an accompanying commentary in which you describe the linguistic changes you have made – and the effects they have created. Would the humour of 'Red Dwarf' be lost if all the characters spoke in formal, Standard English verse? Would informal and dialectal speech be appropriate for a drama set in Canterbury cathedral and culminating in the murder of an archbishop?

ACTIVITY 90   SCRIPTWRITING

Before we turn again to our core text, you may now like to try some scriptwriting of your own – especially if the course you are studying allows you to submit a folder of original writing as coursework.

What follows is merely a list of suggestions – you may be able to negotiate alternative possibilities with your teacher:

- script the opening few minutes of a new soap opera. Decide on your viewing time, target audience, settings and key characters first.
- alternatively, try your hand at a sample script for part of an episode of your favourite existing soap
- if you enjoy humorous sketches, try writing a short sketch of your own and persuading a group of dramatic friends to act it out; work together with some fellow-students and you may have enough material for a short revue
- many films start life as novels. Take a chapter from a novel which you think could be successfully adapted for the screen, and produce your screenplay for it (don't worry too much at first about the technicalities of camera shots etc.)
- radio drama is another possible genre. Investigate how plays work on radio – how voice-overs and sound effects are used, and how it compensates for and exploits the absence of pictures – before trying a short 10–15 minute mini-drama
- write the opening scene of what would turn out to be your own full-length play. As with the new soap-opera option, sketch out your ideas for the whole play first, so that you know who your characters are, what the plot is going to involve, and how it is going to end!

Whichever scriptwriting option you try, write an accompanying commentary in which you reflect in some detail on how you have applied to your own writing some of the discoveries you have made about conversation, discourse and dialogue throughout this chapter.

4.9 Back to the texts: *Translations*

In many ways, the subject of Brian Friel's play is language itself – which makes it an especially interesting text for any combined Language and Literature course. So, not only can we now examine it using our discourse-analysis framework, but we can also find in the play many springboards for other language investigations.

4.9.1 The dramatic script: investigating discourse

We have seen how productive it can be to subject a short passage of dialogue from any play to the kinds of scrutiny to which we first subjected samples of real talk. Equally, we can use the kinds of systematic approach associated with discourse analysis to investigate characters and the way their authors make them behave in dramatic texts.

ACTIVITY 91   ANALYSING DIALOGUE AND CHARACTERS

1 Take any short extract from *Translations* (or any other set play you are studying) and investigate its text and sub-text closely. How would the relationships and attitudes between the characters be 'translated' into a performance? Either direct a rehearsal of the extract or write detailed director's notes for the scene.

2 Investigate a character from the play by surveying (i.e. listing, classifying and counting):

   (i)   the types of utterance (command, question, complaint, apology, etc.) they make. You could construct a bar chart to show the relative frequency with which your character (for example) cracks a joke, makes a complaint or asks a question

   (ii) similarly, survey the types of utterance which other characters make to him/her. A character may be revealed as much by how others speak to them as by their own speech

   (iii) his or her choices of vocabulary (e.g. you could survey Hugh's vocabulary, using an etymological dictionary which reveals the origins of words, to assess his preference for a Latinate, literary register)

   (iv) survey the length and complexity of sentence which a character produces, taking a sample from typical sections of the play

   (v)   survey the various forms of address which your character uses, and which are used towards him/her

   (vi) in all these surveys, distiunguish between the language used at different times in the play, and use the results of your analysis to explain any change or development in the character's behaviour and role.

4.9.2. Translating and translatability

When turning to consider some of the linguistic themes of Brian Friel's play, we need look no further than the title. For a start, what do we mean by 'translation'? Usually, the production in one language of the equivalent meanings of a piece of a text or utterance originally produced in another. However, this is not always a straightforward matter, as the writers of this 'Monty Python's Flying Circus' sketch showed:

A Hungarian tourist enters an ordinary tobacconist's, clutching and reading hesitantly from a phrase book.

Hungarian: *I will not buy this record, it is scratched?*
Tobacconist: *Sorry?*
Hungarian: *I will not buy this record, it is scratched.*
Tobacconist: *No, no . This … tobacconist's.*
Hungarian: *Ah! I will not buy this tobacconist's. It is scratched.*
Tobacconist: *No, no, no … tobacco … er, cigarettes* (holds up a pack)
Hungarian: *Yes!, cigarettes. My hovercraft is full of eels* (pretends to strike a match)
Tobacconist: *Matches, matches?* (showing some)
Hungarian: *Yah! Yah!*(he takes out cigarettes and matches and pulls out loose change; he consults his book) *Er, do you want…do you want to come back to my place, bouncy bouncy?*
Tobacconist: *I don't think you're using that thing right.*
Hungarian: *You great poof.*
Tobacconist: *That'll be six and six, please.*
Hungarian: *If I said you had a beautiful body would you hold it against me? I am no longer infected.*
Tobacconist: (miming that he wants to see the book; he takes the book) *It costs six and six …* (mumbling as he searches) *Costs six and six … ah, here we are … Yandelvayasna grldenwi stravenka.*
(Hungarian hits him between the eyes.)

[from 'Monty Python's Flying Circus', Volume Two,
Programme Twenty-five, 1989]

Translation is difficult enough without the deliberately mischievous intervention of rogue translators! Usually, the intention will be to render the original meanings as accurately as possible – but there may be occasions when the power of the translator to distort or 'put a spin on' the original may be useful – as in the following extract from *Translations*:

Here, the British Captain Lancey is explaining (in English) the survey of the surrounding land which is being carried out, and the bilingual Owen (who is employed as an interpreter by the British) is translating his words for the benefit of the local people (including Hugh, the schoolmaster).

Lancey: *His Majesty's Government has ordered the first ever comprehensive survey of this entire country – a general triangulation which will embrace detailed hydrographic and topographic information and which will be executed to a scale of six inches to the English mile.*
Hugh (Pouring a drink): *Excellent – excellent.*
(Lancey looks at Owen)
Owen: *A new map is being made of the whole country.*
(Lancey looks to Owen: Is that all? Owen smiles reassuringly and indicates to proceed.)
Lancey: *This enormous task has been embarked on so that the military authorities will be equipped with up-to-date and accurate information on every corner of this part of the Empire.*
Owen: *The job is being done by soldiers because they are skilled in this work.*

Lancey: *And also so that the entire basis of land valuation can be reassessed for purposes of more equitable taxation.*
Owen: *This new map will take the place of the estate agent's map so that from now on you will know exactly what is yours in law.*
Lancey: *In conclusion I wish to quote two brief extracts from the white paper which is our governing charter:* (reads) '*All former surveys of Ireland originated in forfeiture and violent transfer of property; the present survey has for its object the relief which can be afforded to the proprietors and occupiers of land from unequal taxation.'*
Owen: *The captain hopes that the public will cooperate with the sappers and that the new map will mean that taxes are reduced.*
Hugh: *A worthy enterprise – opus honestum! And Extract B?*
Lancey: '*Ireland is privileged. No such survey is being undertaken in England. So this survey cannot but be received as proof of the disposition of this government to advance the interests of Ireland.' My sentiments, too.*
Owen: *This survey demonstrates the government's interest in Ireland and the captain thanks you for listening so attentively to him.*

[*Translations*, Act 1]

It is clear from this that Owen – who has recently returned to his native village after six years in Dublin – is deliberately changing Lancey's text in the act of translation. So what exactly are the differences between the original meanings and those which Owen conveys in Irish – and what reasons may he have for doing this?

ACTIVITY 92

Your task is to complete Table 4.9 (page 190) with the parallel version produced by Owen, and explain the differences between it and Lancey's version. The first example has been completed for you.

At least one of the characters present – Manus– knows enough of both languages to realise what Owen is doing, as he challenges him a few lines later:

Manus: *What sort of a translation was that, Owen?*
Owen: *Did I make a mess of it?*
Manus: *You weren't saying what Lancey was saying!*
Owen: '*Uncertainty in meaning is incipient poetry' – who said that?*
Manus: *There was nothing uncertain about what Lancey said: it's a bloody military operation, Owen! …*

[*Translations*, Act 1]

Thus, for personal and political reasons which become clearer as the play goes on, whilst Owen conveys the literal senes of some of the captain's words accurately enough, he is deliberately making his words sound less threatening and politically provocative.

Of course, this skill – putting potentially unfavourable information in a more favourable light – is one which is developed by politicians everywhere, and is described nowadays as 'spin-doctoring'. This can usually be heard in action during any political interview!

Elsewhere, as we saw in the Monty Python sketch, the problems and confusions of translation can become a source of humour in the play. In the following extract

Table 4.9

	Lancey (English)	Owen (Irish)	Differences
(i)	a general triangulation which will embrace detailed hydrographic and topographic information … etc.	a new map is being made of the whole country	Owen avoids the technical (and Latinate) language from the register of cartography (map-making) and so reduces Lancey's lengthy preamble to the more colloquial terms which he imagines are more suitable for his audience.
(ii)	the military authorities will be equipped with up-to-date and accurate information on every corner of this part of the Empire		
(iii)	the entire basis of land valuation can be reassessed for purposes of more equitable taxation		
(iv)	this survey cannot but be received as proof of the disposition of this government to advance the interest of Ireland … etc.		

from *Translations*, Yolland, another English soldier, tries to communicate to Maire his wish to accompany her to a dance. Remember, Yolland is speaking English, Maire Irish, and Owen is attempting to translate between them.

Owen: *Maire says there may be a dance tomorrow night.*
Yolland: (To **Owen**) *Yes? May I come?* (To **Maire**) *Would anybody object if I came?*
Maire: (To **Owen**) *What's he saying?*
Owen: (To **Yolland**) *Who would object?*
Maire: (To **Owen**) *Did you tell him?*
Yolland: (To **Maire**) *Sorry-sorry?*
Owen (To **Maire**): *He says may he come?*
Maire: (To **Yolland**) *That's up to you.*
Yolland: (To **Owen**) *What does she say?*
Owen: (To **Yolland**) *She says …*
Yolland: (To **Maire**) *What-what?*
Maire:(To **Owen**) *Well?*

Yolland:(To **Owen**) *Sorry-sorry?*
Owen: (To **Yolland**) *Will you go?*
Yolland: (To **Owen**) *Yes, yes if I may.*
Maire: (To **Owen**) *What does he say?*
Yolland: (To **Owen**) *What is she saying?*
Owen: *Oh for God's sake!* (To **Manus** who is descending with the empty can.)
You take on this job, Manus.

[*Translations*, Act 2, scene 1]

4.9.3 The Greeks have a word for it: translatability

You may remember we encountered the views of the linguists Sapir and Whorf (page 130), who maintained that the language which we happen to speak limits the kinds of thoughts and ideas which we can have. If this had indeed been true, it would be impossible to 'translate' between languages, since some of the ideas conveyed by one tongue would not be expressible in another.

In practice, translation does enable speakers of different languages to communicate – otherwise organisations such as the European Community and the United Nations would not be able to function! – but that is not to say that it is always easy to express in terms of one tongue meanings deeply rooted in the culture and language of another. As the Irish-speaking Hugh tells Lancey in *Translations*, 'English couldn't really express us'.

We can begin to appreciate some of these difficulties when we look at different translations into English of the same original text. This may be an issue for you if you are studying a text which was first written in a language other than English. Anton Chekhov's *The Cherry Orchard* has been rendered into English by many different translators since its first performance in 1904 (we have already seen an extract from one of these on page 178). Some of these texts claim to be 'translations', others merely 'versions' – but all of them are different.

ACTIVITY 93

1 Before looking at some examples of these differences, let's ask the question 'Why should this be?'.

 If you have tried to learn a second language, and had to translate between this and your 'mother tongue', you may find it useful to reflect on your experiences. If you are lucky enough to be bilingual, even better! Consider also how the following (or any other) factors might affect a translation:
 • when the translation was written
 • the presence in the text of idiomatic expressions (e.g. the equivalent of 'down in the dumps', 'over the moon', etc., which if translated word for word would produce nonsense. Try suggesting to a French speaker that you are so happy you are 'au-dessus de la lune'!)
 • the presence of words which do not correspond exactly to any in English
 • other (grammatical?) differences between the source and target-language.

2 Now let's look closely at three versions of the same scene from *The Cherry Orchard*. Version A is from a translation by Elisabeta Fen (1951), Version B is from Michael Frayn's 1978 translation, and Version C was adapted by Peter

Gill from a literal translation by Ted Braun, also in 1978, and performed most recently by the Royal Shakespeare Company in 1995–6.

In this scene from Act 1, we meet for the first time Trofimov, who arrives at the Andreyevna estate to greet Ranyevskaya (Liubov Andryeevna), the landowner, whose dead son he had formerly tutored. He is still (in his late twenties) a student at the university.

Varia is Liubov Andreyevna's adopted daughter, and Gayev her brother.

Version A
Enter **Trofimov**. He is dressed in a shabby student's uniform, and wears glasses.
Liubov Andryeevna: *What a wonderful orchard! Masses of white blossom, the blue sky …*
Trofimov: *Liubov Andryeevna!* (She turns to him) *I'll just make my bow and go at once.* (Kisses her hand warmly) *I was told to wait until morning, but it was too much for my patience.*
(Liubov Andryeevna looks at him, puzzled)
Varia: (through tears) *This is Pyetia Trofimov.*
Trofimov: *Pyetia Trofimov, I used to be tutor to your Grisha. Have I really changed so much?*
(**Liubov Andryeevna** puts her arms around him and weeps quietly)
Gayev: (embarrassed) *Now, now, Liuba …*
Varia (weeps): *Didn't I tell you to wait until tomorrow, Pyetia?*
Liubov Andryeevna: *My Grisha … my little boy … Grisha… my son …*
Varia: *There's nothing for it, Mamma darling. It was God's will.*
Trofimov: (gently, with emotion) *Don't, don't …*
Liubov Andryeevna: (quietly weeping) *My little boy was lost … drowned … What for? What for, my friend?* (More quietly) *Ania's asleep there, and here I am, shouting and making a scene. Well, Pyetia? How is it you've lost your good looks? Why have you aged so?*
Trofimov: *A peasant woman in the train called me 'that moth-eaten gent'.*
Liubov Andryeevna: *In those days you were quite a boy, a nice young student, and now your hair is thin, you wear glasses … Are you still a student?* (Walks to the door.)
Trofimov: *I expect I shall be a student to the end of my days.*

Version B
Enter **Trofimov**, in a shabby student's uniform and spectacles.
Ranyevskaya: *What an amazing orchard it is! The white masses of the blossom, the pale blue of the sky …*
Trofimov: *Lyubov Andreyevna!*
(She looks round at him)
I'm just going to pay my respects to you, and then I'll go away and leave you in peace. (Ardently kisses her hand) *I was told to wait until morning, but I didn't have patience enough.*
(**Ranyevskaya** gazes at him in perplexity.)
Varya: (on the verge of tears) *It's Petya.*

Trofimov: *Trofimov. Petya Trofimov. I used to be Grisha's tutor … have I really changed so much?*
(**Ranyevskaya** embraces him and weeps quietly.)
Gayev: (embarrassed) *Come on, Lyuba. Come on, now.*
Varya: (weeps) *Petya, I did tell you to wait until tomorrow.*
Ranyevskaya: *My Grisha … my boy … Grisha … my son …*
Varya: *What can we do, Mama? It was God's will.*
Trofimov: (softly, on the verge of tears) *There now … There now …*
Ranyevskaya: (weeps quietly) *My boy died, my little boy was drowned … Why? Why, my friend?* (More quietly) *Anya's asleep in there, and here am I talking at the top of my voice … making a noise … What's this, Petya? Why have you lost your looks? Why have you aged so?*
Trofimov: *You know what some old woman on a train the other day called me? 'That mangy-looking gentleman'.*
Ranyevskaya: *You were still only a boy before, just a nice young student. Now you've got glasses, your hair's gone thin. You're surely not still a student?* (Goes to the door)
Trofimov: *I should think I'm going to be a perpetual student. The Wandering Student, like the Wandering Jew.*

Version C
Ranevskaya: *It's a wonderful orchard, masses of white flowers. Blue sky …*
(Enter **Trofimov**, wearing a shabby student's uniform and spectacles)
Trofimov: *Liuba Andreyevna. I've come to pay my respects.* (She looks at him) *I won't stay. I was told to wait until the morning but I didn't have the patience.* (Kisses her hand warmly)
(**Ranevskaya** looks at him perplexed)
Varya: (through tears) *It's Pyetia Trofimov.*
Trofimov: *Pyetia Trofimov. Grisha's tutor. Have I changed that much?*
(**Ranevskaya** puts her arms around him and weeps quietly)
Gaev: (embarrassed) *Now, now, Liuba.*
Varya: (weeps) *I told you to wait until tomorrow.*
Ranevskaya: *Grisha, my little boy. Grisha, my son.*
Varya: *It was God's will, Mama. There's nothing we can do.*
Trofimov: (tenderly through tears) *There, there.*
Ranevskaya: (weeps quietly) *I lost him. He was drowned. Why, Pyetia, why?* (more quietly) *Anya's asleep in the other room and here I am making all this noise. Why have you lost your looks, Pyetia? Why are you looking so old?*
Trofimov: *On the train a peasant woman insisted on referring to me as the moth-eaten gentleman.*
Ranevskaya: *You used to be such a good-looking boy. The perfect student. Now you've got thin hair and spectacles. Are you still a student?* (Goes to the door)
Trofimov: *I think I shall be an eternal student.*

Your task is to survey and analyse the most interesting differences between these three versions.

Begin by listing the main differences you find and organising them as you go along into categories. You may find it useful to use some of the ones suggested below – but also try to suggest categories of your own.

- characters' names and their spellings (e.g. 'Anya' or 'Ania'?)
- alternative synonyms chosen in each translation (e.g. is the orchard 'wonderful' or 'amazing'? Is Trofimov 'mangy-looking' or 'moth-eaten'?)
- significantly different words in each translation (e.g. does Trofimov kiss Ranevskaya 'warmly' or 'ardently'? Is he a 'perpetual student', a 'Wandering Student', or simply 'a student until the end of his days'?)
- a different idiomatic expression chosen (e.g. does Trofimov 'make his bow' or 'pay his respects'?
- different syntax or sentence structure in each translation (e.g. does Varya rebuke Trofimov by saying 'Didn't I tell you to wait until tomorrow?', 'I did tell you to wait until tomorrow' or 'I told you to wait until tomorrow')
- an omission or addition in one or more of the translation (e.g. the reference to the Wandering Jew).

Now go on to analyse the different meanings and connotations of these variations, and how they might affect our understanding of the scene.

COMMENTARY

One immediate problem facing a translator moving from Russian into English is that the two languages use different alphabets, and so the nearest equivalent letters must be found to convey names. You will see that each translator finds different solutions to this (the direct expression of the sounds of the original language using a different alphabet is known as **transliteration**).

The remarkable richness and density of the English vocabulary (we will learn something of how this has come about in Chapter 5) may mean that there are occasions when a single expression in the original language could equally well be conveyed by several in English, many of them idiomatic. So, Ranyevskaya could be 'talking at the top of her voice', 'making all this noise', or 'making a scene'. Similarly, 'Come on …' and 'There, there …' are both acceptable, if subtly different, expressions of comfort and encouragement.

Elsewhere two syntactic alternatives ('Didn't I tell you …?.' and 'I did tell you …' may both correspond to the original literal sense, and yet there is clearly a slight difference in the degree of rebuke implied by each.

On the other hand, a translator may sometimes feel that the most obvious English equivalent is not suitable. Michael Frayn, the translator of Version B, rejected the phrase 'perpetual student' (as used in Peter Gill's Version C) for Trofimov because, he says:

> it suggests the idea of of his being the unchanging student type. The Russian phrase, vyechniy studyent, has quite a different overtone; it is a variant of vyechniy zhid, literally 'the eternal Jew', but in English the Wandering Jew, who was condemned to wander the earth for all eternity without shelter.

[from the translator's introduction to the Methuen Student Edition of *The Cherry Orchard*, p. xlix]

Throughout this book we have been studying the huge variety within our own language, and its apparently infinite capacity to express a whole range of social meanings as well as simply to communicate information. The task of translating these messages into equivalent meanings and styles in another language is a daunting one. How, for example, would we approach the translation into a foreign language of a text which features a number of different accents and dialects? Michael Frayn himself quotes the comments of a former translator of *The Cherry Orchard* as a reminder of the scale of the translator's task:

> *each character is distinguished by an appropriate speech pattern. Ranyevskaya constantly employs diminutives and uses vague expressions; Gayev employs a mixture of the fulsomely oratorical and the abruptly interrogative ... Pishchik speaks in breathless phrases which are a 'hodge-podge of old-world courtesy, hunting terms and newspaper talk'; Lopakhin's language is socially varied and depends on whom he is addressing; Trofimov's is a* melange *of the poetic, the literary and the political ...*

[from the translator's introduction to the Methuen Student Edition of *The Cherry Orchard*, pp. xxxix–xl]

Finally, before we return to *Translations* itself, we should also note that even within our own native tongue, we may need to translate – between the different registers, styles and codes which coexist in everyday usage. For example, when dealing with patients, a nurse may have to 'translate' a consultant's technical diagnosis of an illness into terms which the patient can understand.

ACTIVITY 94   TRANSLATING THE CODES

Consider what kinds of 'translation' may be needed in each of these situations – and draw up your own 'phrase book' for each one:

1 a teacher is writing a school report to the parents of a pupil who has been described (informally) by staff as lazy, disruptive and badly behaved.

2 The receptionist at a garage has received from the mechanic the results of an MOT test on a vehicle. S/he speaks to the owner of the vehicle, who has limited technical knowledge, to tell him the news.

3 A politician has received some statistical information which suggests the country's economy is in trouble. S/he is to make a party political broadcast.

4.9.4 *Translations*: language, culture and identity

We saw in Chapter 3, Section 3.4 how the poet Seamus Heaney explored the importance of a distinctive language and voice for the identity of a community, and how this has been reflected in campaigns for the preservation of Welsh, Scots Gaelic and even Cornish. As with Irish Gaelic, each of these languages declined in use as a consequence of social, political and economic factors – and in *Translations* Brian Friel turns back the clock to the early nineteenth century (the play is set in 1833), when the decline in the Irish language was gathering speed. The story told by his play touches on many aspects of the relationships between language, power, community and identity – or what is called **sociolinguistics**.

Although English-speaking rule over Ireland was first established as long ago as the twelfth century, it was during the seventeenth century that the extent of English influence was greatly extended (notably through the campaigns of Oliver Cromwell), to the point when Ireland was incorporated into the United Kingdom by an Act of Union (1803).

As the language of the ruling class, English became dominant, and the combination of its political and social prestige, the emigration of Irish people on a large scale, and the devastation which the famine of the 1840s was to bring about, led to a huge reduction in the numbers of native Irish Gaelic speakers. Its revival – in the later part of the nineteenth century and beyond – was part of a broader political movement to resist English rule and assert a distinctive Irish Celtic culture. It is significant that one of the first characters we see on stage in *Translations* is the dumb Sarah, who is being taught to speak by Manus; the need for a language to give a voice to a community, as much as to an individual, is one of the play's key themes.

We soon learn (from Bridget, one of the members of Hugh's hedge-school) that through the new national schools, the English language is being imposed on the country:

> **Bridget:** *And from the very first day you go, you'll not hear one word of Irish spoken. You'll be taught to speak English and every subject will be taught through English'* .
>
> [*Translations*, Act I]

Just as it is the power of the Captain Lancey's military forces which imposes the new Anglicised place-names on the map, so the power of the new education system will play its part in displacing the old language. For the Baile Beag community where the play is set, English is a foreign language that is not the natural expression of its culture and identity. As Hugh says, 'English, I suggested, couldn't really express us.'

On the other hand, elsewhere in the play we hear from Maire that Daniel O'Connell, the Irish political leader who became known as 'the Liberator', had declared that 'the old language is a barrier to modern progress', a view which the forward-looking Owen might appear to support when he describes his job as 'to translate the quaint archaic tongue you people persist in speaking into the King's good English'. Indeed, we have already seen a similar argument being used (by Professor Christie Davies) in the current debate over the status of Welsh (see page 134).

ACTIVITY 95   ENGLISH OR IRISH?

Should the villagers of Baile Beag welcome the opportunity to learn English, or reject it in order to preserve their native tongue?

Alongside the comments above, also consider Hugh's following remarks about Irish Gaelic and any other discussions in the play of the merits of English and Irish. Then, complete Table 4.10 on page 197 by suggesting arguments that could be made on either side of question.

> **Hugh**: [Gaelic] *is a rich language, Lieutenant, full of the mythologies of fantasy and hope and self-deception – a syntax opulent with tomorrows. It is our response to mud cabins and a diet of potatoes; our only method of replying to inevitabilities …*
> *… But remember that words are signals, counters. They are not immortal. And it can happen that a civilisation can be imprisoned in a linguistic contour which no longer matches the landscape of … fact.*
>
> [*Translations*, Act 2, scene 1]

Table 4.10

In favour of learning English	In favour of rejecting English

The language of the tribe

At one point in the play, the Englishman Yolland – who has already begun to develop a sympathetic interest in the local culture and its language – is working with the interpreter Owen on finding an English equivalent of the place name Bun na hAbhann. Yolland can only produce an approximation of the correct pronunciation, and suggests 'let's leave it alone. There's no English equivalent for a sound like that.'

You may be reminded of Seamus Heaney's poem 'Broagh' (see page 132) in which he celebrates both the place and its name, with its final 'gh the strangers found difficult to manage'. For both Heaney and Yolland, the unique identity of the community is bound up with its language and especially in its place-names. Later, as he once again struggles with the pronunciation (of the word 'poteen'), Yolland realises that for all his worthy attempts to learn the language, he will always be an outsider:

> **Yolland**: *Poteen – Poteen – Poteen. Even if I did speak Irish I'd always be an outsider here, wouldn't I? I may learn the password but the language of the tribe will always elude me, won't it? The private core will always be … hermetic, won't it?*
>
> [Act 2, scene 1]

Similarly, when, at the end of the play, Hugh promises to teach Maire English so that she can communicate with Yolland, he says 'I will provide you with the available words and the available grammar. But will that help you to interpret between privacies? I have no idea.'

ACTIVITY 96   DISCUSSION

Let's stop for a moment to consider what Yolland and Hugh mean by the 'private core' and the 'privacies' of a community. It may be helpful to think on a small scale – how do families, close-knit groups of friends, or members of other strongly defined social groups define their identity and values, both through language and otherwise, and so exclude outsiders ?

At the end of *Translations*, does the blossoming relationship of Maire and Yolland promise a hopeful future? The confusions and inadequacies of the processes of translation in the play – and the doubts which both Hugh, and Yolland express about being able to cross the cultural divide – leave their future uncertain. Maire is left at the end of the play to contemplate Jimmy's words of warning:

> **Jimmy**: *Do you know the Greek word* endogamein? *It means to marry within the tribe. And the word* exogamein *means to marry outside the tribe. And you don't cross those borders casually – both sides get very angry.*

[Act 3]

One irony of the play is, of course, that these issues are being discussed in a future in which English has triumphed, and in which the words of Irish Gaelic-speaking characters have to be represented in English. However, Irish English has not only developed as a variety of English in its own right with a rich and vibrant literature (from Sean O'Casey to Roddy Doyle) but has also, thanks to large-scale emigration, come to influence the linguistic forms of communities as far apart as Australia and the United States. In some ways, too, its distinctive features continue to echo the influence of the Gaelic; for example, the so-called cleft **structure** which Jimmy uses when he says 'it's not stripping a turf-bank you'd be thinking about, eh?' reflects Gaelic, rather than English syntactic patterns.

ACTIVITY 97

1 In place of the Gaelic which his Irish characters would have spoken, Friel has used the forms of Irish English to convey their speech. Scour the script of *Translations* and compile a list of characteristic accent and dialect features he has represented.

2 It has been said that 'a language is a dialect with an army', because the 'triumph' of one form of language over another is a matter of economic and political power rather than linguistics. Standard English has become the dominant world-language not because it is the 'best' tongue, but because those who use it have exercised most influence.

Using any reference materials you have available (the Internet, or a CD-ROM archive of recent years' newspaper articles, will be particularly useful) find out what you can about the following examples of dialects/languages under threat in different political circumstances, and present your findings in the form of an article or live presentation:

Quebecois French	Breton
Welsh, Manx	Friesian
Cornish	Catalan
Scots and Irish Gaelic	Basque.

4.9.5 What's in a name?

According to Shakespeare, a rose by any other name would still smell as sweet. Indeed, one of the basic principles of modern linguistics (following the work of pioneer Ferdinand de Saussure) is that the names we give to things – words – are quite arbitrary and entirely unconnected to the things themselves. So, we happen to call a table a 'table', but we might just as easily call it a 'cucumber' (see page 90).

However, some names – especially the names we give to people and places – seem to matter more than others, and *Translations* makes the process of naming – or the 'caerimonia nominationis' as Hugh calls it – a central issue in different ways. In the background of the play is the christening of Nellie Ruadh's child, and the question of how the name reflects the child's paternity; in the foreground is the British map-making team, embarking on a wholesale renaming of Irish place-names to make them intelligible in English. As Owen explains:

> **Owen**: *The captain* [Lancey] *is the man who actually makes the new map. George's* [Yolland] *task is to see that the place-names on this map are … correct. …*
> …
> **Manus**: *What's incorrect about the place-names we have here?*
> **Owen**: *Nothing at all. They're just going to be standardised.*
> **Manus**: *You mean changed into English?*
> **Owen**: *Where there's ambiguity, they'll be Anglicized.*

[Act 1]

ACTIVITY 98   TRANSLATING AND TRANSLITERATING

This process of Anglicisation involves either transliterating (see page 194) the sounds of the names to the nearest English equivalent, or translating the etymology (or literal meaning and derivation) of the name into English. So, in the case of the problematic Bun na hAbhann, Owen explains: '… Bun is the Irish word for bottom. And Abha means river. So it's literally the mouth of the river.' As Yolland points out that 'there's no English equivalent for a sound like that', they settle for Burnfoot – something less than a transliteration (only the first syllable bears any real resemblance to the pronunciation of the original) but which retains something of the word's etymology (since 'burn' – elsewhere in English, 'bourn(e)' – is a stream or river).

Does it seem that translation or transliteration has been used in the examples in Table 4.11 quoted by Lancey?

Table 4.11

Irish	Anglicized	Translation or transliteration?
Lis na Muc	Swinefort	
Bun na hAbhann	Burnfoot	
Drium Dubh	Drom Duff	
Machaire Ban	Whiteplains	
Cnoc na Ri	Kings Head	

Throughout the play, we see examples of this process in action. As Manus joins them, Owen and Yolland seem to be celebrating their work as an act of baptism and creation:

> **Manus**: *What's the celebration?*
> **Owen**: *A christening!*
> **Yolland**: *A baptism!*
> **Owen**: *A hundred christenings!*
> **Yolland**: *A thousand baptisms! Welcome to Eden!*
> **Owen**: *Eden's right! We name a thing and – bang ! – it leaps into existence!*
> **Yolland**: *Each name a perfect equation with its roots.*
>
> [Act 2, scene 1]

However, in referring to the biblical story of creation, Yolland reminds us that in naming something, someone, or some place, we assert our control and authority over it. In the book of Genesis, first we are told:

> *And God said, Let us make man in our image, after our likeness: and let them have dominion over the fish of the sea, and over the fowl of the air, and over the cattle, and over all the earth ...*
>
> [*Genesis*, 1:26]

A few verses later, we hear that Adam asserts this 'dominion' by naming all the creatures which he now has authority over:

> *And out of the ground the Lord God formed every beast of the field, and every fowl of the air; and brought them unto Adam to see what we would call them: and whatsoever Adam called every living creature, that was the name thereof. And Adam gave names to all cattle, and to the fowl of the air, and to every beast of the field.*
>
> [*Genesis*, 2: 19–20]

So, like Adam in Eden, the British map-makers were asserting their authority over Ireland by proposing a new, Anglicised version of the country and its place-names. In the course of the play, the two men develop different, and rather unexpected attitudes towards the task. It is Yolland who becomes sentimentally attached to the country and fears that 'something is being eroded', whereas Owen, the Irishman, is far from being disturbed by the process. Rather, he seems to embrace it as part of a welcome rationalisation and modernisation of his country. When considering what to call a crossroads previously known as 'Tobair Vree', which commemorates an ancient local legend of an old man and a well ('tobair' means 'well', and 'vree' is a corruption of Brian), he argues:

> *What do we do with a name like that? Do we scrap Tobair Vree altogether and call it – what? – The Cross? Crossroads? Or do we keep piety with a man long dead, long forgotten, his name 'eroded' beyond recognition, whose trivial little story nobody in the parish remembers?*
>
> [Act 2, scene 1]

ACTIVITY 99

1 Just as Yolland falls in love with Ireland and its original place-names, so Maire becomes fascinated by the sounds of English. She lists the places near the village in Suffolk where Yolland is from:

> *... one of them's called Barton Bendish – it's there; and the other's called Saxingham Nethergate – it's about there. And there's Little Walsingham – that's his mother's townland. Aren't they odd names? Sure they make no sense to me at all ...* [Act 3]

The writer Bill Bryson shares her fascination, and as well as providing an entertaining survey of American place-names in his book *Made in America* (1995), in *Notes from a Small Island* (1995) he comments with amusement on such British place-names as Scabcleuch, Whelpo, Mockbeggar, Chew Magna, Titsey, Stragglethorpe and Thronton-le-Beans.

Your task is to get hold of a detailed map of your area and try to research the etymological history of some of its more distinctive place-names. Local-history societies and reference libraries will help. Present your findings in the form of an entertaining (but enlightening) article for a local newspaper.

Would you agree with Owen, that such things are not important, or with Yolland, that they should be preserved?

2 Place-names can often become a matter of considerable political sensitivity. For example, whether you refer to the city in Northern Ireland as Derry or Londonderry may reflect your attitude towards the 'troubles' and identify you as supporting either the Unionist or Nationalist position in the dispute.

Using maps printed at different times in the last 50 years, track down other examples of cities whose name-changes have reflected political disputes and upheavals. You could, for example, investigate the changing place-names in Africa and how they reflect the process of decolonisation and independence.

3 Sometimes commercial organisations decide to change the names of their companies or products – presumably in the belief this will improve profits. For example, a chain of car showrooms known simply as 'Cowie's' has recently re-named itself as 'Arriva'.

Collect your own examples of these and try to explain how the new names might serve the company's interests. (You might start with the renaming of the chocolate bar formerly known as 'Marathon' as 'Snickers'!)

4.10 Learning points

4.10.1 Key concepts

As you have progressed through this chapter, you will have learned:

- that language is rule-governed at every level, including the ways we conduct conversations
- to gather your own conversational research data
- to distinguish between natural speech and scripted dialogue
- to apply a discourse-analysis framework to the analysis of transcripts and scripts, including your set text(s)
- that playscripts are blueprints for performances rather than complete texts in themselves
- that different scriptwriters may use different degrees of realism in their dialogue
- to develop your own dialogue-writing skills in different styles and to comment in detail on your linguistic choices
- to reflect on the process of translation and to comment closely on alternative translations of texts

- the historical context of *Translations* and the social and political implications of the linguistic issues it raises
- the etymology of place-names, both in *Translations* and your own area.

4.10.2 Glossary

adjacency pair the basic unit of conversation, consisting of an utterance and its response

agenda the subjects discussed during a conversation

chorus/choric speaking in drama, the use of several actors to represent and speak for a collective group

co-operative principle the underlying understanding between speakers and their observance of conversational rules which enables talk to take place

cues on stage, the line immediately before an entrance or speech; in conversational analysis, the signal that a speaker is coming to an end of a turn

discourse markers phrases within a conversation which draw attention to aspects of the conversation itself

etymology the historical origins and derivations of the meanings of words

forms of address terms which are used in directly addressing participants in a conversation

holding the floor being able to continue speaking in a conversation

idiolect(al) relating to the individual characteristics of a speaker's uses of language

maxims (Grice's) the basic principles on which conversation is based

melodrama a form of drama with crudely portrayed heroes and villains, lots of sentiment, and (originally) unsubtle musical accompaniment

motivation the psychological reasons why characters act and speak as they do

objective theatrical term for the primary aim which a character has in a scene or play

parody a humorous send-up

pastiche an accurate imitation

phatic talk the small talk which frequently opens and closes conversations, whose primary function is social rather than informative

politeness strategies the methods used in conversation to avoid causing offence

pragmatics the study of the meanings and effects of language in use

prosodic features/elements variations in the speed, loudness, pitch, stress and intonation of speech, and the meanings these convey

realism/realistic scripted dialogue creating an illusion of natural speech

seizing the floor successfully interrupting, or gaining a turn in a conversation

sub-text a theatrical term for the meanings, feelings, and intentions underlying a character's words and actions

thought-tracking a theatrical rehearsal technique whereby an actor speaks aloud the unspoken thoughts which s/he imagines the character to be having during a scene

topic management the control or organisation of the subjects discussed during a conversation

transliteration the direct rendering of a word from a different language using an alternative alphabet

turn-taking the basic procedure of talk

4.11 Extension activities

4.11.1 Research and data-gathering

▷ Recent research suggests that men and women learn to behave differently in conversations. You may wish to test this hypothesis by gathering data which allows you to compare similar conversations involving all-male, all-female, and mixed speakers.

▷ Plays and television programmes set in schools are always popular – but how realistic are they?

Subject dialogues from scripts such as 'Grange Hill', and 'Our Day Out' to a detailed study, and compare them with some classroom discourse which you record (with permission!) in your own school or college.

4.12 Further reading

The literature covering the topics we have discussed in this chapter is vast. Some useful starting-points include:

R. Wardhaugh's *How Conversation Works* (Blackwell, 1989), O. Tannen's *Talking Voices* (Cambridge University Press, 1989) and D. Langford's *Analysing Talk* (Macmillan, 1994) all offer full and detailed explorations of conversational analysis.

Specific investigations of the role of gender include J. Coates's *Women, Men and Language* (Longman, 1986) and, more recently, Sally Johnson's and Ulrike Hanna Meinhof's *Language and Masculinity* (Blackwell, 1996).

Alison Ross's *The Language of Humour* (Routledge, 1998) provides a recent survey of this area.

An excellent section on place-names in D. Crystal's *Encyclopaedia of the English Language* (Cambridge University Press 1995, pp. 140–7) provides a survey of this topic; you can pursue special interests in more detail (especially in relation to Translations) in J. Field's *Place Names of Great Britain and Ireland* (David and Charles, 1980).

Shakespeare and language

5.0 Introduction

It is unlikely that you will be taking English Language and Literature at A-level without having to study at least one play by Shakespeare, though as soon as you ask why this particular writer assumes such a prominence, you may well receive a number of different answers (you could try carrying out such a survey for yourself, and see which is the most popular!):

- he wrote great stories
- he was a practical man of the theatre with a fine sense of what worked well on stage
- he created wonderful characters and knew a lot about human nature
- he showed terrific wisdom about life
- he was a great patriot
- he was a revolutionary
- he used language in remarkable ways.

Many of these are true, in their own way – although of all his plays, only *The Tempest* has not been found to be based on someone else's plots, the range of his women characters is rather limited, other playwrights in his own time such as Christopher Marlowe and Ben Jonson certainly approached Shakespeare in theatrical skill and popularity and, like the Bible, his plays can be quoted in support of just about any political ideology or philosophy you like. All of which leaves us with:

- he used language in remarkable ways – which no one has seriously disputed. So, in this chapter, we will see that Shakespeare's plays not only repay close study in their own right, but like our other 'core' texts, raise many important and interesting linguistic issues.

5.1 Shakespeare as discourse: *Othello* and *The Tempest*

Although we will make reference to several of Shakespeare's plays in this chapter, our main texts will be *Othello* and *The Tempest*. Whatever the play you may be studying, however, you should be able to apply many of the investigations to your own set text.

Othello is usually described as one of Shakespeare's great, mature tragedies. It seems to have been first performed in 1604. It depicts the desperate fate of an African general (Othello) who falls in love with and marries Desdemona, the daughter of a Venetian. He is then convinced (by his spiteful and embittered aide, Iago) that she is unfaithful to him. He acts on this conviction and kills her, only to discover, too late, the truth of her innocence. The play ends with his suicide, and as is usual with Shakespeare's tragedies, plenty of work for the undertakers.

Like *Othello*, *The Tempest* appeals to its contemporary audience's interest in the exotic and unusual, but is still a very different play. Sometimes thought to have been Shakespeare's last play (in fact the lesser-known *Henry VIII* seems to have followed it), it tells the story of the former ruler of Milan, Prospero, who has been stranded with his daughter Miranda on an enchanted island. Here, he uses his magical powers acquired through years of study to keep in service the bestial/monstrous Caliban and a spirit, Ariel. Now, many years after being illegally deposed by his brother Anthonio and the rival King of Naples, he has the opportunity to wreak his revenge … or bring about a reconciliation.

5.1.1 Applying the framework: Shakespeare

In Chapter 4 we explored a number of ways of analysing not only natural talk, but also scripted dialogue, and used a discourse-analysis framework to do so (see Section 4.3, pages 157–62). We can equally well apply this framework to the scripts of Shakespeare.

So, we'll begin with a short extract from *Othello*; if you are unfamiliar with the play, see how much you can deduce about the characters and their situation from a close analysis of the discourse – a full explanation follows later.

ACTIVITY 100

1 Your task is to use the headings and prompt questions in the framework to deduce as much as you can about the extract – and how it might be staged.

2 Go on to suggest which actors you might cast in the three roles, on the basis of your deductions about the characters of Brabantio, Iago and Othello.

Brabantio (appears above), at a window
Brabantio: *What is the reason of this terrible summons?*
      What is the matter there?
Roderigo: *Signior, is all your family within?*
Iago: *Are your doors locked?*
Brabantio: *Why? Wherefore ask you this?*
Iago: *'Zounds, sir, you're robbed; for shame, put on your gown!*
      Your heart is burst, you have lost half your soul;
      Even now, now, very now, an old black ram
      Is tupping your white ewe! Arise, arise;
      Awake the snorting citizens with the bell
      Or else the devil will make a grandsire of you,:
      Arise, I say.
Brabantio: *What, have you lost your wits?*
Roderigo: *Most reverend signior, do you know my voice?*
Brabantio: *Not I, what are you?*
Roderigo: *My name is Roderigo.*
Brabantio: *The worser welcome!*
      I have charged thee not to haunt about my doors:
      In honest plainness thou hast heard me say
      My daughter is not for thee; and now, in madness,
      Being full of supper and distempering draughts,
      Upon malicious bravery, dost thou come
      To start my quiet?
Roderigo: *Sir, sir, sir –*
Brabantio: *But thou must needs be sure*
      My spirit and my place have in them power
      To make this bitter to thee.
Roderigo: *Patience, good sir!*
Brabantio: *What tell'st thou me of robbing? This is Venice*
      My house is not a grange.
Roderigo: *Most grave Brabantio,*
      In simple and pure soul I come to you –
Iago: *'Zounds, sir, you are one of those that will not serve God, if the devil bid you.*
      Because we come to do you service and you think we are ruffians you'll have your
      daughter covered with a Barbary horse ...

[Act 1, scene 1, lines 81–110]

COMMENTARY
In fact, you would not have had to arrive very late at the theatre to find yourself
in this situation – working out what you can from the dialogue that has already
started (this extract occurs some 80 lines after the start of the play).

   Using the headings from the framework, compare your observations with the
ones below:

1 Turns
Who speaks, how often, and for how long?
Brabantio seems to be the focus of the scene, as he speaks on every other turn;
Iago only speaks twice, but the fact that of all the utterances, his are the longest,
might have alerted you to his influential role.

What kind of contribution does each speaker make?
There are a great many questions in the extract: the first four turns are questions, and three of them receive no direct answer. This creates an air of confusion and alarm. Brabantio's first four utterances all contain questions and challenges – suggesting alarm, confusion and annoyance. Instead of answering the questions which both Iago and Roderigo put to him, he in turn questions their right to ask such questions of him ('why, wherefore ask you thus?'), and the sanity of the questioners ('what, have you lost your wits?'). Later, Brabantio's utterances are direct assertions of authority ('My daughter is not for thee!') and threat ('My spirit and place have in them power / To make this bitter to thee'). Roderigo, on the other hand, asks two questions and makes three unsuccessful attempts to get to the point. He expects Brabantio to recognise his voice, so his failure to do so is something of a put-down. Iago, by contrast, tries to alarm Brabantio by his short, repetitive speech ('Even now, now, very now', etc.), though his riddling words seem designed to prolong Brabantio's puzzlement (what does he mean by 'Your heart is burst, you have lost half your soul … the devil will make a grandsire of you?'), and it is noticeable that, unlike Roderigo, he does not try to introduce or identify himself.

Who interrupts and gets interrupted?
At first sight, there is only one case of interruption – of Roderigo, by Brabantio – and the difference in status of these two characters will not surprise us once we learn that Brabantio is the father of the girl whom Roderigo has been pursuing! However, you will have noticed that the lay-out of the lines is unusual; some of the lines of verse have been split between two characters, with one speaker completing the line begun by another:

> **Brabantio**: *My house is not a grange.*
> **Roderigo**:   *Most brave Brabantio, …*

Many actors and directors believe that when this occurs in Shakespeare, it is an indication that the successive lines, if not actually overlapping, should at least follow on very smartly from each other. In performance, could – or would? – Roderigo try to cut in slightly on Brabantio at this point?

Who influences the agenda and changes the topic?
We hear that Iago and Roderigo have 'summoned' Brabantio, so they clearly have an agenda of their own – to tell Brabantio about a theft of some kind. Iago is allowed a speech of six lines in which to develop this topic, but his preference for obscure figures of speech allows the conversation to be temporarily hijacked. For once Brabantio realises who Roderigo is, he assumes he knows the reason for his disturbance (Roderigo pestering him about his daughter again!) and pursues his own agenda – to warn Roderigo off. For ten lines (from his speech beginning 'The worser welcome' to his threat 'To make this bitter to thee') he pursues this theme, and Roderigo twice fails to return to the subject of the theft. Where he fails, Iago succeeds, and with the final speech of the extract, not only reclaims the agenda but risks a direct rebuke ('you are one of those that will not serve God if the devil bid you').

2 Relationships

How do the speakers address each other?

When surveying this aspect of the discourse, you may find it helpful to tabulate your findings as shown in Table 5.1.

From this, we note that Brabantio fails to identify either Iago or Brabantio by name, but uses 'you' when addressing both the men (as at the start of the extract) and Roderigo alone – up to the point where Roderigo identifies himself. After this, he simply uses 'thee' and 'thou'.

For a (very attentive!) member of a modern audience, this may be a puzzle – unless we bring to the script not just our awareness of how discourse works, but also some understanding of how language has changed in the centuries since Shakespeare. (We will investigate this topic further in Section 5.3.) In fact, the explanation for Brabantio's 'you's and 'thou's lies in the way these pronouns were used in the past:

- 'you' for addressing more than one person, or for showing respect and formality
- 'thou' (as the subject of a phrase) and 'thee' (as the object) for addressing single people in a more familiar, less formal or respectful style.

In other words, as soon as Brabantio realises who he is talking to, he drops the more polite form and shows his disrespect for (and higher status than) Roderigo by using thou and thee!

For his part, Roderigo limits himself to 'you', and prefaces his remarks with a variety of respectful phrases – 'Most reverend Signior', etc. – which underline his humility and respect. Iago is less obsequious, and uses the basic forms which politeness requires ('Sir' and 'You'), whilst being fairly blunt in other ways.

Do any of the speakers comment on another speaker's contribution?

At first only Brabantio does so, with his 'What, have you lost your wits?', but at

Table 5.1

	Addressee		
	Brabantio	**Iago**	**Roderigo**
Addressor Brabantio	–	you	you (until 'My name is Roderigo') thee, thou
Iago	Sir You	–	–
Roderigo	Signior Most reverend signior you sir, sir, sir good sir Most grave Brabantio you	–	–

the end Iago seems to rebuke Brabantio for his attitude ("Zounds, sir, you are one of those that will not serve God').

3 Lexical and grammatical choices

What distinguishes the vocabulary, phrase and sentence construction of each speaker? As well as using a barrage of abrupt and impatient questions, Brabantio displays his 'honest plainness' in his direct insults of Roderigo ('in madness, / Being full of supper and distempering draughts') and his comparison of him to an unwelcome ghost ('I have charged thee not to haunt about my doors'). Roderigo finds it difficult to get beyond his opening politeness strategies, but Iago's speech is very distinctive. He twice uses what looks like a kind of swear word – "Zounds' – (we'll look at swearing and abuse in more detail in Section 5.6 below), risks using a series of urgent imperative forms ('Put on your gown', 'Awake', 'arise, I say') and twice refers to the devil. In doing what many people might when bringing bad news – avoiding coming too directly to the point – he actually increases the shock of his crude announcement that Brabantio's daughter will be 'covered with a Barbary horse'. (A glance at a good dictionary will alert you to the coarsely agricultural sense in which the word 'covered' is being used here.)

Another aspect of Iago's language is likely to have caught your attention – his first speech ("Zounds, sir, you're robbed') appears to be in verse, whereas his later one ("Zounds, sir, you are one of those') is written in plain prose. Why? Not for the only time in the play, there is a sudden switch from one form to the other which can hardly be accidental. This introduces another complication into the way we examine Shakespeare – how, where, when and why does he switch from the artificiality of verse to the more down-to-earth language of prose? We will return to this issue in Section 5.2.5.

4 Productive, prosodic and paralinguistic features

The productive, prosodic and paralinguistic features you imagine – in other words, the way in which you would wish to see the extract performed – will, of course, reflect your analysis of other aspects of the script. The initial stage direction will have helped shape your ideas about the setting (a street/courtyard outside Brabantio's window?), and you may guess that it must be at night – why else would the speakers not be able to see each other? This may partly explain Brabantio's extreme annoyance (was he in bed?), and influence his vocal and physical performance (as well as his appearance!). You may decide that Iago deliberately remains anonymous (and raise sub-textual questions about his motivation in the scene) and that he may, therefore, conceal himself in the darkness and even disguise his normal voice. You may have considered what kinds of eye-contact takes place between Iago and Roderigo, and at which points.

Try your own different ideas out – and see which work best.

Overview

So, a close scrutiny of the script in this way will reveal a great deal. In fact, Iago has heard that (i) Othello has promoted another soldier (Cassio) 'over his head', and (ii) that Othello has eloped with Desdemona, the daughter of Venetian senator Brabantio, and is trying to exploit the situation to make life difficult for his boss. Roderigo proves a willing stooge, as he is still himself infatuated with Desdemona.

ACTIVITY 101

1 Take a short passage from your own set play and subject it to this kind of detailed discourse analysis – remembering to translate your analysis into some precise suggestions for how the extract would be performed.

(If you are studying *Othello*, try the opening 25 lines or so of Act 2, scene 3, and focus particularly on how the relative status and relationships of Othello, Cassio and Iago are developed; if *The Tempest* is your text, look at the opening of Act 2, scene 1, and consider what the dialogue reveals about the nobles (Alonso, Anthonio, Sebastian, Gonzalo, Adrian and Francisco), their status and their relationships.)

2 If Activity 98 has suggested ways of investigating a short passage of dialogue in some detail, we can also extend similar approaches to the study of **characters** throughout the text. The particular suggestions given here refer to *Othello* and *The Tempest*, but you can apply similar methods to whichever play you are studying.

Othello
(i) Start your investigation of Iago's **attitudes towards women** by collecting all the **terms of address** and **reference** which he uses in the play to and about Emilia, Desdemona and Bianca. You could organise your analysis of them as a wallchart or oral presentation.
(ii) Iago and Emilia seem to belong to a different **social class** from Desdemona and Cassio. Investigate the ways in which this is reflected in the script by using the discourse-analysis framework to compare *either* the language of Iago and Cassio *or* Emilia and Desdemona throughout the play. Use a chart or table to record your findings as you go along.

The Tempest
(i) Investigate how Prospero uses the **language of power** to exercise his authority in the play. You could begin by sampling his speeches to assess what proportion of his sentences are **imperatives**. What forms do they take, and how do they vary according to the person he is commanding?
(ii) Caliban's language is particularly worth investigation. He tells Prospero that his 'profit' from learning to speak English is that he knows how to curse – but how fair a description of his language repertoire is this? Survey his speeches throughout the play and construct a bar chart or other graphic representation which shows the proportion of his language which is devoted to:

- cursing
- complaining
- narrating
- pleading
- describing
- thanking
- worshipping
- rejoicing
- apologising
- other functions.

5.2 Distinctly Shakespeare

Approaching Shakespeare in this way, as we might any other drama text, can take us so far – but it will also be clear by now that the language in his scripts is quite distinctive for a number of reasons:

- it consists of a mixture of **prose** and **verse**
- the verse often contains sentences whose length and **syntax** make them difficult to follow
- much of the language – verse and prose alike – contains a lot of **figurative language** and **imagery**
- the scripts were written 400 years ago, since which time language has undergone considerable change, affecting the meanings and uses of words and grammar.

So, we'll now turn to examine each of these particular qualities.

5.2.1 Shakespeare's verse

First of all, a simple 'odd one out' exercise.

ACTIVITY 102

Look at the lines printed below, which are taken from a number of different plays by Shakespeare. What do all of them – except one – have in common?

> *In sooth I know not why I am so sad*
>
> *Thus do I ever make my fool my purse.*
>
> *Come not between the dragon and his wrath*
>
> *When I have decked the sea with drops full salt*
>
> *Here comes a spirit of his, and to torment me*
>
> *The duke cannot deny the course of law*
>
> *Beseech you sir, be merry; you have cause*
>
> *The quality of mercy is not strained*

COMMENTARY

If you cottoned-on to the fact that the similarity has nothing to do with the meanings of any of the lines, but a lot to do with their rhythm, you'll have spotted the exception quite easily. If you set going a regular beat, using a pencil, a metronome, or even (for a Shakespeare rap!) a drum machine, you should find that most of the lines follow a regular pattern of five beats, or stresses.

Test this out again, and identify the syllable of which line on which the beat seems to fall. So:

> *In **sooth** I **know** not **why** I **am** so **sad***
>
> *Thus **do** I **ever** **make** my **fool** my **purse**.* etc.

The pattern repeats itself with most of the others – every other syllable (making ten syllables in all) carrying the beat. With the exceptional lines, however, if we work hard we can still find the five beats, but there are extra syllables in the line which make it less regular:

*Here **comes** a spirit of **his**, and **to** tor**ment** me*

The basic, regular five-beat unit of the verse is called a **pentameter** (penta = 5), and because its usual pattern is to alternate unstressed and stressed syllables (a pattern known as an **iamb**) we arrive at the best-known metrical unit in poetry, the **iambic pentameter** (see page 118). This is the basic rhythmical unit of a surprising amount of English verse – including the traditional sonnet form. In fact, Shakespeare frequently varies the pattern, sometimes along the lines of the speech (it is Caliban's, in *The Tempest*), as above. Indeed, many of Caliban's lines – even when his speech is presented as verse – do not fit this rhythm (or **scan**) easily. This may be because Shakespeare wants to suggest something of the imperfection in his speech which results from his having learned his language relatively recently, from Miranda and Prospero.

Although he uses rhythmical verse, Shakespeare seldom uses rhyme (though you may find some rhyming couplets at the ends of scenes, and in some of his earlier plays such as *A Midsummer Night's Dream*). The term **blank verse** has been coined to describe this kind of poetry.

ACTIVITY 103

1   It is often said that the iambic pentameter easily fits the natural rhythms of English speech. So, put this to the test and develop your familiarity with its particular metre by:
   (i)   producing some single-line sentences of your own which fit the pattern, e.g.

   *Our **dog** has **had** a **juicy bone** for **tea***

   or

   *I'm **going** to **watch** the **football match** to**night**.*

   (ii)   working in pairs to develop a conversation consisting of single lines of iambic pentameters. For example:

   A: *I'm **going** to the **pub** – d'you **want** to **come?***
   B: *No **thanks**, I've **got** a **lot** of **work** to **do**,* etc.

2   Take a passage of verse from your set play. Discover how well – or not – it fits the iambic pattern by tapping out the beat as you speak it aloud. Where the beat doesn't quite fit, consider whether Shakespeare has deliberately altered the rhythm and the stresses on the line to draw attention to a particular word or idea, or if, as with Caliban's speech, there may be another reason (is the character struggling to express an idea? Or, as with Othello's language in the latter part of that play, is he straining to remain in control of his language and his emotions?).

5.2.2 Deadly syntax?

The order in which Shakespeare arranges the component parts of his sentences can be an initial problem for a modern audience. There are two factors at work here:

- writers of verse tend to take liberties with the usual 'rules' of English syntax in search of the appropriate rhythmical patterns
- as a result of changes which have taken place in English grammar some constructions which were used 400 years ago are no longer common.

So, for example, where Othello tells Desdemona:

> That **hand**ker**chief** /did **an** Egyptian to my **mother give**

the beats fit the regular iambic metre better than

> An Egyptian gave/ that handkerchief to my mother

because it avoids the two successive unstressed syllables 'to' and 'my' which the second version produces.

However, the sentence uses a verb form which is unusual in modern English ('did give' instead of 'gave') and the syntax is quite different from the order we would prefer:

> An Egyptian **gave** that **hand**ker**chief** to my **mother**.

ACTIVITY 104

1 To become more comfortable with Shakespeare's sentence construction, and to understand exactly how it works, try generating some sentences of your own which follow this pattern, rather than the usual modern syntax. Follow these steps:

- produce a sentence which fits the template provided below – a couple of examples are provided in Table 5.2 to get you started
- split the modern verb form by introducing 'do' or 'did' (i.e. an **auxiliary verb**) + the base form of the verb (e.g. 'gave' – 'did give', 'give' – 'do give')
- rearrange it in the sequence **C – B1(Aux) – A – D – B2 (Base)**

Table 5.2

A	B	C	D
An Egyptian My mate Bill All this Shakespeare etc.	gave collected drives	that handkerchief a very large parcel me	to my mother from the office round the bend

Translating these into Shakespearian syntax we get:

> That handkerchief did an Egyptian to my mother give.
>
> A very large parcel did My mate Bill from the office collect.
>
> Me does all this Shakespeare round the bend drive.

We can describe this unusual arrangement using some grammatical terminology. Part **A**, or the **subject** of each sentence, usually comes first in modern English; in this construction it has been displaced by **C**, the **object**. Part **B**, the verb, which here consists of an **auxiliary** and a **main verb**, has been split, with the main element held back until the end of the sentence. This too, is unusual – and can be confusing, as we have to reach the end of the sentence before we discover the nature of the action being described! Part **D**, or the **adjunct**, which provides additional information about the action, has been moved in from its normal position at the end of the sentence.

2   There are, of course, many other unusual sentence patterns in Shakespeare's verse. Look closely at some of the lines from your own set play, and follow these same steps, which should allow you first to imitate and then to describe the construction of the sentence.

Here are a couple of examples from *The Tempest* (Act III, scene 1, line 39 and scene 3, line 83), spaced out to show their component parts:

(Ferdinand)	*Full many a lady*	*I*	*have eyed*	*with best regard*		
(Prospero)	*Bravely*	*the figure of this harpy*	*hast*	*thou*	*performed*	

5.2.3 Figurative language

In Chapter 3, Section 3.0 we looked at the ways in which figurative language is part and parcel even of everyday colloquial speech, even if many of the idoms we use are clichés that we take for granted rather than carefully devised metaphors. The range of metaphors and images which appear in Shakespeare's verse is vast – whole books, such as Caroline Spurgeon's *Shakespearian Imagery and What It Tells Us* (1935), have been devoted to it – but you can begin to investigate the figurative language in your own set play by asking some straightforward questions about how, and why it is being used.

ACTIVITY 105

For your set play, skim through as much of the script as you can and collect examples of the most common strands of imagery, noting down which characters use each image, and in what situation.

    Now assess the dramatic functions of imagery in Shakespeare by considering the importance and relevance of these images in the play. Use the following suggestions as a starting-point:

- does the imagery help remind an audience of the setting of the play? (e.g. there are several sea-related images in plays like *Twelfth Night*, *The Merchant of Venice* and *Othello*). Bear in mind that in Shakespeare's original theatre there was precious little scenery to do the job.
- does it express an aspect of a character's attitudes and values? (e.g. in *Othello*, Iago's frequent reference to animals implies a low and cynical view of human nature in general, and sexual relationships in particular).
- does it express something of a play's overall themes? If so, the imagery may not be restricted to just one or two characters but can run throughout the play. As such, this provides the play with a kind of cohesion, forming a thread of metaphorical meaning which binds together the language of the play, like a pattern in a piece of fabric (e.g. the images of disease which run throughout *Hamlet*) (see also Chapter 3, pages 120–1).

5.2.4. Keywords

Each play, as well as having its own distinctive strands of figurative language, seems almost to have an even more distinctive linguistic fingerprint – sets of keywords which occur frequently in a particular play. CD ROM technology and the Internet can be used to search Shakespeare's complete works and reveal the precise distribution of such words in the plays as a whole and any one of the plays in particular. There is usually something interesting here to investigate further, especially as these keywords are often complex in their multiple meanings, associations and connotations, some of which may no longer be familiar to a modern audience.

ACTIVITY 106   WORDSEARCH

1 If you have access to a CD ROM of Shakespeare's plays or the Internet (http://the-tech.mit.edu/Shakespeare/cgi–din/search.pl), carry out your own search to discover how many times a given word is used in all the plays, and how often in your set text. Some suggestions are offered below – but start from your own intuition about which word(s) seem to crop up frequently in your text.

   The Tempest: brave
   Othello: honest, blood, office
   King Lear: nature, nothing, see, eye
   A Midsummer Night's Dream: moon
   The Merchant of Venice: justice, mercy

2 Even without the benefit of CD ROM or the Internet, you can investigate what seem to be the keyword(s) for your text.

   First, look up the word(s) in the *Oxford English Dictionary* (or *OED* for short) – you will probably need to go to a library for this, as it occupies around twenty large volumes (or a CD ROM). The *OED* lists the various meanings which words have had at different times, and supports each definition with an illustrative example of the word in use. It is, of course, based on recorded uses of the words in written texts.

   Look for the entries which describe the meanings and uses your word had in the late sixteenth and early seventeenth centuries. You may need to know if your word is used as an adjective, noun, or whatever, as the *OED* identifies words by word-class. Every occurrence of 'brave' in *The Tempest* is an adjective, and in the *OED* under 'brave, adj.', you will find these definitions and illustrations:

   1 *courageous, daring, intrepid, stout-hearted* (as a good quality) (Illustrated by quotations from 1485, 1591 and 1642)
   2 *finely dressed; splendid, showy, grand, fine handsome* (Supported by quotations from 1593, 1612 and 1624)
   3 *Loosely, as a general epithet of admiration and praise* (1577, 1600, and many others)

   You would note in passing that the modern sense of the word has narrowed to the first of these but that some unexpected connotations may be attached to the second sense. Now return to your text, and search for each usage of the word. Record each occurrence, all the while considering which of the *OED*'s meanings seem to be at work, and how the different uses of the word in the play are related to each other and to the play's themes.

5.2.5 Verse and prose

As we discovered when examining our first extract from *Othello*, Shakespeare switches from verse to prose at different points in his script. Although this certainly doesn't happen in modern, realistic drama, it is not so different from the way in which, in a musical, characters will move in and out of song. It is not always easy to be sure why verse or prose is preferred at any given time – Table 5.3 lists several possible explanations – and on occasions, the two earliest surviving editions of the play (the Quarto and Folio versions –see Section 5.7.1) don't even agree which parts of the text are prose and which are verse! Some passages which behave like iambic pentameters appear as continuous prose – you might call it poetry in prose clothing.

However, the general principles which seem to operate are these:

Table 5.3

Verse	Prose
Used by central characters	Used by minor characters
Used by higher-class characters	Used by the working-class characters
Used by serious, or 'straight' characters	Used by comical, humorous characters
Used for discussing serious issues	Used for trivial conversation
Used in serious, dramatic or tense scenes	Used in lighter, less intense or comical scenes

Of course, this immediately throws up difficulties. What happens if a comic character is present during a scene of high tension? Or if the leading 'serious' character is in a scene which moves from high drama to light relief? Or, to put it another way around, why do Iago and Caliban, in *Othello* and *The Tempest*, speak sometimes in verse, and sometimes in prose?

ACTIVITY 107

Use Table 5.4 to survey some of the points in your set play when the language switches from verse to prose – and to suggest the reasons for and effects of its doing do.

Table 5.4

Act/scene/line	Context	Reasons and effects

5.3 Changing language

For many people, a first encounter with the language of Shakespeare provides the most direct evidence of an undeniable fact – English, like all living languages, has changed a great deal even in the fifteen or sixteen generations since he was alive. Go back further, to the work of Geoffrey Chaucer, and beyond, to the anonymous surviving literature of the Anglo-Saxon, or Old English period, and the lesson is clearer still. There will come a time – perhaps in the next 400–500 years – when the language of Shakespeare will have been left so far behind by the continually evolving English language, that if students in the twenty-fifth century want to study this old dinosaur of English Literature, they will need to study his texts as they would a foreign language. Performances of the original scripts will become rarer, more academic and specialised events, rather like those of the Medieval Mystery Plays today (see the *Noe* extract on pages 181–2), though we might still get to see alternative, modernised versions like the adaptations of Chaucer's tales which are sometimes staged today.

For the change which language undergoes is perpetual – and we can begin our wider study of this phenomenon by asking how, and why, change affected the English of Shakespeare. Shakespeare himself has had a significant influence on the language, and has contributed many common sayings and expressions such as 'be cruel to be kind' (*Hamlet*), 'a foregone conclusion' (*Othello*) and 'a tower of strength' (*Richard III*). However, the language of each of his plays illustrates some of the changes that were already underway in his lifetime, and which would shape the language we speak today.

In 1623, his plays were gathered together for the first time in the First Folio, and the first page of the first play in the book – *The Tempest* – is reproduced in Figure 5.1 (see page 218).

So – we need to ask three key questions about the process of language change:

- what are the different ways in which the language has changed?
- how have these changes occurred?
- why have such changes occurred in the past – and continue to take place in the present?

As usual, we can organise our analysis at several different linguistic levels:

Graphology and orthography: You will notice from the original opening of *The Tempest* that the words 'Boatswain', 'bestir' and others are printed using a letter that resembles an uncrossed 'f' instead of an 's'; that the punctuation of the extract may not exactly correspond to that used in your modern edition; and that there is some differences in spelling from Modern English – some words retain a final 'e' which has since been lost ('cheere', 'keepe', 'storme', etc.). Having noted this, you will also observe that there is some inconsistency in that the spellings 'cheerely' and 'cheerly' occur immediately adjacent to each other!

Pronunciation: It is impossible to judge, of course, just from the one script, how Shakespeare's pronunciation might have differed from ours, but the way that words are used elsewhere in rhyming verse suggests that the word 'wind', for example, would have been pronounced to rhyme with 'kind'.

Lexis: Some words and phrases are clearly unfamilar (e.g. 'yarely'), or are used in ways that would not seem natural in modern English ('keep your cabins').

1

THE TEMPEST.

Actus primus, Scena prima.

A tempestuous noise of Thunder and Lightning heard: En-
ter a Ship-master, and a Boteswaine.

Master.

Ote-swaine.
  Botes. Heere Master : What cheere?
  Mast. Good : Speake to th'Mariners : fall
too't, yarely, or we run our selues aground,
bestirre, bestirre.   *Exit.*
          Enter Mariners.
  Botes. Heigh my hearts, cheerely, cheerely my harts:
yare, yare : Take in the toppe-sale : Tend to th'Masters
whistle : Blow till thou burst thy winde, if roome e-
nough.
    Enter Alonso, Sebastian, Anthonio, Ferdinando,
          Gonzalo, and others.
  Alon. Good Boteswaine haue care : where's the Ma-
ster? Play the men.
  Botes. I pray now keepe below.
  Anth. Where is the Master, Boson?
  Botes Do you not heare him? you marre our labour,
Keepe your Cabines : you do assist the storme.
  Gonz. Nay, good be patient.
  Botes. When the Sea is : hence, what cares these roarers for the name of King? to Cabine; silence : trouble
vs not.
  Gon. Good, yet remember whom thou hast aboord.
  Botes. None that I more loue then my selfe. You are
a Counsellor, if you can command these Elements to silence, and worke the peace of the present, wee will not
hand a rope more, vse your authoritie : If you cannot,
giue thankes you haue liu'd so long, and make your
selfe readie in your Cabine for the mischance of the
houre, if it so hap. Cheerely good hearts : out of our
way I say.   *Exit.*
  Gon. I haue great comfort from this fellow : methinks
he hath no drowning marke vpon him, his complexion
is perfect Gallowes : stand fast good Fate to his han-
ging, make the rope of his destiny our cable, for our
owne doth little aduantage : If he be not borne to bee
hang'd, our case is miserable.   *Exit.*
          Enter Boteswaine.
  Botes. Downe with the top-Mast : yare, lower, lower,
bring her to Try with Maine-course. A plague———
A cry within.   *Enter Sebastian, Anthonio & Gonzalo.*

vpon this howling : they are lowder then the weather,
or our office : yet againe? What do you heere? Shal we
giue ore and drowne, haue you a minde to sinke?
  Sebas. A poxe o'your throat, you bawling, blasphe-
mous incharitable Dog.
  Botes. Worke you then.
  Anth. Hang cur, hang, you whoreson insolent Noyse-
maker, we are lesse afraid to be drownde, then thou art.
  Gonz. I'le warrant him for drowning, though the
Ship were no stronger then a Nutt-shell, and as leaky as
an vnstanched wench.
  Botes. Lay her a hold, a hold, set her two courses off
to Sea againe, lay her off.
          Enter Mariners wet.
  Mari. All lost, to prayers, to prayers, all lost.
  Botes. What must our mouths be cold?
  Gonz. The King, and Prince, at prayers, let's assist them,
for our case is as theirs.
  Sebas. I'am out of patience.
  An. We are meerly cheated of our liues by drunkards,
This wide-chopt-rascaill, would thou mightst lye drow-
ning the washing of ten Tides.
  Gonz. Hee'l be hang'd yet,
Though euery drop of water sweare against it,
And gape at widst to glut him.   *A confused noyse within.*
Mercy on vs.
We split, we split, Farewell my wife, and children,
Farewell brother : we split, we split, we split.
  Anth. Let's all sinke with' King
  Seb. Let's take leaue of him.   *Exit.*
  Gonz. Now would I giue a thousand furlongs of Sea,
for an Acre of barren ground : Long heath, Browne
firrs, any thing; the wills aboue be done, but I would
faine dye a dry death.   *Exit.*

Scena Secunda.

Enter Prospero and Miranda.
  Mira. If by your Art (my deerest father) you haue
Put the wild waters in this Rore; alay them :
The skye it seemes would powre down stinking pitch,
But that the Sea, mounting to th' welkins cheeke,
Dashes the fire out. Oh! I haue suffered
With those that I saw suffer : A braue vessell

A   (Who

Figure 5.1 The first page of The Tempest from the First Folio

Grammar and syntax: There are differences in the way verb phrases are constructed (e.g. 'you do assist the storm') and in the way questions are formed ('what cares these roarers?') Let's now consider each of these aspects in turn, and review the main differences between Shakespeare's English and our own.

5.3.1 Graphology and orthography

Typographical conventions – the representation of the language on paper by printers – have changed since 1623 in a number of ways. The most obvious difference is when the sound 's' occurred at the start and in the middle of words, printers formerly used the 'long s', as in the First Folio, with the more familiar 's' being used at the ends of words. The practice was dying out by the early nineteenth century, when the modern 's' became standard.

Punctuation has been an ever-changing aspect of written English, and modern editors of Shakespeare may differ considerably both from the Folio version – and each other. Some of the principal developments since 1623 include changes in the use of the colon, semi-colon and dash, more consistent use of commas to mark off the main syntactic divisions in sentences, and the rise (and decline! – see Section 5.3.6) of the apostrophe. In *The Tempest*, you'll observe that apostrophes are used to indicate letters omitted, but as with some aspects of spelling, this is inconsistent – we have both 'lets' and 'let's', for instance.

Spelling in handwritten and printed texts during the early seventeenth century was chaotic and inconsistent, varying not only between different writers and typesetters, but even within the same paragraphs of a text. In the absence of a widely accepted standard (such as our *Oxford English Dictionary*), writers used their own discretion and judgement; the spellings of some words reflected former rather than contemporary pronunciations, whilst others were the idiosyncratic preferences of individuals. Neither are the printed texts which survive free from genuine typesetters' errors.

It was during the eighteenth century – some 100 years or so after Shakespeare's lifetime – that major attempts were made to standardise spelling (and many other aspects) of English. The publication in 1755 of Dr Samuel Johnson's hugely influential *Dictionary* was a landmark, and it was soon succeeded by other dictionaries which eventually succeeded in codifying English spelling.

5.3.2 Pronunciation

Most linguists suggest that the sounds of Shakespeare's English would not have been as different from ours as the sounds of Chaucer – who only died in 1400 – had been from his. This is because the major shift in English pronunciation known as the Great Vowel Shift had taken place during the intervening 200 years, and radically transformed the phonemic strucutre of the language.

Nevertheless, if we were able to revisit one of the original performances of a play by Shakespeare, we would certainly be aware of some minor differences. Take this extract from Act 2 of *Othello*, for instance, where Montano and Two Gentlemen are peering into the stormy seas in search of Othello's fleet. First, read it aloud as you would if it was a passage of modern English:

Montano: *What from the cape can you discern at sea?*
1 Gentleman: *Nothing at all, it is a high-wrought flood:*
      I cannot 'twixt the haven and the main
      Descry a sail
Montano: *Methinks the wind hath spoke aloud at land,*

[Scene 1, lines 1–5]

It is unlikely that you will have made the conversation sound quite as it did in the seventeenth century. This is because:

- the vowel in the word 'sea' would be closer to 'say' than to 'see'. The difference in modern spelling does, in this case, reflect a one-time difference in pronunciation that has subsequently been lost
- the vowel in the word 'flood' (and other words spelt /oo/ like 'food' and 'mood') may at this time have been pronounced either to rhyme with '**t**ub' or with '**y**ou'.
- 'wind', as noted above, would rhyme with 'kind' rather than 'sinned'.

So – try reading aloud the passage again in the light of these changes.

Another significant pronunciation change has affected the position of the stress on words of several syllables which we would pronounce as perse**vere**, **de**monstrate and **as**pect. Evidence in the use of these words in metrically regular poetry suggests that Shakespeare's pronunciation would have been per**se**ver, de**mon**strate and as**pect**.

ACTIVITY 108   STRESSED OUT?

Try out these words with their modern and seventeenth-century pronunciations in the following lines, and comment on the different stress patterns which result:

e.g. modern: *Some **other** Mistress **hath** thy **sweet** aspects*

[*A Comedy of Errors*, Act 2, scene 2, line 115]

Seventeenth century: *Some **other** Mistress **hath** thy **sweet** aspects.*

Note how the modern stressing of 'aspect' creates an awkward succession of two strong beats on 'sweet' and 'asp'; the original pronunciation thus fits the iambic pattern of alternate stressed and unstressed syllables more smoothly:

And this may help to thicken other proofs
That do demonstrate thinly

[*Othello*, Act 3, scene 3, lines 431–2]

I will persever in my course of loyalty

[King Lear, Act 3, scene 4, line 23]

However, the *OED* suggests the word 'aspect' was already being stressed '**as**pect' by 1609, and many polysyllabic words may have been undergoing the same kind of fluidity in Shakespeare's time as 'controversy' is today.

Indeed, a passage from one of Shakespeare's earliest comedies, *Love's Labour's Lost*, indicates that just as today, such variations in pronunciations of words were a source of controversy and argument. In this extract, the schoolteacher Holofernes deplores some current developments:

> *I abhor such fanatical phantasimes, such insociable and point-devise companions; such rackers of orthography, as to speak 'dout' fine when he should say 'doubt'; 'det', when he should pronounce 'debt' – d,e,b,t, not d,e,t. He clepeth a calf 'cauf', half 'hauf'; neighbour vocatur 'nebour'.*
>
> [Act 5, scene 1, lines 18–25]

So, just as we may argue about the relevant merits of '**con**troversy' or con**tro**versy, Holofernes deplores the linguistic changes he hears going on around him. However, it is clear from his use of 'clepeth' (i.e. 'calls', but archaic even at the time) and the pedantic 'vocatur' (i.e. Latin for 'is called') that he is shown to be a backward-looking linguistic conservative, only one of many who confuse fighting losing battles over language usage with saving civilisation from certain decline.

Subsequent attempts in the great era of standardisation – the eighteenth century – to control the pronunciation of the language included John Walker's *Pronouncing Dictionary of English* (1774), and the nineteenth and twentieth centuries were to see the emergence of Recieved Pronunciation (see Section 2.6) as a prestige accent which was held up as a desirable norm and imitated in elocution classes. However, pronunciation has proved much less amenable than spelling to standardisation, and many local and national variations have continued to flourish.

5.3.3 Lexis

It is perhaps the vocabulary of a language which provides the most immediately striking evidence of change. When comparing texts written at different times, we might expect to find:

- words which have fallen out of use
- words which have entered the language. In English new words have come in at an explosive rate. They include **borrowings** from other languages, **recombinations** of established words and their prefixes and suffixes (e.g. the multiple variations on 'hamburger'/'beefburger'/'veggieburger' etc.), brand-new **coinings** associated with technological developments (e.g. 'microwave') new shortened forms and **acronyms** (e.g. 'CD ROM'), and an endless stream of the sometimes short-lived forms of new slang with every generation and cultural movement
- words whose **meanings** have changed
- words whose **usage** has changed (i.e. they are not used in the same phrases or constructions as they once were)
- words whose **status** has changed (e.g. from slang to standard, or from general to specialised).

So, let's now investigate some of the vocabulary used by Shakespeare in a passage from *Othello*. Here, Othello has been disturbed and arrives to quell a drunken brawl which has broken out among his troops on Cyprus:

> **Othello**:   *Now, by heaven,*
> *My blood begins my safer guides to rule*
> *And passion having my best judgement collied,*
> *Assays to lead the way. 'Zounds, if I once stir,*
> *Or do but lift this arm, the best of you*
> *Shall sink in my rebuke. Give me to know*
> *How this foul rout began, who set it on,*
> *And he that is approved in this offence,*
> *Though he had twinned with me, both at a birth,*
> *Shall lose me. What, in a town of war*
> *Yet wild, the people's hearts brimful of fear,*
> *To manage private and domestic quarrel?*

(Act 2, scene 3, lines 200–11)

As with most investigations of English lexis, the *OED* needs to be our trusty guide here. It will confirm, for example, that 'collied' is now 'archaic' and 'dialectal', that its last recorded written use was in 1855, and reveal that its meaning is 'darkened', 'blackened' or 'murky'. More interesting still, the *OED* traces the etymology of the word and connects it with 'coal' and 'collier'. So, here we have a black man, fearing that 'passion' has 'blackened' his best judgement! If you are studying the play, you will begin to understand the significance of this in the context of its many other 'blackness' references. We will also learn that 'assay' is a word with several meanings, but the one most likely here, to 'try' or 'attempt', is a variation on the word 'essay' which is now obsolete.

Some words which we recognise but which appear to have a different meaning include 'approved' and possibly 'wild'. 'Wild' is a word with an extremely complex history – its entry in the *OED* occupies seven whole columns – and in the context of *Othello*, it is fascinating to discover that one of its many meanings around 1600 was 'giving way to sexual passion, licentious, loose'. Although it is still widely used today, the word has not retained all of these associations and our understanding of its use in Shakespeare is clearly enhanced by this kind of research. The *OED* also reveals that 'approve' formerly had several meanings other than the modern one, including 'to show to be true, to confirm, to display to advantage, to show or prove a person to be something'. In the context of the speech, we might use instead a form of the related word 'prove' (as in, 'he that is proved to have committed this offence').

The progress of 'approve' is an example of what is known as the **narrowing** of the range of meanings of a word.

ACTIVITY 109   HAVE A NICE DAY!

The contrary development (i.e. **broadening**), where a word which formerly had a few very specific meanings develops much wider and more general applications, is perhaps best illustrated by the fate of the word 'nice'. Use the *OED*, or any other etymological dictionary, to trace the history of this currently all-too-generalised word, and survey your Shakespeare text to discover how the earlier meanings of the word are being used.

In our speech from *Othello*, there are several examples of words being used in unfamiliar constructions. Whilst 'give', 'me', 'to' and 'know' are all very common modern English words, we would not now combine them into this particular phrase (or **collocation**). Equally, the most usual preposition which we use with 'night' would be 'at'; in modern English, 'in' would also require the definite article (i.e. 'in the night').

Strange as it sounds, perhaps the most difficult words to deal with are those which appear at first glance to be absolutely familiar. For sometimes closer inspection can reveal that although their primary meaning (or **denotation**) has remained the same, the baggage of associations and **connotations** which they import to a text have changed significantly.

The word 'blood' in this speech (and its association with passion) is one such case. The *OED* confirms that not only can it carry associations of guilt and unlawfulness (you might think of how it is used throughout *Macbeth*), but that it was the 'seat of emotion and passion', and often associated with uncontrolled feelings, especially anger. Elsewhere it can imply specifically sexual passion. Equally, the word can stand for one's family and genetic inheritance (as in 'royal blood'). All of these associations are likely to complicate and enrich our understanding of how the word is used throughout *Othello*. The word 'honest', also frequently used in the play (but not in this passage), is another example. At first glance it seems straightforward enough, but it was actually a minefield of ambiguity in the early seventeenth century. For at the time, according to the influential critic William Empson's essay on the subject ('"Honest" in *Othello*', in W. Empson, *The Structure of Complex Words*, 1964) the word 'carried an obscure social insult as well as a hint of stupidity'.

ACTIVITY 110
Othello

1 If *Othello* is your text, make your own survey of the entries in the *OED* for 'blood' and 'honest', and survey each use of the words in the play. Write an essay on the significance of the two words, bringing out how your linguistic research has affected your understanding of Shakespeare's meanings.

2 Whatever your set play happens to be, select a short passage and use the *OED* to investigate the range of contemporary meanings and associations of some of the keywords which it contains.

5.3.4 Grammatical change

Although less immediately obvious than lexical change, the change which affects the grammar of the language is equally remorseless and on-going. We have already seen evidence of the disappearance of 'thee' and 'thou', and the distinctions with 'you', from the mainstream of English (see Section 5.1, page 208). In *The Tempest*, for example, Miranda usually addresses her father as 'you'; for his part, he addresses Ariel and Caliban as 'thou'. These forms are now only preserved in archaic usage and some regional dialects (for example, in south Yorkshire). Thus, the distinction between singular and plural, and intimate and formal, which is preserved in the French 'tu' and 'vous', has been lost – though the Irish-influenced 'yous' preserves, in some dialects, the single/plural distinction. It is, of course, still possible to make such distinctions of formality, familiarity and politeness in other ways – for example in the title and forms of address which we use.

In fact, the decline of 'thee' and 'thou' was well underway during Shakespeare's day, and not all of the variations in the use of the form can be explained as easily as in the passage from *Othello* which we considered.

ACTIVITY 111

For your own set play, take a scene and survey the uses of thee/thou and you. For each case where the forms are used, try to decide:

For *thee/thou*:

● is it singular?
● does it also indicate friendly intimacy?
● is it being used between characters of equal status?
● is it being used insultingly or contemptuously?
● none of these?

For *you*:

● is it plural?
● if singular, does it reflect respectful politeness?
● is it used by a person of junior to a person of senior status?
● none of these?

Some promising scenes to investigate might be the opening scene of *King Lear*, the scenes in *Hamlet* in which the prince speaks with the Ghost, or the scene in *Much Ado About Nothing* after Hero's humiliation in which Benedick and Beatrice declare their love for each other.

There have been, of course, many other types of grammatical change. The following extracts from *The Tempest* illustrate several of these.

Inflection and progressive tenses

As Prospero begins to tell the story of his banishment from Milan, he asks Miranda, his daughter:

> *Dost thou attend me?*
> [Act 1, scene 2, line 78]

and later
> *Thou attendst not?*
> [*Ibid*, line 87]

In both cases it is likely that in modern English we would say 'are you attending?' – two developments in the way we use verbs are shown here.

First, we have lost the ending(or **inflection**) of /st/ on the second person of the verb, which had been part of an older grammatical system from Anglo-Saxon times. Instead, we would say 'do' and 'attend'. Another part of this older system was the third person ending /eth/, which was formerly the alternative to /s/ in verbs like 'droppeth' (i.e. 'drops'). In Shakespeare's time, this change was well underway, and you will find both of these forms – sometimes even within the same speech, as in this example from *The Merchant of Venice*:

> *The quality of mercy is not strained;*
> *It dropp**eth** as the gentle rain of heaven*
> *Upon the place beneath. It is twice blest;*
> *It bless**eth** him that give**s** and him that take**s**.*

[Act 4, scene 1, lines 183–6]

(In some ways, the eventual triumph of /s/ over /eth/ was unusual, as /s/ was from the less fashionable and influential northern dialects, whereas -/eth/ was part of the the southern variety which generally tended to become the favoured standard form. See Section 5.3.5.)

Secondly, in the 400 years since Shakespeare, English has developed a wide range of progressive tenses – those which use the present participle /ing/. So, if a character in a modern play were to be asked, as Hamlet is, 'what do you read, my lord?', he might answer, 'Well, I usually read the odd newspaper, mainly the sports pages, and the occasional magazine'. He would, in other words, assume he was being asked about his reading habits. However, in Hamlet, it is clear from the context of this line that Polonius is asking Hamlet about the letter he has in his hand at that moment, a situation in which we would now use the progressive 'what are you reading?'.

Auxiliary verbs

Consider these sets of questions from early in *The Tempest*:

Boatswain: *what cares these roarers for the name of king?* [Act 1, scene 1, line 15]
what do you here? [line 34]
have you a mind to sink? [line 35]
Miranda: *had I not / Four or five women once that tended me?* [Act 1, scene 2, line 46]
Prospero: *What seest thou else … ?* [Act 1, scene 2, line 50]
Miranda: *What foul play had we … ?* [Act 1, scene 2, line 61]
How came we ashore? [Act 1, scene 2, line 158]
Prospero: *Shrug'st thou, malice?* [Act 1, scene 2, line 372]

These forms would no longer be recognised as Standard English; instead, we now form questions by introducing the word 'do' – as an **auxiliary verb** – and changing the verb to produce:

what do these roarers care for the name of king?

So, can we conclude that this change has taken place between Shakespeare's time and our own? As usual, it is not this simple. In the same play, and very close to these examples, we also find:

Boatswain: *Do you not hear him?* [Act 1, scene 1, line 12]
Miranda: *Wherefore did they not / That hour destroy us?* [Act 1, scene 2, line 138]
Prospero: *Dost thou forget /From what a torment I did free thee?* [Act 1, scene 2, line 250]

So, we seem to witnessing here a point in the development of the language where there is variation between the form which eventually emerges as the dominant one (using the auxiliary 'do'/'did')and the older form.The development of the auxiliary verb in English has also affected the way in which we form negative sentences. Consider these examples, also from *The Tempest*:

Boatswain: *Trouble us not* [Act 1, scene 1, line 16]
Prospero: *I know not how much tribute* [Act 1, scene 2, line 124]
Speak not you for him … [Act 1, scene 2, line 467]
Francisco: *I not doubt / He came alive to land* [Act 2, scene 1, line 118]

So, if Shakespeare were to arrive, via a time machine, what could we tell him about how he must change the way he forms negative statements in English? We would have to tell him that during the intervening centuries, the auxiliary verb has become a compulsory part of such statements, producing instead 'don't trouble us' and 'I don't know'.

You might also find elsewhere in Shakespeare negative expressions which would be seen as 'incorrect' in modern Standard English – sentences such as 'I cannot go no further' (Celia, in Act 2, scene 4 line 9 of *As You Like It*). Although this double negation survives in much regional dialect speech (see Chapter 2, Section 2.6.3, page 59), it has long since drifted out of accepted 'standard' use, partly driven by the desire in the eighteenth century to codify and rationalise the grammar of English.

On the other hand, there are cases of the auxiliary being used where we would no longer do so – as in these examples:

Boatswain: *Keep your cabins; you do assist the storm* [Act 1, scene 1, line 12]
Ferdinand: *The ditty does remember my drowned father* [Act 1, scene 2, line 410]
Gonzalo: *The truth you speak doth lack some gentleness* [Act 2, scene 1, line 135]

Although we still have the option of using the auxiliary 'do' in straightforward declaratives like these, it is now reserved either for counter-accusations or denials ('I **did** hand it in!'), or very emphatic statements ('I **do** love you, you know!').

ACTIVITY 112

Survey your own set text for examples of such language change in action. Which of the forms seems to be more frequent in your text(s)?

Just as the appearances of several influential dictionaries was to help codify and standardise the orthography and vocabulary of the language in the eighteenth century, the appearance of grammar books such as Robert Lowth's *Short Introduction to English Grammar* (1762) and Lindley Murray's *English Grammar* (1794) tried to do the same job for its grammar. Then, as now, such attempts led to great argument: should the people who write such books try to lay down rules of good English (an approach which is described as **prescriptive**) or just reflect the ways in which the language was actually being used (a **descriptive** approach)?

During the eighteenth century, the prescriptive approach was certainly very powerful, and writers liked to look to written Latin as an ideal model for English rather than the spoken language.

ACTIVITY 113

Apart from Shakespeare, you may well be studying other pre-twentieth-century texts. As we approach our own century, you are likely to notice fewer grammatical differences – but there may be some, especially in the ways in which verb tenses are formed and used.

Survey a text which you are studying for some of these (the novels of Charles Dickens are especially interesting for the range of forms of language he puts into the mouths of his characters – though the narrative metalanguage is invariably in the 'standard' English of his day).

5.3.5 How and why?

As soon as we begin to note the extent to which language changes, two questions inevitably arise: how and why does it do so?

How?

Some changes may result from decisions which speakers deliberately take as a result of influence – perhaps they adopt a particular 'buzzword', or mimic the pronunciation of some admired figures – but many more seem to 'just happen'.

We have already seen from our brief analysis of Shakespeare's language that at any given time, there will appear in the language a variety of forms. This diversity is known among linguists as **synchronic variation**. Over time, some of these variations will survive and prosper to the point of displacing the others – as has happened with the 'triumph' of /s/ as the third-person verb inflection (see above, pages 224–5) Others will become much less widely used, and eventually disappear. These alterations over time are referred to as **diachronic variation**. Some writers have compared the process to that of natural selection, whereby animals evolve depending on which of the many variations in their forms proves most successful for the needs of their species.

The linguist Jean Aitchison suggests that the spread of a particular form of language – a pronunciation, word, meaning or grammatical construction – follows a gradual curve, starting with a very slow process of 'catching on' among small groups of people before 'taking off' and spreading more rapidly (*Language Change: Progress or Decay?*, 1991).

Why?

So – why should one variation prove more 'successful' than another, and spread throughout the language? In biological terms, the feature of an animal which develops in this way turns out to be of advantage to the species in the survival stakes. How does this work for language?

We can understand the reasons under two headings:

Sociolinguistic reasons:
(i)   The American linguist William Labov has shown in studies of change in contemporary American English that even a minor detail of pronunciation (such as the pronunciation of the rolled, or **rhotic** /r/ among middle-class New Yorkers, or the pronunciation of the vowel in 'house' among the residents of the island of Martha's Vineyard) can start to spread throughout a community if it is regarded in high enough esteem, and associated with the prestige of groups to which other speakers aspire to belong. So – if you decided today to initiate some language change by inventing a new word, or introducing a new pronunciation, you would only have a chance of success if the group of people to which you belong has some kind of social influence, prestige or power.
(ii)   Sometimes other languages can have a significant impact. We have already seen how some of the forms of Irish Gaelic influenced the variety of English spoken in Ireland (see Chapter 4, Section 4.9.4, page 198 ff.), and many characteristic modern American-English features are the result of the presence in the USA of large numbers of speakers of other languages.
(iii) As a community develops, it needs its language to develop with it, and to meet its changing needs. This is most clearly seen in the ways in which new

words enter the language – not just driven by technological developments (though these are hugely important, especially in the realm of Information Technology) but by new ideas and social practices. For example, in recent years, the noun 'statement' has been converted into a verb 'statemented', to describe the documentation of children with special learning needs; and the term 'spin-doctor' has become almost universal in the political language of the 1990s to describe the party managers and advisers who carefully manipulate the information which politicians give in public.

Linguistic reasons:
Some linguists also believe that underlying these social causes of language change are more deep-seated tendencies in language itself. These can be summarised as:

(i)   a tendency for the language to become more efficient and require less effort of its speakers. In English this is most noticeable in the loss of what was once a complex system of inflections.

(ii) A tendency to produce 'chain reactions' to changes within the system. The classic example in English is the Great Vowel Shift mentioned above (Section 5.3.2, pages 219–21).

5.3.6 Language change today – are things getting worse?

Even as you read this, language is continuing to change, and just as in the past, such changes became a battleground for controversy and debate about the 'corruption' or development of the language, so contemporary linguistic change is frequently the subject of heated academic debate and dire warnings that deteriorating standards of everyday usage are threatening the very existence of civilisation as we know it.

ACTIVITY 114

Here is just a small selection of some of the developments which seem to be affecting the language at the moment: What do you think will happen in each case – and is it a good or a bad thing if it does?

Orthography: The apostrophe, much abused and misunderstood (especially by greengrocer's – sorry, greengrocers), is often omitted from company names, logos (or should that be logo's?) and shop fronts. Some people even advocate its abolition – it is complicated and usually unnecessary. So, will it disappear from use?

Spelling: The desire for some reform of what many would describe as a chaotic, and certainly rather complex English spelling system, has a long and honourable history. It extends back to Webster's first American dictionary of 1828. The writer George Bernard Shaw advocated a system based entirely on phonetics, and American English tends to stick more closely to pronunciation. Now, with the increased influence of American English in the media and via the Internet, forms such as 'program' are seen in English. How long before we lose the distinction between 'television programme' and 'computer program'? Will forms like 'center' and 'theater' replace the English varieties?

Pronunciation: Trends in pronunciation can 'take off' surprisingly quickly. If you hear a 1950's news broadcast, you will notice that even in the space of 40 years the sounds of RP have changed, and some observers have detected the spread of an accent which they call 'Estuary English' in the Southeast (think of the comedian Danny Baker and you have it). Meanwhile, the shifts in the positions of stress on some words continues and 'older' pronunciations of words such as 'forehead' (i.e. 'forred') and 'waistcoat' (i.e. 'weskit') are displaced by 'modern' ones ('forehead' and 'waistcoat').

Lexis: The continuous influx of new words and meanings is overwhelming. Some dictionaries – like the most recent *Oxford Dictionary of New Words* (1997) – try to keep up, but the endless creativity and productivity of English – especially for generating new varieties of slang – will always defeat the lexicographers. Although many of the new usages will prove to be short-lived, and disappear as fashions change, we can never be sure which ones. Meanwhile, there is some evidence that we may be losing some of the regional dialect vocabulary of the past (see Melvyn Bragg's article in Chapter 2, Activity 29, pages 67–8).

Grammar: arguments rage about the acceptability or otherwise, in Standard English of such constructions as 'split infinitives' (as in 'to boldly go') though few teachers would now describe this as an 'error'. Equally controversial is the debate about the status of grammatical patterns found in regional dialects (such as double negatives, as used by Shakespeare!). Meanwhile the language continues to produce its own variations and developments; in current 'football speak', for example, we are finding a new use in oral narratives of the **present perfect tense** (formed by the present tense of have + the **past participle**, to form 'he has scored …'). Thus, instead of:

> *well, Wilko just cleared the lines and found Mickie on the wing, he took on his man and hit a great cross for me to get on the end of …'*

we may now find:

> *well, Wilko's just cleared the lines and he's found Mickie on the wing, he's taken on his man and he's hit a great cross …*

Perhaps we can see here the influence of the 'Action Replay'; encouraged by the replay to give a running commentary on events in which the present perfect would be the natural choice, speakers have subsequently adopted the same tense even when there is no visual replay present. So even 'Match of the Day' can influence language change.

For some people, linguistic change will always seem like a deterioration in standards, and they may attack new usages as 'sloppy', 'lazy', or even worse 'American'. Others will welcome it wholeheartedly as evidence of progress – the language is 'getting better', so our English today is actually superior to the tongue of Chaucer. The truth is probably neither; a language will simply continue to adjust itself so that it meets the needs of its speakers at any given time; as long as does so, it is neither improving nor deteriorating, but evolving. If it fails to do so – as Hugh suggests about Irish Gaelic in *Translations* (see Chapter 4, page 196) – it starts to die.

5.4 'You taught me language': language, power and the colonies

As well as illustrating many aspects of language change in action, *The Tempest*, like Brian Friel's *Translations*, also raises a number of other sociolinguistic issues. One question which any production of the play has to address is 'Who, or what, is Caliban?' There are, broadly speaking, two traditions for representing this character:

- he is a grotesque, semi-mythical, and only partly human character. This view is based on his unusual parentage (the devil for a father and a witch!) and the several references to him as being ugly or monstrous in appearance (he is often referred to as 'monster' and ' moon-calf')

- he is a human islander whose appearance is unusual to the Europeans who discover him partly because they have not encountered such people before. This view is based on the fact his mother at least was human and we only hear from Prospero that his father was indeed 'the devil'. The play was written at a time when Europeans were indeed exploring distant parts of the world and making contact for the first time with their native inhabitants. In the travel writing of the time, just as writers such as Paul Theroux and Michael Palin do today, many travellers published detailed accounts of their journeys which were hungrily devoured by a curious public, and these natives were sometimes represented as savages, sometimes as gentle and innocent. In Caliban, we can see both of these views, but his name is almost an anagram of 'cannibal', the word coined (and used by Othello) to describe 'savage' man-eating tribes.

However we see Caliban, in either case, there are some interesting language issues raised by the script. We hear that on arriving on the island, Prospero and Miranda adopted him and, as they might have said, tried to 'civilise' him. This naturally included teaching him their language. So Caliban himself remembers:

> *When thou cam'st first*
> *[Thou woudst] … teach me how*
> *To name the bigger light, and how the less,*
> *That burn by day and night.*
>
> [Act 1, scene 2, lines 261–4]

But had Caliban himself acquired a language – his own – from his own mother, as you would expect of any human child? Not according to Miranda. She reminds him:

> *I pitied thee,*
> *Took pains to make thee speak, taught thee each hour*
> *One thing or other. When thou didst not, savage,*
> *Know thine own meaning, but wouldst gabble like*
> *A thing most brutish, I endowed thy purposes*
> *With words that made them known.*
>
> [Act 1, scene 2, lines 353–9]

In other words:

- Caliban was only capable of some pre-linguistic meaningless sounds (the term which modern linguists use to describe the playful sounds made by infants before they learn to speak is **babble**)
- until he was taught Miranda's language, he was not even conscious of what he meant. As Sapir and Whorf were to argue 300 or so years later (see Chapter 3, page 130), as language shapes the thoughts we are capable of having, an absence of language must mean an absence of thought.

Should we believe Miranda? After all, she takes Ferdinand to be a 'spirit' simply because she has never seen a young white male before, and could it be that Caliban's 'gabble' was actually a kind of native language of Caliban's own? Caliban's reply would indicate not:

> You taught me language; and my profit on't
> Is, I know how to curse.

> [Act 1, scene 2, line 367.]

Nevertheless, the play may make us think of the many colonial situations where contacts between powerful invaders and native inhabitants led to the introduction of European languages, the development of pidgins and creoles (see Chapter 2, Section 2.6.7, page 70) and, in some cases, the loss of the native tongue(s). This is a story that would be played out all over the world, whether it be the loss of many of the languages of native North Americans or the aboriginal inhabitants of Australia and New Zealand.

5.5 Persuasion and rhetoric

The plot of *Othello* hinges on the devastating skill with which Iago convinces Othello of his wife's unfaithfulness. However, Iago is by no means the only character into whose mouth Shakespeare puts eloquently persuasive language. Indeed, many of Shakespeare's plays depend upon such an act of persuasion – and several of his characters are among the most effectively persuasive speakers who have ever lived! Table 5.5 (page 232) gives a list of these great persuaders. You can probably add to this list for whichever play you are studying.

The way they all do it is, of course, through language, and though it may seem a long way from Lady Macbeth to the advertisements of Saatchi and Saatchi, we can see in persuasive language ancient and modern the emergence of remarkably similar strategies and techniques.

First, though, we'll turn back to *Othello*.

5.5.1 'Rude am I in my speech': Othello the persuader

In the course of a single scene and with nothing but insinuation and circumstantial evidence, Iago succeeds in transforming a blissfully (and very recently) married man into a volcano of jealous fury. Ironically, however, it is Othello who first emerges (in Act 1) as an assured persuader when defending himself against the charge that he had used witchcraft to seduce Desdemona from

Table 5.5 Shakespeare's Great Persuaders

Persuader	Persuadee	To ...
Lady Macbeth	Macbeth	Kill King Duncan
Iago	Othello	Believe Desdemona is unfaithful
Goneril and Regan (Cordelia is too honest!)	King Lear	Give them his land
Henry V	The English Army	Beat the French
Portia	Shylock	Show mercy on the merchant, Antonio
Mark Antony	The Roman crowd	Oppose the conspirators who killed Julius Caesar

her father, Brabantio. This is his address to the assembly of Senators and Officers of the Venetian State:

> *Most potent, grave, and reverend signiors,*
> *My very noble and approved good masters:*
> *That I have ta'en away this old man's daughter*
> *It is most true; true, I have married her.*
> *The very head and front of my offending*
> *Hath this extent, no more. Rude am I in my speech*
> *And little blest with the soft phrase of peace,*
> *For since these arms of mine had seven years' pith*
> *Till now some nine moons wasted, they have used*
> *Their dearest action in the tented field,*
> *And little of this great world can I speak*
> *More than pertains to feats of broil and battle,*
> *And therefore little shall I grace my cause*
> *In speaking for myself. Yet, by your gracious patience,*
> *I will a round unvarnished tale deliver*
> *Of my whole course of love, what drugs, what charms,*
> *What conjuration and what mighty magic –*
> *For such proceeding I am charged withal –*
> *I won his daughter*

[Act 1, scene 3, lines 77–94]

ACTIVITY 115

What makes this such an effective speech in his own defence? In answering this question, consider:

● the logic, structure and sense of the speech – try to reduce the key points to a flow-chart

- his address of his audience, and his portrayal of his own character
- the use of patterns and verbal techniques in his use of language
- the tone of the speech (suggest the prosodic features which you imagine hearing your Othello use).

COMMENTARY

The chart in Figure 5.2 illustrates the structure of the speech; additional comments are suggested alongside.

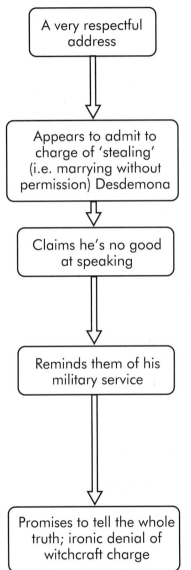

A very respectful address

Othello adopts the civilised courtesies of Venetian speech – could such a refined and humble person be associated with witchcraft? – but also uses two common techniques in persuasive speaking: (i) the list of 3 ('potent', 'grave', and 'reverend') and (ii) a pair of semantically related words 'in tandem' ('noble' and 'approved').

Appears to admit to charge of 'stealing' (i.e. marrying without permission) Desdemona

Were they expecting a denial? If so, his open admission might disarm them! In doing so, he skilfully manipulates the syntax of two successive phrases so as to produce two 'true's together, and in effect, says the same thing twice ('That I have ta'en away this old man's daughters/It is most true; true, I have married her').

Claims he's no good at speaking

We may suspect the sincerity of people who are too obviously polished as performers of speeches; Othello suggests that just as he used no witchcraft to woo Desdemona, he will use no artful speaking to woo his listeners. Nevertheless, he draws attention to the word 'rude' (i.e. unskilled) by avoiding the more usual syntax of 'I am rude in my speech' and preferring 'rude am I in my speech'.

Reminds them of his military service

Othello gives himself an implied character reference which, in a subtle way, is a kind of moral blackmail – 'how dare you show such ingratitude for all the wars I've fought on your behalf by bringing such ridiculous charges!' (Othello is not beyond this tactic at the end of the play: to Lodovico he pleads, 'Soft you, a word or two before you go./I have done the state some service and they know't' [Act 5, scene 2, line 336].) His use of a visual image – the tented field – is a more effective tool than simply using the more abstract 'battlefield'.

Promises to tell the whole truth; ironic denial of witchcraft charge

'unvarnished' harks back to 'rude am I in my speech'; the metaphor is rather domestic and humdrum, implying that his story will be as natural as untreated wood, not polished and covered with a veneer of gloss. Only at the end of the speech does he make the denial we have been expecting, and he is, perhaps, in his repetitive listing of 'what drugs, what arms, what conjuration and what mighty magic', using irony gently to mock the charge he faces.

Figure 5.2

Thus, Othello, after claiming to be 'rude ' in his speech, uses a variety of sophisticated strategies and techniques to persuade the Venetians of his integrity.

5.5.2 Oratory and rhetoric

We can often compare the skills of persuasion used by Shakespeare's characters with the speeches of 'real-life' experts in the art of **oratory** (i.e. the art of effective public speaking).

For example, we can consider two well-known speeches, both associated with commemoration. One of these is the address which Abraham Lincoln gave at the cemetery of Gettysburg in 1863, commemorating the dead of the American Civil War; the other, Mark Antony's passionate tribute to the recently assassinated leader in *Julius Caesar*.

Here is Lincoln's speech:

> *Fellow-countrymen – Four score and seven years ago our fathers brought forth on this continent a new nation, conceived in Liberty, and dedicated to the proposition that all men are created equal.*
>
> *Now we are engaged in a great civil war, testing whether that nation, or any nation so conceived and so dedicated, can long endure. We are met on a great battlefield of that war. We have come to dedicate a portion of that field, as a final resting-place for those who here gave their lives that that nation might live. It is altogether fit and proper that we should do this.*
>
> *But, in a larger sense, we cannot dedicate – we cannot consecrate – we cannot hallow this ground. The brave men, living and dead, who struggled here, have consecrated it, far above our poor power to add or detract. The world will little note, nor long remember, what we say here, but it can never forget what they did here. It is for us, the living, rather, to be dedicated here to the unfinished work which they who fought here have thus far so nobly advanced. It is rather for us to be here dedicated to the great task remaining before us – that from these honoured dead we take increased devotion to that cause for which they gave the last full measure of devotion – that we here highly resolve that these dead shall not have died in vain – that this nation, under God, shall have a new birth of freedom – and that government of the people, by the people, for the people, shall not perish from the earth.*

> [Abraham Lincoln, The Gettysburg Address, 19 November 1863,
> in B. McArthur (ed.), *The Penguin Book of Historic Speeches*, 1996]

So what is it that made this so effective? The speech has been much-admired and analysed, and some of its classic oratorical features are:

- there is a clear and straightforward structure. Lincoln first looks back to the founding fathers of America, then compares the sacrifice of those who have recently died, and then looks to the present generation to build the nation's future

- the insistent use of the first person plural 'we', which creates solidarity between speaker and listener

- the repetition of several related keywords such as 'nation', 'liberty'/'freedom' and 'dedicated'/'devotion', helps the speech hang together, or cohere, and reinforces its main themes

- the register is lifted by the rather archaic ('four score and twenty'), biblical ('brought forth', 'shall perish from the earth') and religious ('consecrate', 'under God', etc.) language.

- the speech is frequently based on pairs of carefully balanced opposites, or **antitheses**. These may be pairs of words like 'living'/'dead' and 'add'/'detract', or whole phrases and sentences. Note how closely these pairs of phrases parallel and balance each other:

(i)

those	who here gave their lives
that that nation	might live.

(ii)

The world	will little note, nor long remember	what we	say here
but it	can never forget	what they	did here

- Lincoln's meanings are occasionally reinforced by the use of pairs of semantically related words (e.g. the collocation 'fit and proper') in tandem

- As in Othello's speech, some of the ideas are arranged in lists of three:
  (i) 'a new nation, conceived in Liberty, dedicated to the proposition'
  (ii) 'we cannot dedicate – we cannot consecrate – we cannot hallow this ground'.

Here, the three phrases follow parallel structures (and so this kind of repetition is known as **parallelism**), and the three words are linked semantically ('hallow' and 'consecrate' are near synonyms) and even phonetically ('dedicate'/'consecrate').

- Indeed the climax of the speech is, in effect, a list of three within a list of three. The final prolonged sentence can be split into the three clauses introduced by 'that':
  (i) 'that from these honoured dead we take increased devotion to that cause for which they gave the last full measure of devotion'
  (ii) 'that we here highly resolve that these dead shall not have died in vain'
  (iii) 'that this nation, under God, shall have a new birth of freedom – and that government of the people, by the people, for the people shall not perish from the earth'

The third and final of these contains one of the most quoted lists of three in the language:

'government   of the people
by the people
for the people'

This triadic structure is a strong one whether at the level of the phrase, as here, or even at the level of narrative structure. Folk tales (see Chapter 1, Section 1.1, page 12) and jokes often follow a similar pattern.

Now let's compare Shakespeare's – Mark Antony's – oratory in *Julius Caesar*. Brutus is the leading figure among the senators who carried out the assassination on the grounds that Casesar was becoming too powerful and was ambitious to establish himself as an emperor. Mark Antony was a close supporter of Caesar.

Friends, Romans, countrymen, lend me your ears;
I come to bury Caesar, not to praise him.
The evil that men do lives after them;
The good is oft interred with their bones;
So let it be with Caesar. The noble Brutus
Hath told you Caesar was ambitious.
If it were so, it was a grievous fault;
And grievously hath Caesar answer'd it.
Here, under leave of Brutus and the rest –
For Brutus is an honourable man;
So are they all, all honourable men –
Come I to speak in Caesar's funeral.
He was my friend, faithful and just to me;
But Brutus says he was ambitious,
And Brutus is an honourable man.
He hath brought many captives home to Rome,
Whose ransoms did the general coffers fill;
Did this in Caesar seem ambitious?
When that the poor have cried, Caesar hath wept;
Ambition should be made of sterner stuff.
Yet Brutus says he was ambitious;
And Brutus is an honourable man.
You all did see that on the Lupercal*
I thrice presented him a kingly crown,
Which he did thrice refuse. Was this ambition?
Yet Brutus says he was ambitious;
And sure he is an honourable man.
*a Roman feast day

[Act 3, scene 2, lines 75–101]

ACTIVITY 116

These two speeches are both acts of commemoration designed to stir the emotions of the audience. Nevertheless, they are clearly rather different in their strategies. Identify any similarities and differences between their approaches and their use of language.

You should consider:

- the effect of repetitions in Brutus' speech
- the use of paired antitheses and synonyms
- the use of **rhetorical questions** (i.e. questions aimed to provoke agreement rather than an actual answer) – a common tactic of speakers, but not used in Lincoln's speech.

Perhaps the best-known wartime orator of our own century is Winston Churchill; here is one of many powerful speeches made both to Parliament and (via radio) to the country. The date was 18 June 1940: France had just surrendered to the German occupying forces, the USA was still not involved in the war, and Britain was isolated.

What General Weygand called the Battle of France is over. I expect that the Battle of Britain is about to begin. Upon this battle depends the survival of Christian civilization. Upon it depends our own British life, and the long continuity of our institutions and our empire. The whole fury and might of the enemy must very soon be turned on us. Hitler knows that he will have to break us in this island or lose the war. If we can stand up to him, all Europe may be free and the life of the world may move forward into broad, sunlit uplands. But if we fail, then the whole world, including the United States, including all that we have known and cared for, will sink into the abyss of a new Dark Age made more sinister, and perhaps more protracted, by the lights of perverted science. Let us therefore brace ourselves to our duties and so bear ourselves that, if the British Empire and its Commonwealth last for a thousand years, men will say, 'This was their finest hour'.

[Winston Churchill, 18 June 1940, from B. McArthur (ed.), *The Penguin Book of Historic Speeches*, 1996]

ACTIVITY 117

1   By now you will recognise many of Churchill's characteristic techniques.Comment briefly on the following:
    - his use of paired antitheses
    - his use of paired synonyms
    - his use of lists and parallelism
    - his use of metaphorical language
    - any other feature which contributes to the effectiveness of the speech.

2   Now let's go back to Shakespeare, and to another powerful wartime speech – Henry V's speech to his troops before the Battle of Harfleur.

    Which oratorical techniques are used to good effect, and what do you find interesting about the differences in tone between the two speeches?

> *Once more unto the breach, dear friends, once more;*
> *Or close the wall up with our English dead.*
> *In peace there's nothing so becomes a man*
> *As modest stillness and humility;*
> *But when the blast of war blows in our ears,*
> *Then imitate the action of the tiger:*
> *Stiffen the sinews, summon up the blood,*
> *Disguise fair nature with hard-favour'd rage;*
> *Then lend the eye a terrible aspect;*
> *Let it pry through the portage of the head*
> *Like the brass cannon: let the brow o'erwhelm it*
> *As fearfully as doth a galled rock*
> *O'erhang and jutty his confounded base,*
> *Swill'd with the wild and wasteful ocean.*
> *Now set the teeth and stretch the nostril wide;*
> *Hold hard the breath, and bend up every spirit*
> *To his full height. On, on, you noblest English,*
> *Whose blood is fet from fathers of war-proof—*
> *…*
> *I see you stand like greyhounds in the slips,*
> *Straining upon the start. The game's afoot:*
> *Follow your spirit; and upon this charge*
> *Cry 'God for Harry! England and Saint George!'*

[Act 3, scene 1, lines 1–34]

3 Comment in detail on the techniques used in the following famous political speeches of the 1960s, making connections with the techniques used in Shakespeare's speeches where you can.

Extract A

The American Civil Rights leader Martin Luther King, 28 August 1963, addressing a huge crowd in Washington DC, USA:

I am not unmindful that some of you have come here out of great trials and tribulations. Some of you have come fresh from narrow jail cells. Some of you have come from areas where your quest for freedom left you battered by the storms of persecution and staggered by the winds of police brutality. You have been the veterans of creative suffering. Continue to work with the faith that unearned suffering is redemptive.

Go back to Mississippi, go back to Alabama, go back to South Carolina, go back to Georgia, go back to Louisiana, go back to the slums and ghettos of our northern cities, knowing that somehow this situation can and will be changed. Let us not wallow in the valley of despair.

[in B. McArthur (ed.), *The Penguin Book of Historic Speeches*, 1996]

Extract B

President John F Kennedy's Inaugural Address, 20 January 1961:

… And so, my fellow Americans: ask not what your country can do for you – ask what you can do for your country. My fellow citizens of the world: ask not what America will do for you, but what together we can do for the freedom of man. Finally, whether you are citizens of America or citizens of the world, ask of us the same high standards of strength and sacrifice which we ask of you. With a good conscience our only sure reward, with history the final judge of our deed, let us go forth to lead the land we love, asking His blessing and His help, but knowing that here on earth God's work must truly be our own.

[from B. McArthur (ed.), *op. cit.*]

Oratory or rhetoric?

Many of the techniques we have focused on here are not limited to public speeches; in fact, they can assist any piece of language in its effectiveness in making an impact on the reader or listener. In a sense, all language aims to be persuasive – it has to persuade its audience that what you have to say is important, interesting and true. (Indeed, as I write this last sentence, I am aware that quite unconsciously, I have resorted to a list of three.)

So – in your speaking and your writing, in your essay-writing and presentations, and in your introductions and your conclusions, try framing your ideas using some of these tried and tested techniques. (Did you spot them?)

ACTIVITY 118

Perhaps it is in the world of advertising that we see persuasion going on at its most blatant. However, there are many other types of text whose aim is at least partly persuasive.

1 Gather together a selection of advertisements and other persuasive texts, and survey the techniques and strategies which they use. You might include

newspaper editorials, letters to the editor, charity appeals, recruitment literature produced by your school or college, or political broadcasts.

2 Produce as a piece of original writing a persuasive text of your own. Some possibilities are:

- a speech to your class or students' union
- a newspaper editorial
- an advertisement campaign for a charity
- a letter to your local council or MP
- a letter of complaint to your school or college on an issue which you feel strongly about
- a press release promoting your favourite but still unsigned band.

5.6 'The red curse rid you!': taboo, insults and abuse

The dialogue of both *Othello* and *The Tempest* is littered with abuse of various kinds, and indeed, such is the colourful variety of insults thrown at each other by characters throughout Shakespeare that collections of them can now be purchased separately and games constructed around them! Although some of these abusive terms may now seem quaint, the offensive language we find in Shakespeare reminds us of several things:

- abuse and vulgar language have always been, and will always be, an important aspect of conversational discourse
- the words which people find particularly offensive are associated with particular areas of human life (e.g. sex, excretion, bodily parts and religion)
- women and members of different racial groups have often been the targets of abusive language
- though the kinds of words which cause offence may change, our susceptibility to verbal offence remains.

We can place the words which we consider to be 'bad words' or 'swear words' on a spectrum, ranging from the mildly offensive to the most viciously unpleasant. These words, which are 'not to be spoken' (i.e. taboo), as we shall discover, actually fulfil a variety of linguistic functions.

5.6.1 Two colourful cursers: Iago and Caliban

The first word which Iago uses in *Othello* is ''Sblood' – a contraction of 'Christ's blood' – and as he is the equivalent of an NCO (non-commissioned officer) in the army, we would not be surprised by a colourful repertoire of swearing, in particular a tendency to blasphemy, which is sustained throughout the play. An Act of Parliament (the Act of Abuses of 1606) which prohibited the use of swear words on stage may have inhibited his author somewhat – and we will see when considering the text of *Othello* in Section 5.7 that Iago's language was cleaned up for the edition which was published in 1623, much as some films today are cut and dubbed for family viewing. Nevertheless, the particular character of Iago's vulgarities is revealing.

ACTIVITY 119

1 Survey the use of blasphemous phrases such as "Sblood' and "Zounds' in the play. What proportion of them is spoken by Iago? (Most modern editions have restored the blasphemies which the 1623 edition removed.)

2 You may already have discovered a good deal about Iago's **misogynistic** (i.e. hostile to women) attitude if you carried through Activity 101 (page 210). Review here the terms of abuse (such as 'guinea-hen', 'foolish wife', etc.) he uses in his references to women. At what point in the play does Othello himself first use such a term (e.g. 'whore), and how significant is this?

3 Another group of abusive phrases is racist in nature. Gather the racially abusive terms used by Iago (or anyone else) about Othello in the play.

4 How important a clue to Iago's character is Shakespeare providing with his use of such language?

COMMENTARY

If you charted the frequency of blasphemies and other apparent swear words, perhaps you found that early in the play, they are mainly the prerogative of Iago, but as his influence over Othello grows, the Moor himself begins to use Iago's favoured curses – a sure sign that what Iago calls his 'medicine' is indeed 'infecting' Othello.

Iago's references to women indicate his deeply cynical view of human sexual relationships – as further investigation of his crudely sensual and food-related imagery reveals. So, when Othello describes Desdemona as a 'devil', a 'subtle whore', 'impudent strumpet' and 'cunning whore', you could say he is accepting not only Iago's slander of Desdemona but a whole misogynistic mindset. He has learned not just to speak Iago's language (and, like Caliban, to curse with it) but to see the world his way.

The racially offensive references to Othello consist of:

- language which draws attention to Othello's physical difference (e.g. 'Thicklips')
- language which insists on his colour
- language which represents Othello as an animal (e.g. 'Barbary horse', 'old black ram') and implies a bestial, sensual nature
- language which exploits a mythical association of blackness with evil, and the devil.

Many of us may no longer believe in the literal reality of a devil, but a brisk flick through a dictionary of idioms will reveal that our metaphorical use of the colour black still has pejorative connotations:

to be as black as one is painted
the black sheep of the family
accident black spot
the pot calling the kettle black
black Tuesday (i.e. a stock market crash).

Should we consider such uses of the word 'black' offensive, and avoid them? This has sometimes become something of a controversial issue. We saw when discussing the *Adventures of Huckleberry Finn* in Chapter 2 how sensitivities to race-related language issues are constantly evolving, and some attempts to remove unnecessarily pejorative references to 'black' have been attempted – often to meet with the scorn of the popular press and its criticism of so-called 'political correctness'.

It is also interesting that Othello is generally referred to as 'the Moor'; like Shylock in *The Merchant of Venice*, it is his racial difference which defines him in the eyes of the Venetians.

Caliban in *The Tempest* is also defined by his racial difference from the white Europeans whom he encounters. As a character, he could hardly be more different from Iago, however, except in this respect – the first line which he speaks on stage (if we overlook his offstage 'There's wood enough within') is a curse, directed at both Prospero and Miranda:

> *As wicked dew as e'er my mother brushed*
> *With raven's feather from unwholesome fen*
> *Drop on you both; a South-west blow on ye,*
> *And blister you all o'er.*

[Act 1, scene 2, lines 322–5]

As with all curses, its impact cannot be explained by its literal sense alone, nor just by its sounds, but by a combination of the two. References to mothers are not uncommon in curses (though they more typically involve an insult directed at the mother of the cursed!), and the general drift of the sense here isn't far off the modern 'drop dead!'.

Phonetically, certain sounds combine and repeat to produce the venom which it is hard to avoid when delivering the lines. 'Th' and 'f' persist throughout the speech ('mo**th**er', '**f**eather', '**f**en', 'bo**th**',)and a pair of 'bl's ('**bl**ow and **bl**ister') provide the punch at the end. It is worth noting that the phonemes usually represented by the letters 'f' and 'b' both occur frequently in modern English 'swear' words.

As you will have discovered if you followed through Activity 101 on page 210, although Caliban's speech is a lot more varied than he would have Prospero believe when he says 'my profit on't is I know how to curse!', he certainly does have a rich repertoire of curses. As he has acquired his English from Miranda and Prospero, we might ask where he has learned his curses from! Perhaps we should not forget that he is also on the receiving end of some stinging insults, which it is helpful to consider in deciding exactly how the character should be played.

ACTIVITY 120

1 Survey the curses Caliban uses throughout the play, and try to define their characteristic qualities. Pay attention both to their meanings (if the source of Iago's invective is Christian blasphemy, racism and misogyny, what is his?) and their sounds which make them effective.

2 Now investigate the insults and abuse hurled on Caliban by other characters in the play by completing Table 5.6 on page 242.

Table 5.6 The abuse of Caliban

Character	Insult/abuse	Act/scene/line
Prospero		
Miranda		
Trinculo		
Stephano		
Others		

5.6.2 Cursing, swearing, abuse and taboo in modern English

We can define these important related terms as follows:

To curse: To speak words against another person which are intended to bring them harm. (E.g. 'May you rot in hell!')

To swear: To give vent to an intense emotion using unpleasant or offensive language. (E.g. 'damn!' (mild) to f— hell!' (strong).)

To abuse: To insult by using offensive language. (E.g. 'you little sh—!')

Taboo: Words or phrases which are usually avoided in polite society.

Often, of course, these categories may overlap – we may use taboo words either to abuse others or to swear out loud.

Such words as these are always a touchy subject. We may smile at the 1606 Act of Abuses which temporarily robbed Iago of his ability to use such terms as "Zounds!", but as recently as 1914, the use of the word 'bloody' on an English stage (in George Bernard Shaw's play, *Pygmalion*) was the cause of a major controversy. As the century has worn on, 'bloody' has become commonplace (even Royalty have been heard to use it in public), but in 1976, a similar level of outrage resulted from the use of the so-called 'f-word' on tea-time television by the Sex Pistols in an interview with presenter Bill Grundy. In the 1980s, a television broadcast of Tony Harrison's poem 'V' (which contains many examples of both the f- and c-word) provoked questions in parliament and as we have seen, the award of the Booker Prize to James Kelman's *How Late It Was How Late* caused yet more controversy because of the nature of its language. More recently still, a college students' production of *The Tempest* at which younger pupils were present received complaints because it included Trinculo's complaint that he 'smelt all horse piss'.

It's strange to consider how much fuss can be caused by the combination of three or four phonemes! Nowadays, however, people are likely to be offended by 'bloody' and even the f-word is commonly heard on films (and television too, after the 9 o'clock 'watershed'). However, as some taboos have weakened, others have grown more intense; it may well be, for instance, that the terms which our grandparents would have used to describe people of different races are now considered taboo. The changing nature of taboo and swearing is, after all, another aspect of the way linguistic change is subject to social influences such as those identified in Section 5.3.

ACTIVITY 121

So what language do we use nowadays to curse, to swear and to cause offence – and what are our strongest taboos?

1 Either individually or in groups, brainstorm all the words/phrases you can think of which you would consider to be taboo under the following categories:

   (i)   insulting terms which a male would make to or about a male
         female – female
         male – female
         female – male

   (ii) abusive equivalents to 'please go away', 'a load of rubbish'

   (iii) taboo expressions which are used as exclamations at moments of high tension or excitement.

   Please note: some of the language we are examining here is, by definition, offensive to some people. You will need to show sensitivity in the way you discuss and refer to them.

2 Now try to draw some conclusions from the (doubtless) large amount of colourful data this exercise has produced. What does it reveal about us, our values and our prejudices?

   (i)   What does your gender-related data reveal about male and female values and attitudes?

   (ii) What seem to be the principal, and strongest sources of taboo language in our culture? Consider the importance of:
         ● sexual activity   ● excretion
         ● genitals   ● religion
         ● other body parts   ● family members.

   (iii) Consider what makes the stronger taboo words so powerful and so satisfying – when used as exclamations. We have already considered meanings; now think about these words phonetically. Are there particular phonemes, or combinations of phonemes (see Caliban's curse on page 241) which seem to occur frequently?

   (iv) Finally, review your own, and other people's attitudes, towards swearing. These are some of the questions you could put:
         ● what do you consider to be swearing?
         ● would you consider terms of racial or sexist abuse swearing?
         ● in what circumstances do you swear?
         ● are there some swear words you would never use?
         ● what do you think about 'bad language' on television and on film?
         ● would you expect to find swear words in a textbook, or a text which you were studying?

COMMENTARY
Insults

The large number of terms such as 'whore', 'strumpet' (formerly), 'tart', 'slut' and (more recently) 'slapper', as compared to terms such as 'stud', reflects a long-standing dualism of standards in our attitudes towards male and female sexuality. There is some evidence that 'tart' is now beginning to be used to describe promiscuous males, but if our attitudes really have changed, the language has some way to go to catch up. Males may abuse each other with terms associated with masturbation. More harmless, and less sexual insults may focus on physical appearance ('fatty', 'four-eyes', 'pizza-face', etc.) or personality/intelligence deficits ('divvy', 'nomark', 'idiot', etc.), though even these may vary in usage between males and females.

Taboo words

Most English speakers identify two words as significantly stronger than the rest – those beginning with 'f-' and 'c-'. (The strength of the taboo on these words is reflected in the fact that we might hesitate to print them in an educational textbook!) Which is worse? Certainly, the f-word is more versatile; it can occur in several word-classes, and perform a variety of grammatical and semantic functions. In their book *Bad Language* (1990), Lars Gunnar Andersson and Peter Trudgill list thirteen different meanings it can convey, and other studies have been carried out into its many and varied grammatical uses within a sentence! The c-word – usually felt to be the stronger – is heard less on films, and hardly ever on television.

So, sexual activity and the bodily parts associated with it supply our strongest taboos. This is sometimes taken as evidence that we are, as a culture, somewhat obsessed with the subject of sex – an impression which it is not easy to deny to judge from the amount of sexually related material used in advertising, the film industry and most notably, on the Internet. Yet for a long time in our society, overt discussion of sexuality and sexual behaviour was rare, and though this has begun to change in the last 30 years (the poet Philip Larkin famously began his poem 'Annus Mirabilis' with the lines 'Sexual intercourse began in 1963'), this repression has a lot to do with the strength of this taboo.

However, some sexual words (such as 'bonk') are relatively mild, and many of the words used to describe male sexual organs border on the comical. Those for females are fewer, and less jocular, but women's breasts also enjoy a large and often humorous repertoire of associated slang. A word such as 'boobs' is now so commonplace that it can hardly be considered taboo at all, which may reflect changing social attitudes and fashions.

Excretion – which is generally a private act – provides a large number of rather less powerful if still effective taboos. Once again, however, there is a range from the genuinely offensive to the childishly silly (such as the words actually used with young children, like 'wee wee') via a middle ground of humorous euphemism.

Religion – in the case of English, Christianity – has provided many of the swear words (like Iago's "S'blood' and "Zounds', which both refer to the crucifixion) which have come to be seen as fairly mild. We have become a secular culture, and the diminishing importance of religion in many people's lives is reflected in the diminishing power of, and high level of toleration for expressions such as 'God', and 'Bloody Hell!', though expressions involving either 'Jesus' or 'Christ' still retain their capacity to offend.

Families tend not to figure strongly in English swearing in the way in which they do elsewhere – though 'bastard' is an exception, with its implications about one's mother and father. American expressions combining 'mother' with other obscenities are crossing the Atlantic via the medium of film, but some of the most powerful mother-related taboo language remains in the countries of Mediterranean Europe. If it is true that the kinds of swear words we have, and the ways in which we use them, says something significant about the kind of society we are, then we might expect different languages to have different kinds of swear word, according to their particular taboos, values and preoccupations. Unsurprisingly, this is exactly what we find: in countries with a strong Catholic tradition, for example, expressions which refer to the Virgin Mary and mothers in general – particularly in combination with the equivalent for 'whore' – are among the most powerful.

Common aspects

What do our most powerful taboo expressions have in common, phonetically? Many are, it is true, the proverbial four-letter words. More significant is their brevity – usually a single syllable – and their preference for a single short vowel (such as the ones usually represented by 'u', 'i', and 'a') sandwiched between consonants. You may have noted how frequently the sound 'k' occurs as either the initial or terminal consonant in examples such as 'dick', 'cack' as well as in the stronger words) and how 'b' is often the initial consonant in some of the milder expletives. Yet, for all this, we know that we cannot just invent swear words, and even if the combination of sounds 'Bock!' has all the phonetic ingredients of a good English swear word, unless it has some of the taboo associations we expect, and unless English speakers agree that it really *is* a bad word, we would find it hard to use spontaneously the next time we hit our thumb with a hammer.

Differences

The findings of your survey of views will, of course, vary – but depending on what? Is there a difference in attitude between male and females? Is there evidence of the traditional attitudes that 'nice girls don't swear' and that men should only swear when 'ladies' aren't present? Is it a matter of a generation gap, with younger people swearing more and being more tolerant?

Most of us will swear from time to time – though the milder 'Damn' and 'blast' or 'oh bother!' of some speakers may scarcely make the needle flicker on the linguistic scale of someone who routinely uses the f-word. Some research has shown that swearing can be infectious – as with accent and dialect variation (see Chapter 2, Section 2.6), we can demonstrate our convergence towards a social group by adopting its favoured swear words and swearing patterns – or abstaining from them altogether, if that is what we perceive is the favoured behaviour. However, learning how to swear in a foreign language is notoriously difficult!

ACTIVITY 122

In Chapter 4, we imagined the dilemma of an alien visitor who had mastered the vocabulary and grammar of English but who needed instructing on the nature of conversational rules.

Having made sound progress, our guest now wishes to understand the protocol surrounding our swear words – and to grasp the grammatical rules for forming phrases involving some of the more common. For example, he might wish to know:

How can I insert a swear word into sentences like 'The spaceship broke down', 'There was a snarl up coming through the asteroid belt' and ' You would not believe what I have just seen!'

Write a letter, offering what guidance you can, along the lines of the one in Chapter 4, Section 4.1.5 on page 152.

5.7 Back to the texts: *Othello* and *The Tempest*, texts and performances

Let us now return to our 'core' texts and apply some of our linguistic awareness and approaches to the scripts themselves, and the performances to which they give rise.

5.7.1 Shakespeare's texts

If you have been using more than one edition of your set play in your class, you may have come across some points in the script where the different versions apparently disagree. This is due to the ways in which the texts of the plays have been passed down to us. Shakespeare himself may seem to have had little or no direct influence on the printing of his plays in his lifetime, and some of the plays appeared in several versions. It is a matter of some debate how reliable and accurate these single-play editions (called 'Quartos' because of the size of paper they were printed on) are. After his death, some of his former colleagues assembled his collected works in an edition which became known as the 'First Folio' (1623); for some plays – *The Tempest* among them – this is the first known publication, and most subsequent editors have stuck closely to that text. Even with the First Folio, however, there are suspicions of misprints and typographical errors which some modern versions have attempted to 'correct'.

For the plays which also survive in Quarto editions (such as *Othello*), the issues are more complex (there are particularly interesting differences between the Folio and Quarto texts of *Romeo and Juliet*, *Hamlet* and *King Lear*). Here, modern editors (and directors of performances) have to judge which of the versions to follow – hence some of the discrepancies you may find.

Textual variants in *Othello*

The earliest surviving version of *Othello* is the Quarto (Q) published in 1622, six years after Shakespeare's death. The version which appeared in the Folio (F) the next year differs from it in hundreds of places. The possible reasons for this discrepancy are a matter of academic controversy – that the two texts could be based on Shakespeare's own successive drafts of the play, in which he amended and improved his script is only one of many competing theories. Subsequent editions of the play have tended to blend the two, thus producing many different versions, none of which is likely to have been the one actually produced by Shakespeare!

Many of the textual differences between the Q and F versions are quite minor and not very significant; however, in other cases, which of the variant versions you accept may make a real difference to our understanding of the play, and how it is performed. For example, look at the following alternative versions of the moment when Othello, convinced of his wife's unfaithfulness, is consumed with a desire for vengeance. What difference do these variations make?

Quarto

Othello: *Arise, black vengeance, from thy hollow Cell,*
Yield up, O love, thy crown and hearted throne
To tyrannous hate! Swell, bosom, with thy fraught,
or 'tis of aspics tongues!

Iago: *Pray be content!* (Othello kneels)

Othello: *O blood, Iago, blood!*

Iago: *Patience, I say, your mind perhaps may change.*

Folio

Othello: *Arise, black vengeance, from the hollow hell,*
Yield up, O love, thy crown and hearted throne
To tyrannous hate! Swell, bosom, with thy fraught,
For 'tis of aspics' tongues!

Iago: *Yet be content!*

Othello: *O blood, blood, blood!*

Iago: *Patience, I say, your mind may change.*

[Act 3, scene 3, lines 448–53]

First, 'Thy hollow Cell' develops the personification of the abstract idea 'black vengeance' and makes better sense than 'the hollow hell'.

Second, Iago's 'Pray be content' in Q seems to act as the cue for Othello to kneel – a stage direction absent in F. We know Othello must kneel at some point, as Iago says twelve lines later 'Do not rise yet' – but exactly when is open to question.

Thirdly, if Othello deliberately addresses Iago in 'Blood, Iago, blood', he is clearly still conversing with him; 'blood, blood, blood! however, could almost be spoken to himself as he becomes consumed with rage, and the actor (if not already kneeling) may be turned away from Iago at this point.

ACTIVITY 123

1   Listed in Table 5.7 on pages 249–51 are some of the alternative readings provided by the Quarto and Folio versions of the play. Complete the table by explaining the difference between each one, how each might affect your understanding and a performance of the play, and which you think works best.

Some sample commentaries and prompt questions are suggested.

2   If your set play is not *Othello*, consult the Arden edition of your play to discover its textual history. (If it is one of the plays which has survived Quarto and Folio versions, the footnotes to the text will identify the differences.)

Collect examples of some of these discrepancies and carry out a similar exercise.

Table 5.7

Context	Q	F	Comment
On several occasions, the Q text contains blasphemies which are absent from F – possibly as the author(s) of F had to observe the prohibition of swearing on stage introduced by the 1606 Act of Abuses (see page 239). Some of these are listed here	**Iago:** *'Sblood, but you'll not hear me ...* [Act 1, scene 1, line 4] **Iago:** *'Zounds, sir, you're robbed ...* [Act 1, scene 1, line 81] **Iago:** *'Zounds, sir, you are one of those ...* [Act 1, scene 1, line 107] **Othello:** *'Zounds, if I once stir ...* [Act 2, scene 3, line 203] **Iago:** *By the mass, 'tis morning;/Pleasure and action make the hours seem short* [Act 2, scene 3, line 373] **Othello:** *'Zounds! What dost thou mean?* [Act 3, scene 3, line 157] **Othello:** *The handkerchief!* **Desdemona:** *I'faith you are to blame.* **Othello:** *'Zounds!* [Act 3, scene 4, lines 97–9] **Othello:** *Lie with her, 'zounds, that's fulsome!* [Act 4, scene 1, line 33]	**Iago:** *But you'll not hear me ...* **Iago:** *Sir, you're robbed ...* **Iago:** *Sir, you are one of those ...* **Othello:** *If I once stir ...* **Iago:** *In troth, 'tis morning ...* etc. **Othello:** *What dost thou mean?* **Othello:** *The handkerchief!* **Desdemona:** *I'faith you are to blame.* **Othello:** *Away!* **Othello:** *Lie with her, that's fulsome!*	(Is anything lost from the characterisation of Iago – and his influence on Othello – by the removal of the blasphemies?)
In the opening scene, Brabantio accuses Roderigo of disturbing him after eating and drinking too much	*Upon malicious knavery does thou come /To start my quiet* [Act 1, scene 1, line 99]	*Upon malicious bravery dost thou come / To start my quiet*	(How might each of these alternatives be spoken, and what do you think lies behind this discrepancy?)

Table 5.7 (cont.)

Context	Q	F	Comment
Othello explains to the Venetian senators how Desdemona fell in love with him after listening to his traveller's tales	*My story being done / She gave me for my pains a world of sighs* [Act 1, scene 3, line 160]	*My story being done/ She gave me for my pains a world of kisses*	(How might our perception of Desdemona be affected by the choice we make here?)
Later in the same scene, Desdemona is acknowledging her love for Othello	*My heart's subdued / Even to the utmost pleasure of my lord* [Act 1, scene 3, line 252]	*My heart's subdued / Even to the very quality of my lord*	(A subtler difference, perhaps – but how might your characterisation of Desdemona be influenced by one or the other reading?)
Iago is observing Cassio talking with Desdemona, and begins to plan how to gain his revenge	*Ay, smile upon her, do: I will catch you in your own courtesies* [Act 2, scene 1, line 169]	*Ay, smile upon her, do: I will gyve* thee in thine own Courtship.* (*place in chains or fetters around the ankles)	(Using a dictionary (preferably the *OED*), investigate the relationship between courtship and courtesy. What is stronger – 'catch you' or 'gyve you'?)
Iago persuades Cassio to ask Desdemona to plead to Othello on his behalf	*This brawl between you and her husband entreat her to splinter* [Act 2, scene 3, line 317]	*This broken joint between you and her husband entreat her to splinter …*	(Which version allows the metaphor to be developed?)

Table 5.7 (cont.)

Context	Q	F	Comment
Iago tries to make Othello suspicious as they see him leaving Desdemona	Iago: *I cannot think it That he would sneak away so guilty-like Seeing you coming* [Act 3, scene 3, line 38]	Iago: *I cannot think it That he would steal away so guilty-like Seeing you coming*	(It's a close call – but which word, 'sneak' or 'steal', fits Iago's purpose best, and how would each affect how the actor playing Cassio actually exits?)
Othello confronts Desdemona with his accusation, complaining that she has made him a laughing-stock	**Othello:** *but alas, to make me A fixed figure for the time of scorn To point his slow unmoving fingers at – oh, oh.* [Act 4, scene 2, lines 56–8]	**Othello:** *but alas, to make me The fixed figure for the time of scorn To point his slow and moving finger at.*	(What is the image or metaphor underlying Othello's speech and in which version is this clearer? How might the 'oh oh's affect the way the speech is played?)
Othello prepares to kill Desdemona, and approaches her as she sleeps.	**Othello:** *A balmy breath that doth almost persuade Justice her self to break her sword once more.* [Act 5, scene 2, lines 16–17]	**Othello:** *O balmy breath that dost almost persuade Justice to break her sword. Once more, once more:*	(There are many differences in the punctuation of the two versions, and most editors will modernise the text in this respect. Here, though, it makes a crucial difference to the meaning! Which do you think makes most sense in the context of the whole speech?)

5.7.2 Shakespeare made easy?

Most modern editions of Shakespeare's plays will have modernised the text to some extent – as we have seen, conventions of spelling and punctuation were very different in the seventeenth century, and few modern readers or actors would find it easy to work with the cramped typography of the First Folio. Equally, you will no doubt be using an edition which helps you through some of the linguistic difficulties of the play by providing a glossary and/or commentary on some of the more obscure words and passages.

Attempts to make Shakespeare more accessible to younger students have taken many different forms and the *Shakespeare Made Easy* series presents you with parallel versions of the scripts – Shakespeare's original, and a modernised paraphrase. The example shown on page 253 is from *The Tempest* (edited by Alan Durband, 1990), where Ariel, Prospero's obedient spirit, reports how s/he has created the magical storm at sea as Prospero had commanded. Read the two versions and then carry out Activity 124 below.

ACTIVITY 124

1 Identify the changes made by the moderniser and group them into linguistic categories. You could use these as some of your headings:
   - substitution of words and phrases
   - replacement of figurative with literal language
   - modification to the forms of words
   - reconstruction of the syntax of phrases and sentences
   - addition of explicit explanation (e.g. Neptune the sea-king).

2 Now consider, for each of these categories, the reasons for and effects of each of the changes – and classify these. Some possible headings might include:
   - words no longer in common use or whose modern meanings are different from the one intended by Shakespeare (you may need to use the *OED* here)
   - words or phrases which may be too 'difficult' for the intended audience (GCSE students and younger)
   - the adaptation is in prose, not verse
   - some grammatical constructions are either no longer common in modern Standard English, or may give difficulties to younger readers
   - some references are less likely to be understood by a modern audience.

3 Having analysed the differences between the two versions, you might like to weigh up the advantages and disadvantages of the modernised version. Clearly, the clarity of the literal sense of the passage has been gained, and we can now follow the sense more easily.

   But what has been lost? In a sense, is what is going on here a kind of 'translation' (see Chapter 4)?

Shakespeare Made Easy

Prospero: *Come here servant. Come! I am ready now. Approach, my Ariel, come!*

(Ariel, a spirit, enters)

Ariel: *All hail, great master! Learned sir, hail! I come to do your bidding, whether it be to fly, to swim, to dive into fire, to ride on the billowy clouds. Ariel and all his fellow spirits are at your command.*

Prospero: *Spirit: have you fully enacted the tempest that I ordered?*

Ariel: *In every detail. I boarded the King's ship. At the prow; amidships; on the poop; in every cabin – as a fireball I struck terror. Sometimes I'd split up, and burn in several places: on the topmast, the yardarms, the bowsprit; I'd appear as separate flames, then meet and join as one. Lightning flashes, which precede fearful claps of thunder, were never more sustained and numerous to see. Fire and explosive blasts seemed to besiege mighty Neptune, the sea-king, making his bold waves tremble, and his dreaded trident shake.*

Prospero: *My most excellent spirit! Who could be so courageous, so resolute, that this uproar had no effect on his mind?*

Ariel: *Everyone felt a touch of madness and behaved erratically. All except the sailors plunged into the foaming brine, and abandoned ship, it being all on fire at the time with me.*

Shakespeare

Prospero: *Come away, servant, come. I am ready now.*
Approach, my Ariel, come

(Enter Ariel)

Ariel: *All hail, great master! Grave sir, hail! I come*
To answer thy best pleasure; be't to fly,
To swim, to dive into the fire, to ride
On the curled clouds, to thy strong bidding task
Ariel and all his quality.

Prospero: *Hast thou, spirit,*
Performed to point the tempest that I bade thee?

Ariel: *To every article.*
I boarded the king's ship; now on the beak,
Now in the waist, the deck, in every cabin,
I flamed amazement; sometime I'd divide,
And burn in many places; on the topmast,
The yards and bowsprit, would I flame distinctly,
Then meet and join. Jove's lightnings, the precursors
O' th' dreadful thunder claps, more momentary
And sight-outrunning were not; the fire and cracks
Of sulphurous roaring the most mighty Neptune
Seem to besiege, and make his bold waves tremble,
Yea, his dread trident shake.

Prospero: *My brave spirit!*
Who was so firm, so constant, that this coil
Would not infect his reason?

Ariel: *Not a soul*
But felt a fever of the mad, and played
Some tricks of desperation. All but mariners
Plunged in the foaming brine, and quit the vessel,
Then all afire with me.

[Act 1, scene 2, lines 189–212]

COMMENTARY

Substitution of words and phrases

This is the largest category and includes examples such as:

'come away' ⟶ 'come here'
'grave' ⟶ 'learned'
'answer thy best pleasure' ⟶ 'do your bidding'
'be't' ⟶ 'whether it be'
'curled clouds' ⟶ 'billowy clouds'
'To every article' ⟶ 'In every detail'
'would I flame distinctly' ⟶ 'I'd appear as separate flames'
'Jove's lightnings' ⟶ 'lightning flashes'
'the precursors of dreadful thunder claps' ⟶ 'which precede fearful claps of thunder'
'brave' ⟶ 'most excellent'
'this coil' ⟶ 'this uproar'
'all but mariners' ⟶ 'all except the sailors'
'quit the vessel' ⟶ 'abandoned ship'.

Replacement of figurative with more literal meanings

Sometimes, where Shakespeare has used metaphorical language, the adapter has, in the interests of clarity, opted for a more literal phrase. So, instead of the ships being personified as a creature with a 'beak' and a 'waist', these ideas are replaced with the very literal and more technically nautical 'prow' and 'amidships'. Similarly, the metaphorical 'Infect his reason' is replaced by the literal 'had no effect on his mind', and the complex 'I flamed amazement' is amplified as 'As a fireball I struck terror'.

Modification to the forms of words

This kind of adjustment can be seen in:

'hast thou' ⟶ 'have you' (see Section 5.1, page 208)
'seem to besiege' ⟶ 'seemed' (here, the adapter keeps the narrative consistently in the past, not slipping into the present tense as Ariel does in the original)
'make' ⟶ 'making'
'dread' ⟶ 'dreaded'.

Omissions

Some details have been omitted completely from the simplified version:

'Jove's lightnings' ⟶ 'Lightning flashes'
'Yea' ⟶ (not present).

Reconstruction of the syntax of phrases and sentences

In some places the syntax has been rearranged and the constructions modernised:

'more momentary and sight-outrunning were not' ⟶ 'were never more sustained and numerous to see'
'to thy strong bidding task Ariel and all his quality' ⟶ 'Ariel and his fellow spirits are at your command'

'the fire and cracks / Of sulphurous   → 'fire and explosive blasts seemed to
   roaring the most mighty Neptune   besiege mighty Neptune'
   / Seem to besiege'
'Not a soul but felt a fever of the mad' → 'everyone felt a touch of madness'.

Addition of explicit explanation
We are given help with a couple of phrases:

   'Neptune' is given as 'Neptune, the sea-king'
   'cracks of sulphurous roaring' is given as 'explosive blasts'.

Explanations and effects
Words and phrases no longer in common use, or whose modern meaning and use are different from the one intended by Shakespeare
The adapter has usually aimed for a straightforward clarification of the senses by choosing the modern equivalent. Many of these words still exist in English, but their meanings and usage have changed. In some cases, the literal meaning of the modern word is very similar, but the connotations are different; 'grave', for example, can still mean 'very serious', but largely in the contexts of accidents and medical bulletins, rather than the sense of 'serious-minded' in which it is used by Ariel. 'Brave', as we have seen, is something of a keyword in the play, and its many former meanings have narrowed the sense of 'courageous', which is not what Prospero intends here.

Words and expressions may be too 'difficult' for the intended audience (GCSE students and younger)
This consideration has clearly influenced the replacement of figurative with literal language in places, and (possibly) the substitution of the less-common 'mariners' with 'sailors'.

'Difficult' constructions
The rearranged syntax of some sentences will clearly be more familiar to a modern, younger reader/audience, and comprehensible but slightly archaic constructions using 'but' where we would more usually say 'except' ('not a soul but felt', 'all but mariners') have been replaced.

The adaptation is in prose, not verse
Whereas the modern version is in prose, the versification of the original may have partly accounted for some of the less familiar syntax.

Obscure references
Not unusually for its time, Shakespeare's text contains several references to classical myths and legends which may have been more widely familiar than is now the case. Allowing for this change, the modernised version either adds an explanation that Neptune was the 'sea-king', or omits the reference completely (as with Jove's lightning).

Gains and losses
You will have your own ideas about this! As with all simplifications, and some would say even translations, it is impossible to paraphrase the original and keep exactly the same sets of meanings and experiences as the original contains. It may also make us ask again, what is so special about Shakespeare in the first place? If it is largely his plots and his characters we are interested in, then for improved

comprehension perhaps we should be able to see the modernised version performed on stage. However, if the distinctive quality of Shakespeare is centred in his uses of language, as we originally suggested, then we would have to say that for all the help such versions may give us in understanding his stories, something vital is inevitably lost.

ACTIVITY 125

1 Carry out a similar analysis of these two versions of one of the best-known speeches in *The Tempest*.

Here, having conjured his spirits to perform an entertainment, or Masque, for Ferdinand and Miranda, Prospero reflects on life itself, comparing its short-lived glories to 'this vision' which he has just made vanish.

Shakespeare	Shakespeare Made Easy
Our revels now are ended. These our actors *As I foretold you, were all spirits, and* *Are melted into air, into thin air:* *And, like the baseless fabric of this vision,* *The cloud-capped towers, the gorgeous palaces,* *The solemn temples, the great globe itself,* *Yea, all which it inherit, shall dissolve,* *And, like this insubstantial pageant faded,* *Leave not a rack behind. We are such stuff* *As dreams are made on; and our little life* *Is rounded with a sleep.* [Act 4, scene 1, lines 148–158]	*… [O]ur entertainment is over. Our* *actors, as I said before, were all spirits,* *and have melted into air; thin air. And* *just as this was all an illusion, so lofty* *towers, gorgeous palaces, solemn* *temples, the earth itself and all, indeed,* *who live on it, will disappear; and just* *as this insubstantial performance faded* *away, likewise not even a cloud will be* *left behind. We are made of the same* *stuff as dreams, and our short lives are* *rounded off with a sleep.*

2 'Translate' a section from your own set text – you could try putting it not only into clear, modern Standard English, but also into a regional dialect, or with a much younger audience in mind. (We'll discuss the issues surrounding regional English and Shakespeare in Section 5.7.5.)

5.7.3 Tales from Shakespeare

In the past, writers such as Charles and Mary Lamb have tried to introduce children to Shakespeare in another way – by transforming the plays into short prose narratives. Here, for example, is the opening of their versions of *The Tempest* and *Othello*:

The Tempest

There was a certain island in the sea, the only inhabitants of which were an old man, whose name was Prospero, and his daughter Miranda, a very beautiful young lady. She came to this island so young, that she had no memory of having seen any other human face than her father's.

They lived in a cave or cell, made out of a rock: it was divided into several apartments, one of which Prospero called his study; there he kept his books, which treated chiefly of magic, a study at that time much affected by all learned men: and the knowledge of this art he found very useful to him: for being thrown by a strange chance upon this island, which had been enchanted by a witch called Sycorax, who died there a short time before his arrival, Prospero, by virtue of his art, released many good spirits that Sycorax had imprisoned in the bodies of large trees, because they had refused to execute her wicked commands.

[from Charles and Mary Lamb, *Tales from Shakespear*, Tale the First, 1807]

Othello

Brabantio, the rich senator of Venice, had a fair daughter, the gentle Desdemona. She was sought by divers suitors, both on account of her many virtuous qualities and for her rich expectations. But among the suitors of her own clime and complexion she saw none whom she could affect: for this noble lady, who regarded the mind more than the features of men, with a singularity rather to be admired than imitated, had chose for the object of her affections a Moor, a black, whom her father loved, and often invited to his house.

[from Tale the Nineteenth]

ACTIVITY 126

1   How well suited are these versions of the stories to the needs of young readers? Have the Lambs succeeded in including any echoes of Shakespeare's language in their narratives? Compare the Lambs' 'The Tempest' with this passage from Jennifer Mulhearn's version in the Cherrytree Press's *Shakespeare for Everyone* series:

Twelve years before, when Miranda was a small child, Prospero was Duke of Milan, a rich Italian city. But Prospero spent his time studying magic and left the government of the city to his brother Antonio. Antonio cheated him and at last, helped by Alonso, King of Naples, had his brother banished. Prospero and his tiny daughter were set adrift in a leaky boat. But Gonzalo, a lord of Naples, made sure they had food, clothes and Prospero's magic books which helped them survive until they landed on this island.

[*The Tempest, Shakespeare for Everyone*, pp. 11–12, 1993]

2   The Lambs' *Tales* first appeared early in the nineteenth century, when a lot of children's literature was characterised by its attempt to teach children moral lessons. Identify in these passages any language which is being used to serve a moral purpose.

In what other ways does the language seem dated?

3   Produce your own version of the narrative of whichever play you are studying for younger readers, modernising and controlling the language carefully, but remaining faithful to the characters and storyline.

Aim to make your text accessible to children with a reading age of between 9 and 12, and carry out an initial survey of some 'style models' in the form of popular books enjoyed by children of this age (your local children's library should be able to help). As with all your original writing assignments, also produce a commentary in which you examine and evaluate in some detail the language you have chosen to use.

5.7.4 Multi-media Shakespeare

Shakespeare has been adapted for a range of 'new' media. His texts have appeared in comic-book format, with the lines emerging inside speech bubbles, and Shakespeare has proved a popular source for film-makers. In recent years there have been successful versions of *Romeo and Juliet, Hamlet, Othello, Henry V* and *Much Ado About Nothing* in the commercial cinema, and a series of half-hour animations for television and video.

These adaptations usually involve varying degrees of text-editing – but the skills of selecting parts of the text, and cutting others without damaging the sense, fluency or coherence of the script is not as easy as it looks.

Here are examples of the fairly radical cutting which was needed to reduce the BBC's *Animated Tales* to half an hour. The task fell to Leon Garfield, who transformed some of the text into narrative and used images and voice-overs to convey essential parts of the story as well as simply pruning the text.

This extract from *The Tempest* corresponds to the passage we examined in *Shakespeare Made Easy*; that from *Othello* (when Othello demands Desdemona to produce the handkerchief which Iago has placed in Cassios' lodging) is printed in parallel to the full text of the original:

The Tempest

> **Prospero**: *Come away, servant come. I am ready now. Approach, my Ariel, come!*
> A strange creature manifests itself out of the air, a bright, trembling, vague creature, neither beast nor human, but endlessly changing between them.
> **Ariel**: *All hail, great master! Grave sir, hail!*
> **Prospero**: *Hast thou, spirit, performed to point the tempest that I bade thee?*
> **Ariel** (proudly): *To every article! I boarded the King's ship, now on the beak, now in the waist, in every cabin, I flamed amazement!*
> **Prospero**: *My brave spirit!*
> **Ariel**: *Not a soul but felt a fever of the mad, and played some tricks of desperation!*
>
> [from L. Garfield (ed.), 'The Tempest', *Animated Tales*, 1992]

Othello

Shakespeare's original text

Othello: *I have a salt and sorry rheum offends me,*
Lend me thy handkerchief.
Desdemona: *Here, my lord.*
Othello: *That which I gave you.*
Desdemona: *I have it not about me.*
Othello: *Not?*
Desdemona: *No, faith, my lord.*
Othello: *That's a fault. That handkerchief*
Did an Egyptian to my mother give,
She was a charmer and could almost read
The thoughts of people. She told her, while she kept it
'Twould make her amiable and subdue my father
Entirely to her love; but if she lost it
Or made a gift of it, my father's eye
Should hold her loathed (loathly) and his spirits should hunt
After new fancies. She, dying, gave it me
And bid me, when my fate would have me wive,
To give it her. I did so, and – take heed on't!
Make it a darling, like your precious eye!–
To lose't or give't away were such perdition
As nothing else could match.
Desdemona: *Is't possible?*
Othello: *'Tis true there's magic in the web of it.*
A sibyl that had numbered in the world
The sun to course two hundred compasses,
In her prophetic fury sewed the work;
The worms were hallowed that did breed the silk,
And it was dyed in mummy, which the skilful
Conserved of maidens' hearts.
Desdemona: *I'faith, is't true?*
Othello: *Most veritable, therefore look to't well.*
Desdemona: *Then would to God that I had never seen it!*
Othello: *Ha! Wherefore?*
Desdemona: *Why do you speak so strangely and so rash?*
Othello: *Is't lost? Is't gone? Speak, is't out o'the way?*
Desdemona: *Heaven bless us!*

[Act 3, scene 4, lines 52–82]

Animated Tales version

Othello: *I have a salt and sorry rheum offends me; lend me thy*
handkerchief.
Desdemona: *Here, my lord.*
Othello: *That which I gave you.*
Desdemona: *I have it not about me.*

Othello: *That's a fault. That handkerchief did an Egyptian to my*
mother give. She told her, while she kept it, 'twould subdue my
father entirely to her love; but if she lost it or made a gift of it,
my father's eye should hold her loathly …

Desdemona: *Then would to God that I had never seen't!*

Othello: *Is't lost? Is't gone?*

[from L. Garfield (ed.), 'Othello', Animated Tales, 1994]

ACTIVITY 127

1 Compare the edited-down versions with the originals. What principles does Leon Garfield seem to have been following, and how has he ensured that the scenes still flow smoothly?

2 Inevitably, most of the longer speeches in the *Animated Tales* have been reduced to just one or two lines. In the case of the *Othello* extract, what has an audience lost, and how has the trimming of Othello's speeches affected the pace and suspense in the scene?

3 In performance, some directors choose to edit-out whole scenes and even characters – Rosencrantz and Guildenstern are occasional absentees from productions of *Hamlet*, for instance.

   For your own set play, are there any episodes or characters which the play could do without? Pursue this question in the form of a 'balloon debate', with each person arguing the case why a particular character should not be 'thrown out of the balloon' (i.e. edited out of the script). Candidates for the 'chop' might include:
   - the Porter in *Macbeth*
   - Rosencrantz, Guildenstern and the Gravedigger in *Hamlet*
   - Bianca and Roderigo in *Othello*
   - Adrian and Francisco in *The Tempest*.

4 Take a scene from your set play and produce your own edited-down version which could be used in a half-hour adaptation. Aim to reduce it to no more than one third of its length.
   In your accompanying commentary, discuss the technical problems of making sure the text still coheres, and how you overcame them.

5 Editing texts in this way is a useful skill, and one which some examinations test. So, extend your editing skills to other texts, and produce 'boiled-down versions' of:
   - news articles
   - editorials
   - persuasive speeches – try it on one of the examples we looked at in Section 5.5.2, pages 234–8.

5.7.5 Regional English and Shakespeare

Imagine we are to cast a production of *Othello*, *The Tempest*, or whatever your set play happens to be. Some of our actors are only comfortable working with a particular accent. Thus, our potential Hamlet, a star male performer from Barnsley, speaks in broad South Yorkshire, the older actor who has auditioned as Prospero is a natural 'Brummie', and our Desdemona, from Basildon, has a strong Essex accent.

   Would this casting make sense? It would certainly not be the traditional representation of these characters – the popular stereotypes and attitudes associated with regional varieties which we explored in Chapter 2 are difficult to avoid, and many theatre companies will tend to exploit them rather than go against the grain. So, whilst non-RP regional accents are often heard in Shakespearian performances, they are likely to be spoken by the Gravedigger, the Clown/Fool, servants, and characters from a lower social class. Thus, as Leeds-born poet Tony Harrison remembers in his poem 'Them & [Uz]', at school he only ever got to read the comic parts:

I played the Drunken Porter in Macbeth.
'Poetry's the speech of kings. You're one of those
Shakespeare gives the comic bits to: prose!

[from Tony Harrison, *Selected Poems*, 1984]

In the modern professional theatre, the larger, more serious roles – Hamlet, Prospero, etc. – are usually played in a form of unmarked RP. Is this because, as with BBC newsreaders, we couldn't take them seriously in any other accent? Or rather because RP will reflect their social class – after all, most of Shakespeare's leading characters are at least upper middle-class and, in present-day terms, are unlikely to use a strong regional voice (in fact, the logic of this argument would imply that the Dukes, Kings, and assorted aristocrats who throng Shakespeare's plays should actually be played using marked RP!).

ACTIVITY 128

1 Recent filmed versions of *Othello* have presented Iago with Cockney and Yorkshire accents. How appropriate do you consider either of these to be, and for what reasons?

2 If we chose to exploit the popular associations of English regional accents, suggest the appropriate accents for the characters in your own set play.

However, not everyone accepts this conventional way of doing things. They point out that RP is largely a nineteenth- and twentieth-century invention; that Shakespeare came from the rural West Midlands and that his company was based in London, and so the plays are likely to have been written and performed with whatever those accents sounded like in the sixteenth and seventeenth centuries; and that if you want to hear how Shakespeare really sounded you would need to visit some remote North American communities where, it is alleged, the speech-forms of sixteenth century Warwickshire have been preserved.

So, there are some professional companies – such as Barry Rutter's Halifax-based Northern Broadsides –who flout the conventions and make more liberal use of non-RP accents.

ACTIVITY 129

The characters of Caliban and Othello present particular problems. Suggest the kind of accent you would want your actors to use in these roles, and justify your choice by close reference to the text. Here are some issues to consider:

Caliban
- Do you want to suggest Caliban's foreignness? If so, what kind of foreign accent would you use?
- Having learned language from Miranda, what would his natural accent be?

Othello
- How long has Othello lived among Venetians – and would he have acquired the local accent?
- How would his officer class-status influence this question?
  If you decide to reflect his origins in his accent, precisely what kind of accent is implied by his being described as a 'Moor'?

5.7.6 Reviewing performances – a framework

Shakespeare remains an extremely popular choice with theatre companies and you should be able to experience at least one 'live' performance of your set play during your course. Failing that, the reviews of productions which appear regularly in the press can at least give you a window onto the ways in which directors, designers and actors have interpreted the plays.

The following is an edited version of a review by Susannah Clapp of a recent production of *Othello*:

> 'Iago is out of control, and it scares him'
> Sam Mendes has directed a powerful Othello. *His production … gains in intensity from taking place within the small area of the Cottesloe Theatre; … It gains in pace and clarity from Anthony Ward's beautiful, tactful design. A tiled floor stretches in front of honey-coloured wood: louvred doors and pillars serve in turn as a veranda, a series of rooms, an arcade. There is wicker furniture, a gramophone, a great deal of cigarette-smoking and torrential rain. This could be the Twenties, or the late Forties.*
> …
>
> *As in any good Shakespearian production … unexpected passages are given fresh life. Maureen Beattie's forceful Emilia – moving persuasively from disappointment to despair – and Clare Skinner's dainty Desdemona, a child-bride in satin pyjamas, constitute a warning female commentary, a visual reproach to the military boisterousness that surrounds them. A vocal reproach, too. Men, Emilia explains to Desdemona, are 'stomachs', made for eating up women: 'and when they are full / They belch us.' Beattie seizes on these lines and with great effectiveness, makes them ring like a rallying cry. …*
>
> *As Iago, Simon Russell Beale is superb. … He is a complete soldier – his hands habitually behind his back, his shoulders stiff – and he conducts his plan for Othello's destruction like a military campaign. … As soon as he has fixed on a course of action, however drastic, he permits no second thoughts, but sits back and lights up. There are occasional glimpses –never overstressed – of something out of control which frightens him. … When he declares, 'I hate the Moor', he flings a file across the floor: he recovers himself a moment later and before retrieving the object, straightens his tunic.*

[from *The Observer*, 21 September 1997]

ACTIVITY 130

1 The review highlights several aspects of the production which made the reviewer see the play afresh. Use as starting-points for your own discussion of the play the descriptions in Table 5.8.

Table 5.8 Responding to reviews

Reviewer's observation	Issues raised
Maureen Beattie's forceful Emilia moving persuasively from disappointment to despair.	Has Emilia struck you as a 'forceful' character? In what ways does she show 'disappointment' and 'despair' at different points in the play?
Clare Skinner's dainty Desdemona, a child-bride …	Evaluate the evidence in the text for playing Desdemona as either a very young or a more mature character.
…a warning female commentary, a visual reproach to the military boisterousness surrounding them … Beattie seizes on the lines 'and when they are full/ They belch us' and with great effectiveness, makes them ring like a rallying cry.	What does this imply about the importance which this production places on the issue of relationships between men and women in the play? How far is Othello a play about women abused by men in a man's world?
Iago conducts his plan for Othello's destruction like a military campaign … There are occasional glimpses – never overstressed – of something out of control which frightens him.	What evidence is there in the script for these aspects of Iago's character?

2 We can also consider a review as a piece of writing with a multiple purpose. In what ways is such a text

- informative
- persuasive
- entertaining?

3 Think about the ingredients for a newspaper review such as this – identify in Susannah Clapp's review:

- visual detail about design elements (set, costume, etc.)
- selection of some specific dramatic moments for comment
- interpretation of some aspects of the performance
- evaluation of individual performances and the production as a whole.

4 Survey a range of play and film reviews from different newspapers and magazines, then write your own review of the next play or film you see – tailoring the length, format and style to your intended medium and audience.

5.8 Learning points

5.8.1 Key concepts

In this chapter you should have learned:

- to analyse Shakespeare's script as discourse
- to recognise some of the distinctive features of Shakespeare's uses of language
- to recognise evidence of, and the nature of, language change
- to recognise some persuasive and rhetorical techniques in Shakespeare and elsewhere, and to apply some of these to your own writing
- to understand the nature of swearing and taboo
- to consider in detail the semantic and dramatic effects of variations in Shakespeare's texts
- to comment on aspects of the plays in performance.

5.8.2 Glossary

acronym   an abbreviated term, pronounced as if it is a word (e.g. NATO)

adjunct   a word or phrase that describes an action

antitheses   pairs of opposites, often (in rhetoric) balanced with each other

auxiliary verb   the additional verb (such as 'do') used alongside the main verb in the formation of negatives, questions and some tenses

blank verse   verse with a regular metre but no rhyme

broadening   the process whereby the range of meanings of a word increased over a period of time

connotation   the implied associations and secondary meanings of a word

denotation   the primary and literal sense of a word

diachronic variation   the variation and change which affects language over a period of time

iambic pentameter   a line of verse consisting of five pairs of stressed and unstressed syllables

imperatives   commands

inflection   an ending attached to words which varies according to tense, plurality, gender or other grammatical aspects

narrowing   the process whereby the range of meanings of a word becomes more restricted over a period of time (compare **broadening**)

object   in a sentence, the person, place or thing which is affected by an action

oratory   the art of effective and persuasive public speaking

parallelism   the repetition of similar phrase or sentence structures for rhetorical effect

past participle   the part of a verb used in the construction of perfect tenses, e.g. 'He has *broken* a glass'

personification   the description of an inanimate object in terms which imply it has human qualities

prescriptive grammar (as opposed to descriptive) grammar which aspires to establish 'right' and 'wrong' practice

present participle   the part of the verb used in the construction of the progressive tenses (e.g. 'I am *hoping* to see you')

present perfect tense   as in 'We have *eaten* too much'

progressive tenses   tenses such as 'I am running', 'They were sleeping', 'She will be joining us', using the -ing form of a verb

rhetorical questions questions posed in such a way as to allow only one possible answer, and for persuasive effect

rhotic accent accents in which the 'r' sound is pronounced with a distinct 'roll'

scan/scansion the accurate observance by a line of verse of a regular metre

subject the element in a sentence which is the agent of an action

synchronic variation the variation within the forms of a language which occurs at any given time

5.9 Extension activities

5.9.1 Original writing

Having come this far, you are now in a position to reflect on some of the discoveries which you have made and the skills you have developed as a result of following a course in both Language and Literature.

As an original writing assignment, design and write a leaflet or hand-out which your school or college might use to inform potential students of the nature of the course. In it you should try to summarise

- what the course is about
- how the study of language and literature relate to each other
- what students should expect to learn from the course.

5.10 Further reading

Some enjoyable and accessible ways of exploring the distinctive qualities of Shakespeare's language are to be found in Rex Gibson's *Shakespeare's Language* (Cambridge University Press, 1997). You can take your explorations further by following some of the exercises set out in Cicely Berry's *The Actor and His Text* (Harrap, 1987).

Comprehensive accounts of the development of English can be found in Robert McCrum et al.'s *The Story of English* (Faber, 1986) and Baugh and Cable's standard work *The History of the English Language* (Routledge, 1951). R. Trask's very accessible Language Workbook on *Language Change* (Routledge, 1994) can guide you through this subject, and the issues of how and why language changes are definitively covered in Jean Aitchison's *Language Change, Progress or Decay* (Cambridge University Press, 1991).

The subject of swearing and taboo is entertainingly surveyed in Lars-Gunnar Andersson and Peter Trudgill's *Bad Language* (Blackwell, 1990) and Stephen Burgen's *Your Mother Tongue* (Victor Gollancz, 1996). W. F. Hill's and C. J. Öttchen's *Shakespeare's Insults* (Mainsail Press, 1991) surveys the range of colourful curses to be found throughout his plays.

There is, of course, a huge amount of literature on all aspects of Shakespeare; for a highly practical actor's and director's view of how his language actually works on stage, turn to John Barton's *Playing Shakespeare* (Methuen, 1994).